# PATRONS

My deepest thanks to everyone who backed this project when the dream was not yet reality. Your support means a lot to me.

| | |
|---|---|
| Dylan Wilson | David Le Lievre |
| Aaron Lindsay | James Mok |
| Stephen Old | Gary Shove |
| Steve Boggs | Andrew Bowes |
| Katie McFarlane | Barry O'Sullivan |
| Cameron Marcroft | Alex McLeod |
| Marty Kerr | Peter McFarlane |
| Dave Billington | Angela McFarlane |
| Dave Murdoch | Ian d'Young |
| Hohepa Thompson | Levi Allan |
| Ben Reid | Stephen McCarthy |
| Brad Westgate | Sean Cope |
| Jonathan Kane Houldsworth | Charles Goodson |

## Special thanks

**Nicole Beaver**
Teacher
For wise words along the journey.

**Nic Malone**
Associate Professor of Anthropology
For anthropological advice.

**Gary Shove**
Publisher
For believing in the vision.

## Early backers

Scott Illingworth, Alfred Lee, Geoff Cawson, Clint Bratton, Sam Bryden, Ryan Dupen, Dave Crosbie, Haydn Scott, Christiaan Van Noppen, Andrew Rolf, Dom Harvey, QD, Aimee McFarlane, Mike & Leah McFarlane, Tony Clewett, Ana Dermer, Mike Falloon, Kurt Bradley, Kent Briggs, Karl Bonnici, Conrad Heaven, Aaron Dong, Nicholas Rowan, Rich Lowe, Mathew O'Dwyer, Jackie Messam, Cameron Bower, Rachael Weaver, Mark Jephson, Ben Speedy.

To my family, thank you.

This book had been simmering in my mind for over a decade, an idea waiting for its time to come.

The moment finally arrived with the advances in AI, which allowed this long-held concept to be turned into reality.

But here's a question: did I write this book, or am I merely the conduit for a more advanced form of intelligence?

Intrigued by this thought, I decided to turn the tables, through an experiment called Primal Prompting – a process where the observed behaviour of primates, specifically gorillas in the Democratic Republic of the Congo, were allowed to change aspects of the story.

How? Flick to the final pages to find out more.

Why? Because if I didn't write every word myself, then perhaps AI too, should yield to another kind of wisdom.

Yet, in a sense, the story you're about to read has already been written. As it's essentially a history of humanity – a tale of power, corruption, and survival. My intention was to simply traverse the highs and lows of civilisation, retracing a path long since been cut, by those who came before me.

In blending human insight, artificial intelligence, and primal instincts, Monumental turned into more than a story; it became a reflection of who we are, where we've been, and where our next steps might take us. This is no ordinary narrative, it is a shared story, told through many voices – from the ancient to the artificial.

Follow this symbol to see where the primitive world has influenced the future.

# MONUMENTAL

## POWER, CORRUPTION & THE STRUGGLE FOR A JUST SOCIETY

## BOOK I. RISE OF CIVILISATION

# BOOK II. FALL INTO CORRUPTION

*A Controll emerges from his lair, causing*
*aplings to scatter in all directions. 1465.*

# THE DARKEST DEPTHS

Now, dear reader, gather 'round and listen close, for I'm about to spin a tale as old as time itself. It's a yarn about the wicked ways, darkest desires, and the primal urges that lurk within, that can just 'bout tear down an entire civilisation if left unchecked.

You see, deep within the heart of Monkey Mountain, there lurked a trio of sinister characters: Vulgar, Klepto, and Brutus. Now, folks, these weren't your run-of-the-mill critters. They had a real hankerin' for power that'd make a hyena on the hunt look timid.

Hidden away in the shadows, they were slicker than an eel in a pond. Their intentions were about as mysterious as the darkest night in the wilderness, and they kept themselves hidden from sight most of the time. These three terrors lived hidden beneath the watchful eyes of the mountain's primate inhabitants. They weren't keen on sunlight, but they sure had a knack for stirring up trouble. They thrived on chaos, fed on dissent, and sowed discord among the unsuspecting mountain folk.

Their craving for control led them down a crooked path. They spun webs of deception, warped the minds of those seeking power, and took advantage of the honest folk's weaknesses. They'd go to great lengths to rule Monkey Mountain, come hell or high water.

Yet it wasn't always this way. Once upon a time things were much different round these parts.

BOOK I
# RISE OF
# CIVILISATION

As the wild gives way to order, and the solitary become a tribe, so begins the story of civilisation. It is a journey born from necessity – a desire to rise above chaos, to build something enduring in the face of nature's indifference. Around the first flames of community, bonds are forged, stories told, and the foundation of society takes shape.

This is the beginning of our story – a tale of how the scattered found unity, how survival gave rise to ambition, and how the first steps toward building a greater world were taken. It is the story of civilisation's rise, filled with hope, ingenuity, and the relentless hunger for a better future.

# CHAPTER I
# OF NATURAL ORIGIN

# IN THE BEGINNING

I.Y

# PRIMATES

I.II

# NATURAL SELECTION

I.III

# ADAPTION

I.IV

# & MUTATION

# COOPERATION

I.V

# PREDATORS

I.VI

# THE TRIBE

I.VII

# HUNTER GATHERERS

I.IX

# Dawn Breaks

◆◇◆◇◆◇◆◇◆◇◆

As the first light crept across this newly minted day, it warmed the valleys and peaks, stirring animalia of all ilk from their slumber.

This particular morning heralds the commencement of our epic fable, yet to be writ. Where air, earth, water and flame converge, not as isolated forces but as actors in a cosmic play, each moving to a rhythm older than time itself.

Where nature and nurture shall wrestle with one another, in a world brimming with promise and possibility, the perfect backdrop for this story, soon to unfold: a tale of power, ambition and the restless spirit of creatures seeking to rise above the wild chaos of the jungle. What follows in these pages is the chronicle of that journey – a climb from simplicity to complexity, from survival to meaning, and from the ground beneath their feet to the summit of a mountain built with both hard work and hope.

This world, fresh and unspoiled, was the starting point. And soon, like all things in nature, will change over time.

*A verdant jungle scene, where birds glide above fruit-laden trees in perfect harmony. 1320.*

# APLINGS

Tucked within the vast wilderness, beneath towering canopies and woven into the tangled undergrowth, lived the distant ancestors of our unfolding story.

These nimble little critters didn't bother with brawn or bluster. No sir, they thrived with quiet persistence, moving through the natural order like a note perfectly placed in a grand symphony.

In this untouched haven, the primates lived as nature intended – content, unburdened by ambition or regret. Time passed gently, and they existed only in the now, free from the weight of tomorrow or the shadows of the past.

But as it always goes, even in the most peaceful of places, a question stirs beneath the surface: Why is it that some creatures are satisfied to stay just as they are, while others are driven to become more? What strange spark sets certain beings apart, urging them to build, to reach, and to carve something greater out of the simple rhythm of life? And what awaits those who step off the easy path, where triumph and failure are always only a hair's breadth apart?

*Two primates perch among fruit-laden branches, quietly reflecting the harmony between life and abundance. 1580.*

*Two giraffes reach high to feed, embodying the quiet intimacy of shared survival.* 1605.

# Natural Selection

Out here in the natural world, there's a curious law at work that don't follow no blueprint – natural selection, or what folks like to call survival of the fittest.

It ain't guided by design, just a slow, blind shuffle where only the traits that help a creature scrape by get passed along. Those that don't? They fade into the undergrowth like yesterday's leaves.

Every critter you see – whether it's a prowling panther or a band of sharp-minded primates – bears the marks of this process, chiseled through generations. The ones with keener senses, stronger limbs, or a knack for teamwork? They're the ones that stick around. Just look at giraffes – those long necks didn't sprout overnight. It took ages of culling till only the tall ones could reach the treetop buffet, while the shorter ones went hungry.

Nature doesn't play favorites, but useful traits stick. A faster leap or smarter plan means the difference between seeing tomorrow or not. Bit by bit, creatures sharpen into better versions of themselves. The world of creatures you see now ain't perfect – they're just the lucky few who adapted well enough to survive another day.

# THE ART OF EVOLUTION

**B**ehold the evolutionary patterns of life, working together like a river reshaping its banks over time.

Mutation is where it starts – a random twist in the genetic current. Most changes pass without effect, but now and then, one carves a new path, offering an edge: sharper vision, stronger limbs, or resilience to drought.

Adaptation directs the flow. When a mutation helps a creature survive and thrive, it sticks, passed down through generations. Over time, these small changes accumulate, molding creatures to fit their environments. Take the varied beaks of birds – finches with thick beaks crack seeds, while those with slender beaks pluck insects from tight crevices. Each shape tells the story of countless mutations, carried forward because they gave the birds an edge in their search for food. But the world is always shifting, and survival demands flexibility. In this ever-changing game, adaptation offers no perfection – only a chance to keep moving, like water finding a new route through unexpected bends. Those who adjust endure; those who don't are swept away.

*A vibrant assembly of birds, each beak uniquely shaped for its purpose, reflecting the diversity born from adaptation. 1610.*

*An oxpecker perches atop a rhino, feeding on ticks and offering early warnings, embodying nature's cooperative balance. 1605.*

# THE STRENGTH OF SYMBIOSIS

I f there's one thing that nature wants to teach us, it's that no one makes it alone.

Cooperation ain't just some polite habit – it's a survival strategy, plain and simple. You see, life on this planet has a way of rewarding those who figure out how to scratch each other's backs. Take the oddball friendship between the oxpecker and the rhino. The oxpecker gets scraps of food to eat and a safe place to roost, while the rhino – bless its thick-skinned heart – gets a free cleaning service and an early warning system, when his little pal spots danger on the horizon. It's a tidy arrangement where everybody wins.

This same spirit runs deep in primate societies, where cooperation isn't just helpful – it's essential. Sharing food, raising the young, and fending off predators together means the group thrives, even when the individual might not. One watches while another eats, and if danger comes knocking, they all know what to do.

Over generations, teamwork becomes baked into the very bones of those who practice it. Nature, for all its indifference, keeps what works and trims what doesn't. And what works – whether between bird and beast or within a troop of primates – is sticking together. Because in a world full of predators and pitfalls, survival often belongs to those who learn how to help each other out.

*A dangerous pack of predators prowls the undergrowth,*
*each competing for survival in the unforgiving dark. 1625.*

# LAW OF THE JUNGLE

O nce our primate ancestors staked their claim in the jungle, it didn't take long for predators to start prowling.

Big cats, slinking through the undergrowth; sharp-eyed birds of prey, watching from above; and snakes, silent and coiled, waiting for an opportune moment. These wild animals made no secret of their hunger. Alone, an apling was an easy meal – one misstep, and they'd be snatched away. To survive, they had to out-think the threats around them.

Dealing with predators forced 'em to be resourceful. They learned to read the jungle's warning signs – rustling leaves, sudden silence, or the faint growl of something lurking nearby. They developed a system, with some standing guard while others slept or searched for food. When danger struck, they worked together to drive predators off. Over time, they even began creating safe zones, choosing sleeping spots high in the trees or building barriers to keep prowlers at bay. Every predator encounter sharpened their instincts and their tools. It wasn't enough to be strong; they had to be quick-witted, adaptable, and united. Through these challenges, they turned survival into a skill, proving that the jungle didn't just belong to the strongest – it belonged to those with quickest wits.

# THE TRIBE UNITES

Cooperation became a turning point in evolution, shifting primates from solitary wanderers into tightly-knit tribal communities.

Within these tribes, working together for defence and sharing resources not only for survival but as a gesture of mutual care meant greater security and efficiency. Over time, members took on specialized roles – some gathered food, others hunted or crafted tools – ensuring that every task was handled with skill, boosting the group's overall well-being.

Beyond mere survival, gestures like sharing food strengthened bonds within the tribe, creating a network of interdependence. Success bred more cooperation, creating a positive cycle. Those who thrived within this framework were more likely to survive, reproduce, and pass on the social instincts that held the tribe together. With each generation, these cooperative behaviours became more refined, embedding themselves deeper into the social fabric.

In time, tribes evolved into the building blocks of something far greater. These early communities laid the foundation for organized societies, demonstrating that cooperation wasn't just a survival tactic – it was the key to progress. What began with simple teamwork became the groundwork for the complex structures of civilisation that would follow.

*A vibrant gathering of aplings, each playing their part in a close-knit tribe where strength lies in unity. 1630.*

*A tribe of aplings set out with spears in hand, marking the dawn of innovation and new horizons. 1640.*

# TOOLS OF SURVIVAL

As primates organized into tribes of hunter-gatherers, they tapped into the power of innovation, reshaping their way of life.

The crafting of tools and weapons marked a pivotal step forward, giving them the ability to hunt a wider range of prey and push into new territories. Simple sharpened stones and sturdy branches soon gave way to more advanced implements like spears and bows, giving them the upper hand against creatures that once sent 'em scrambling for cover.

These inventions didn't just fill bellies – they opened up new horizons. With better weapons in hand, the tribes could roam farther, hunt bigger, and stake claims on land that was once out of reach. Territories expanded, resources grew, and with them came safer places to raise young and strengthen the tribe. Each hunt and tool-making session honed their skills and deepened their bonds, turning scattered groups into well-oiled survival machines.

The farther they spread, the more they learned, and before they knew it, these once-simple hands had laid the first stones of something much bigger. Innovation became their compass, guiding them toward a more stable, prosperous life – and setting the stage for the primitive past to make way for the apling future.

CHAPTER II

# THE HEARTH OF WISDOM

# FABLES

*Apling elders gather under the moon to share*
*stories and spark a new era of evolution. 1623.*

# FIRELIGHT FABLES

In the midst of that wild jungle, where the aplings had been making do for generations, something happened that shook things up good and proper.

The shift from just scraping by to building something bigger started with a spark – both literally and figuratively. One stormy night, a bolt of lightning came crackling down from the heavens, striking an ancient tree and setting it ablaze. And, oh boy, that fire was the kind of thing that leaves a mark.

At first, the fire was nothing but trouble – a wild, roaring beast that spooked every critter in earshot, including the aplings. But the elder aplings, sharp as ever, watched from the shadows. They noticed that as fearsome as the flames were, they kept the real monsters of the night, those prowling predators, well out of sight. Sensing there might be more to this fiery stranger, three of the tribe's leaders – Bug, Belle, and Bada decided to get a closer look.

Bug, with his scraggly fur, wise old eyes, and steady, imposing presence, was the first to catch on. He sat back with a calm gaze and a chest that rose and fell in composed confidence, exuding the aura of one who had seen many seasons. "Now, this here flame," he said, scratching his chin, "ain't just some dangerous thing. It's a friend, if we treat it right." Under his guidance, the aplings started gathering wood and learning to tame the fire. Soon enough, they figured out how to cook their food on it, making their meals tastier and easier on the belly.

Belle, known for her gentle ways and thoughtful words, saw another gift in the fire. "It ain't just for keeping the critters at bay," she said. "Let's gather round it, stay warm, and tell our stories. When we sit in the light, we can see each other's faces and let our words carry through the night." And just like that, the aplings started gathering every evening, weaving together tales, lessons, and dreams.

THIS HERE FLAME AIN'T JUST SOME DANGEROUS THING. IT'S A FRIEND, IF WE TREAT IT RIGHT.

*Around the fire, Bug helps wisdom to take shape, marking the first steps toward a shared future. 1651.*

*By gazing into the fire, the aplings discover not just survival, but self-awareness. 1672.*

Then there was Bada, who knew the jungle better than anyone. He saw the fire as more than just warmth or a weapon. "This flame," he said, "is the heart of our wisdom. Around it, we'll build a hearth – a place where we can come together, learn, and grow into something greater."

And so, the Hearth of Wisdom came to be. It wasn't just a spot to cook or chase off the night's terrors – it became the very centre of their lives. They gathered there to eat, swap stories, and share what they knew. The fire grew into more than a tool; it became a spark for something bigger: a light to guide them from surviving into thriving, from the wild into something resembling civilization.

Among the ones who sat close to the fire's glow were Hooma and Pap, two young aplings bound together by curiosity and care. Their lives were stitched from shared adventures, and they'd promised to live, love, and grow together – maybe even, one day, bring new life into the world themselves.

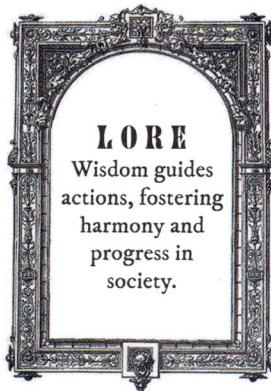

### LORE
Wisdom guides actions, fostering harmony and progress in society.

33

# THE ANIMAL KINGDOM

The discovery – and taming – of fire was a real turning point in the aplings evolution, no doubt about it.

This wasn't just some lucky stroke that helped them scrape by a little easier; it was the moment they stepped up and out of the jungle's ranks. That flickering flame didn't just mean warmth or cooked meals – it lit the way to something new, a line in the sand between the aplings and the rest of the animal kingdom.

The elders, sharp as a tack and always looking deeper, were the first to grasp what fire really meant. It wasn't just for scaring off predators or roasting roots; it was the key to unlocking a whole new way of living. Around the hearth, they began to see themselves differently. The fire stretched their day beyond the sun's setting, giving them time – precious time – when every other creature tucked itself away, blind in the dark.

As the flames danced and the moon watched overhead, the aplings leaned into the night's first real conversation about the world they'd found themselves in. They weren't just animals foraging and fleeing, and they knew it. Hooma, Pap, and the others could feel it in their bones – they were set apart from the wild things that scurried in the brush. And so, by that fire's glow, Bug and the elders started a new kind of discussion, one that would echo through many nights to come: just what was it that made them different from the rest of the animal kingdom?

*In the vast animal kingdom, diverse species coexist, each playing a unique role in the intricate web of life. 1607.*

## THEY BEGAN TO FASHION THEMSELVES A LANGUAGE AS INTRICATE AS A SPIDER'S WEB, FULL OF TWISTS AND TURNS.

## LANGUAGE & COMMUNICATION

The gatherings around the Hearth of Wisdom were the most splendid spectacles you ever did see, where the aplings took a mighty leap beyond the ordinary grunts and growls of other creatures. They began to fashion themselves a language as intricate as a spider's web, full of twists and turns. These clever aplings wove their words into grand tapestries of tales and ideas, sharing wisdom and painting pictures with their speech that could make the heart sing and the mind dance.

## ADVANCED COGNITIVE ABILITIES

Keeping the fire alive showcased the aplings' knack for planning and foresight, setting them apart from their animal kin. It wasn't just tossing sticks onto the blaze; it required careful thought and strategy. As they fed the flames and gathered around it, their minds buzzed with activity, diving into problem-solving and abstract reasoning that would leave a fox scratching its head.

## CULTURE & SYMBOLIC REPRESENTATION

The Hearth of Wisdom became a cultural hub where the aplings created and transmitted complex practices. They told stories, performed rituals, and engaged in music and dance, all imbued with symbolic meanings. These cultural expressions showcased their ability to use symbols to represent abstract ideas and beliefs, something the rest of the animal kingdom did not exhibit.

## ADVANCED TOOL USE & TECHNOLOGY

While most animals muddled along without any tools, the aplings' time around the fire sparked the creation of advanced gadgets and gizmos. They crafted tools and utensils that made their daily chores easier and added convenience to their communal life. The fire itself was a technological wonder, changing their world and capabilities. It set them on a path of never-ending innovation.

## SELF-AWARENESS & INTROSPECTION

The flickering flames of the Hearth of Wisdom offered a perfect backdrop for self-awareness and introspection. As they stared into the fire, they started pondering their existence, their place in the world, and their relationships with one another. This kind of deep thinking marked a big leap forward in their evolutionary journey.

## MORAL & ETHICAL REASONING

Discussions around the fire often veered into matters of right and wrong, sparking moral and ethical reasoning. Bug and Belle debated how best to live together, share resources, and treat the natural world. These fireside chats laid the groundwork for the more complex ethics which were still to come, steering the aplings' behavior in ways far beyond mere survival.

## CUMULATIVE LEARNING & KNOWLEDGE TRANSMISSION

One of the most remarkable things about the Hearth was its role in cumulative learning and passing down knowledge. The elders' stories and lessons didn't stop with one generation – they were handed down like precious heirlooms, each new batch of aplings adding to the wisdom of those before them. This build-up of cultural and technological know-how set the aplings apart from other creatures.

## MANIPULATION OF THE ENVIRONMENT

The ability to tinker with their environment really pointed to a dramatic difference to their animalia kin. With their mastery over fire, they could change their surroundings in ways no other animal could dream of. Pap mastered starting, controlling, and taming fire, while Hooma used its heat to cook meals. This knack for shaping the world around them showed just how unique they were, turning the wild chaos of the jungle into a place of their own making.

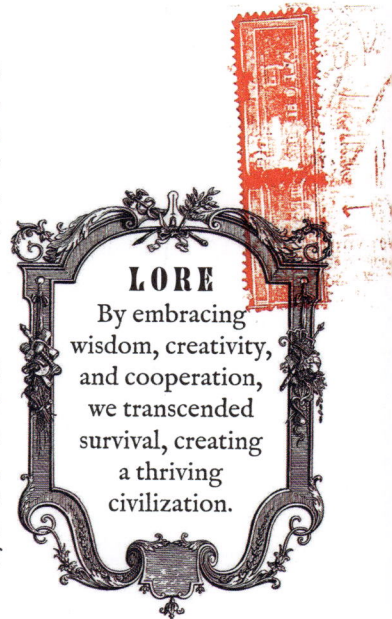

**LORE**
By embracing wisdom, creativity, and cooperation, we transcended survival, creating a thriving civilization.

*The owl watches from the branches, reminding the*
*aplings to seek wisdom above all else. 1714.*

# THE QUEST FOR KNOWLEDGE

In the glow of the Hearth, the elders shared more than stories. They delved into the depths of a thing they called philosophy, exploring the trickiest questions that defined their existence.

This was not just idle chatter but a profound quest for understanding, aimed at laying the foundation for a society built on knowledge, ethics, beauty, and good governance. They reckoned that, like the wise owl, they must seek wisdom tirelessly if they were to succeed in their quest for understanding.

On one particular night, as the fire crackled and the stars twinkled overhead, Bada began to speak about knowledge. "Consider, my friends," he began, "what it means to know something. How do we come to understand the world around us?" The aplings, their faces lit by the flickering flames, listened intently. Knowledge, as Bada explained, was not just about survival. It was about understanding the deeper truths that lay beneath the surface of everyday life.

He spoke of how their senses provided immediate information – like the scent of rain or the sound of a predator's growl – but emphasized that true knowledge went beyond these sensory inputs. "Our minds," he continued, "can think, question, and imagine. We can seek out patterns and meanings, test our ideas, and learn from our experiences." This pursuit of knowledge was a communal effort, with stories and lessons passed down from one generation to the next, creating a rich tapestry of shared wisdom.

*Seeing and feeling the heat of the fire. 1375.*

## THE NATURE OF REALITY

As the conversation about knowledge drew to a close, Bug took up the mantle to explore the nature of reality. "This fire before us," he gestured, "we see its light, feel its heat, and hear its crackle. But is this all there is to reality?" The aplings pondered this question, understanding that their senses were just one window into the world.

Bug spoke of the unseen forces that governed their lives – the wind that rustled the leaves, the spirits of the forest, and the cycles of the moon. These, he explained, were all parts of a greater reality that extended beyond the physical world. "Our reality," he said, "is a blend of what we can perceive and what we cannot. It includes our dreams, our fears, and our beliefs. It is a tapestry woven from both the tangible and the intangible."

## THE MORAL COMPASS

With the foundation of knowledge and reality laid, Bada steered the conversation towards ethics. "How should we live?" he asked, his voice firm and steady. "What is right, and what is wrong?" All the folk leaned in, wondering if the answers to these questions would shape their lives and their community even more.

Bada spoke of the importance of compassion, honesty, and justice. "In our interactions, we must strive to be fair and kind. We must share our resources, help those in need, and treat each other with respect." The elders debated various scenarios – how to handle conflicts, how to distribute food during scarcity, and how to ensure that the weakest among them were cared for.

"Ethics is like the roots of a tree," Bada added. "Without them, we cannot stand strong. Our actions must be guided by principles that uphold the dignity of all living beings and the integrity of our environment." Hooma, Pap and the other aplings nodded, agreeing to create a society where ethical behavior was the norm, and where moral dilemmas were resolved through wisdom and empathy.

## THE PURSUIT OF BEAUTY

As the night deepened, the conversation turned to aesthetics, the philosophy of beauty and art. Belle, an elder known for her artistic talents spoke up, her eyes gleaming with passion. "Beauty," she said, "is not just about what pleases the eye. It is about what touches the soul and lifts the spirit."

She pointed to the fire, noting how its light danced and flickered, creating a mesmerizing display. "Our surroundings," she continued, "should inspire us. The way we build our shelters, the songs we sing, and the stories we tell should all reflect the beauty of our world." The aplings discussed the importance of harmony with nature, ensuring that their creations enhanced the natural landscape rather than destroying it.

Belle spoke of art and ceremony, of dances under the moon and sculptures carved from wood. These artistic expressions, she said, were essential to their cultural identity. They would create spaces of tranquility and inspiration, where the mind could wander and the heart could find peace. "Beauty," she concluded, "is a reflection of our deepest values and aspirations. It is what makes life worth living."

## THE ART OF GOVERNANCE

Finally, as the fire burned low, the discussion turned to politics – the art of governance. Bug stood to speak once again. "Politics," he began, "is about how we organize our collective life. It's how we make decisions, distribute resources, and ensure the welfare of all."

The aplings listened as he touched upon the principles of a just society. "Our governance," he said, "must be based on participation, fairness, and respect for all voices. Leadership is not about dominance, but about stewardship – guiding rather than ruling, serving rather than subduing." "Our mountain," the elder concluded, "will stand as a monument to our societal aspirations. It will reflect our quest for knowledge, our understanding of reality, our ethical commitments, and our love of beauty.

*Like tree roots, Wisdom and the pursuit of truth provide stability. 1632.*

41

# THE MEANING OF LIFE

A s the night deepened, shadows stretched long and lazy beyond the Hearth, which crackled happily away – like it had a secret it was just 'bout ready to spill.

The faces of the gathered aplings glowed in the firelight, their eyes wide with curiosity, their minds hungry for answers to the oldest question in the jungle: what's it all about?

Belle stoked the fire and leaned in closer, her fur catching the light as embers drifted in the breeze. "In these flames," she began, her voice soft and steady like rustling leaves in a sleepy forest, "we see the dance of life itself. Why do we strive? Why do we love? Why do we dream?" The aplings hung on every word, even the jungle itself seemed to hush itself to listen in.

Hooma, nestled close to the fire, rested her hands protectively over the curve of her swollen belly, wondering to herself if tonight's tales might explain a thing or about the mysteries of life? How everything seemed to connect – from the caterpillar to the butterfly. Prodding the fire again, Belle looked up and said, "speak now friends, if you have any notions on what life is – and how to live it?"

## CRAFTING OUR OWN PURPOSE

Sartorio, the ancient, rose up, cleared his throat and began. "The jungle doesn't hand us meaning, my friends. We carve it out ourselves, like a path through the thickest vines. Each choice, each action, shapes our purpose. We have the freedom to decide what matters, but with that freedom comes the weight of responsibility. We must be mindful to craft lives that are meaningful, or risk wandering lost among the trees."

*A vibrant butterfly flutters gracefully, its delicate wings symbolizing the beauty, transformation, and fragility of life. 1520*

## THE SIMPLE JOY OF LIVING

**HEDONISM**

Next, Cureus, ever the optimist, grinned as he shared his thoughts. "Some say life is about seeking joy and avoiding pain, like plucking the sweetest fruits while sidestepping the thorns. Happiness and pleasure are no small things. By filling our days with laughter and light, we can live a life worth remembering."

## THE PATH OF VIRTUE

**EUDAIMONIA**

Stotles, another elder, stood tall, his voice steady. "The ancients believed in flourishing through virtue," he said. "Eudaimonia, they called it – the pursuit of excellence. By nurturing our strengths and living with integrity, we grow into the fullest versions of ourselves. It is not enough to simply live; we must strive to live well."

## A HIGHER CALLING

**FAITH & SPIRIT**

Aquinas, known for her spiritual insights, added softly, "For many, the meaning of life is found beyond ourselves – in the divine, in a higher purpose. Faith gives us direction, moral principles guide our way, and belief in something greater offers a deeper sense of peace."

## MASTERING THE SELF

**STOICISM**

Then came Aurelius, his voice measured and steady. "Life is not about bending the world to our will but about mastering ourselves. Stoicism teaches us to focus on what we can control – our thoughts, actions, and choices. By embracing virtue, practicing discipline, and accepting what we cannot change, we find strength and peace, no matter the chaos around us."

## OUR PLACE IN EVOLUTION

**NATURAL WORLD**

Darwinis chimed in, offering a perspective rooted in the natural world. "We are here because our ancestors survived – adapted to the challenges of the wild. In understanding our place in nature, we find meaning in our resilience, our ability to grow, and the survival that stretches back through the ages."

*A delicate butterfly drawn to a lone flame, symbolizing the fragile pursuit of truth and enlightenment. 1720.*

## THE STRENGTH OF COMMUNITY

CONNECTION

Finally, Belle smiled gently. "One of the richest sources of meaning," she said, "is the love we share with others. By helping our fellow aplings, by building bonds of friendship and care, we create a life that is not just full, but purposeful. It is in connection, in community, that we truly thrive."

As the fire's glow softened and the night grew still, the aplings sat mesmerized by the wisdom that had passed between them. It was beginning to dawn on 'em, that life's meaning wasn't a single path, but a maze of virtues, choices, joy, and love. Hooma, feeling the stir of life within her, smiled quietly. She felt reassured that her offspring would be born into a tribe, rich with wisdom and connection, where the meaning of life was something anyone could pursue, no matter which direction it took you.

**HAPPINESS AND FULFILLMENT ARE WORTHY GOALS.**

45

An apling strides through the jungle. Eyes focused and movements
purposeful, embodying a sense of mission and direction. 1720.

# LIVING WITH PURPOSE

N ight after night the elders gathered the aplings around the Hearth. Tonight, they were setting their sights on something higher than the moon and stars overhead.

Bada, with a twinkle in his eye, proclaimed, "We must rise above the untamed chaos of the jungle. Our purpose is to seek meaning in life, and to do so, we must build a civilisation that reflects our highest aspirations."

Bug nodded, adding, "We shall construct a mountain around this very Hearth of Wisdom, a monumental embodiment of our quest for knowledge, meaning, safety, and security for all. It must be more than just a physical structure; it will be a symbol of our collective journey towards higher ideals."

Belle chimed in, "We will infuse this mountain with all the philosophical and ethical virtues the elders have discussed. Each stone and pathway will be symbols of our commitment to wisdom, justice, and beauty." Yes sir, the vision was clear: a society built not just to survive, but to thrive, embodying the principles that set them apart from their animal kin. And so it was to be, the aplings set their minds and hands to the task of building their future.

## WE MUST RISE ABOVE THE UNTAMED CHAOS OF THE JUNGLE.

"But what exactly is purpose?" piped up Pap from the shadowy edge around the hearth's glow. "Surely my purpose is different to yours. Just as every apling's purpose is different from the tribe's, and the tribe's is different from this mountain you speak of?"

"Well let us consider the various types of purpose one may find in their life." said Bada. "Who has ideas about what in heck's name purpose might be?"

47

# AT THE HEART OF OUR EXISTENCE LIES THE DRIVE TO SURVIVE & REPRODUCE.

## LIFE'S BASICS: SURVIVAL & REPRODUCTION

Sartorio went first, grunting that their basic biological imperatives were most important. "At the heart of our existence lies the drive to survive and reproduce. These imperatives ensure the continuity of life, and in fulfilling them, we partake in the grand cycle of nature. Yet, is survival alone enough to give our lives meaning?"

## SELF-ACTUALIZATION & GROWTH

Another elder, Maslolo, ever the sharp one about apling potential, jumped in next. "Sartorio, survival is all well and good, but life's purpose stretches way beyond just making it through the day. We've got to aim for self-actualization, realizing our potential and ideals. Real meaning springs from becoming the best version of ourselves, broadening our horizons, and chasing after wisdom and personal growth."

*A wise owl guards a basket of bones, a solemn reminder that knowledge and mortality are forever entwined. 1783.*

## FINDING MEANING & FULFILLMENT

Franklus chimed in, "Indeed, Maslolo, but self-actualization alone doesn't cut it. We also need to find meaning and fulfillment in our everyday lives. Setting and achieving meaningful goals, following our passions, and contributing to something bigger than ourselves – that's what really gives us a sense of purpose and makes life richer."

## CONNECTION & RELATIONSHIPS

Confucius, the elder who was always preachin' about social harmony, jumped in next. "Franklus, finding meaning and fulfillment is all wrapped up in our relationships and connections. It starts right at home, with family, where we nurture the next generation. Loving others and building meaningful bonds begin there, growing outward to include our friends and neighbours. Being part of a community is key to living with purpose. By helping each other and making a positive impact, we create a life that's truly rich in significance. It's in these close-knit ties that we find our true worth and pass on our values, ensuring our wisdom and purpose endure through the ages."

## THE PATH HOME

As the evening's discussions wrapped up, Hooma felt that familiar stirring within. Pap, noticing her discomfort, gently helped her to her feet. The moonlight lit their path back to their shack, each step seemed to echo the night's reflections on life's meaning and purpose. The elders' words lingered, especially the talk of connection, growth, and fulfillment.

Lost in thought, Pap walked silently beside Hooma, his mind turning over the ideas shared around the Hearth. The wisdom of the ancients weighed on him, stirring questions he could feel deep in his bones. As the jungle closed in around them, Pap felt that the path ahead – wherever it led them in life, would be shaped by the thoughts that'd started rattling 'round his head.

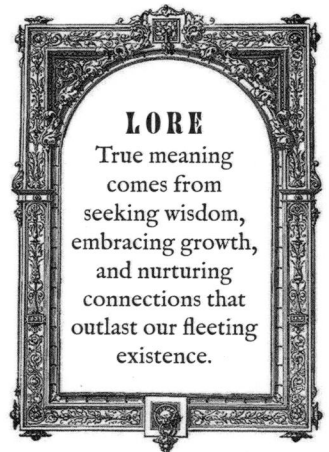

### LORE
True meaning comes from seeking wisdom, embracing growth, and nurturing connections that outlast our fleeting existence.

CHAPTER III
# MAKETH THY MOUNTAIN

NATURAL ORDER

# SETTLERS
# VILLAGE
# AGRARIANISM
# FEUDALISM
# MONARCHY
# EMPIRE
# MERCANTILISM
# INDUSTRIAL ERA
# MODERN AGE

*Village of aplings, fortified against predators behind a fence built for their safety. 1654.*

# NOMADIC NO MORE

**N**ow it seemed like the days of wandering through the wild were done and dusted.

The tribe had made up their minds – this spot, now seen as the heart of their settlement, was where they'd build their home. No more drifting through the jungle with eyes peeled for food and shelter. They weren't just settling down; nope, they were laying the groundwork for something far grander – a mountain that would one day rise high above the canopy, brushing shoulders with the heavens.

Hooma, belly heavy with the little one soon to arrive, sat near the centre of their emerging village, watching Pap and the others busy as ants at work. "Our little one deserves a place to grow strong," she whispered, resting a hand on her belly. Pap, wiping sweat from his brow, shot her a tired but proud smile before getting back to it. Around them, the village stirred with life, each apling adding their bit to this new world.

They wove branches and vines into a sturdy fence, not just around the Hearth but encompassing the entire community, like a protective embrace. Above it, watchtowers stood like silent guardians, keeping a keen eye on the jungle. The fear that had driven them to wander now felt like a distant memory. This wasn't just a camp – it was a stronghold, a place where hope had taken root.

Each day, the settlement grew. What had started as a loose gathering of huts had transformed into a fortified village. More than survival, their purpose evolved into crafting a legacy – a place of unity and shared purpose. The aplings worked tirelessly, not just to survive, but to create a future where their children could thrive. This was no longer just a place to rest – it was the foundation of civilisation. Every stone laid in place was a step toward building their mountain that would one day protect their kin for generations to come.

**WATCHTOWERS STOOD LIKE SILENT GUARDIANS, KEEPING A KEEN EYE ON THE JUNGLE.**

And soon, Hooma and Pap's child would be born into this new world – a home built to endure, rising steadily with each new stone, reaching ever closer to the stars above.

DANGER → DEFENCE → COOPERATION → SECURITY

# The Simple Life

Then sun rose from its slumber, casting golden rays across the land, whilst the aplings bustled about, their little cluster of huts coming to life like bees around a hive.

Survival wasn't the aim anymore – they were building something lasting. "A fence'll keep them critters out, but a village makes us a family," hollered Bug, his voice carrying through the cool morning air. They built their huts in a circle with the Hearth at its heart, each shelter planted like a seed of the future. "We ain't just buildin' huts – we're planting roots," one cheerful fella declared, hammer in hand.

Roles and duties sprouted fast, like mushrooms after rain. Some aplings threw themselves into building, hammering with each strike echoing through the forest. Others turned to healing, teaching, or farming, each finding their place in the rhythm of life. "We need more than hunters," one apling called out. "We need every skill we've got!" Days filled with the clang of tools, children's laughter, and the hum of gardens growing. Each harvest became a celebration, where labour was shared, bounty enjoyed, and life blended with the rustling jungle.

One night brought a moment destined to be told for generations. Hooma, feeling the stirrings of life within her, went into labour. The village gathered close by the Hearth, waiting with bated breath. When the news came, it was twice as sweet. Not one, but two little 'uns were born, moments apart – twins!

The air crackled with excitement as Bada, being a tribal leader, stepped forward to welcome them. Holding the first baby high, his voice rang out. "This boy be called Kratos, for he is Power, the force that drives us forward." Then, cradling the second, Bada smiled. "And this one shall be named Demos, for he is the People – the heart of our tribe." The village roared with joy, knowing these brothers, wherever life took them, were destined to help shape the future of the mountain.

*An apling family huddles beneath the shelter of their humble hut, the weight of survival resting quietly on their shoulders. 1654.*

*An apling shepherd tends to his herd. 1208.*

# WORK THY LAND

O nce their village was firmly settled, the aplings turned their eyes to the soil beneath their feet.

It was high time to move beyond the hunter-gatherer ways of old and dive headfirst into the art of cultivation. The shift from chasing wild fruit to planting seeds marked a mighty step forward – the kind that would push them further up the great mountain of civilization.

Under the sun's warm gaze, the aplings cleared patches of wild growth, taming the jungle bit by bit into neat fields. They planted their seeds with the kind of care a mother gives her babe, tending to the earth like it was something sacred. The Hearth, burning at the heart of the village, remained more than just a gathering spot – it became the beacon by which they steered their farming efforts. Each night, folks would huddle around it to swap stories of their day's toil and share what the changing seasons had taught them.

Their days were filled with the steady rhythm of farm work. Hands that had once scavenged now grew rough and skilled, coaxing life from the land with every turn of the soil. They watered, weeded, and watched, learning the language of the earth – when to sow, when to reap, and when to let things be. The hum of growth filled the air, and the promise of harvest spread through the village like a quiet joy.

Every morning, Pap made his way into the fields, working the land to bring food back for his young brood. The shift to farming brought more than just full bellies; it gave the tribe a sense of stability they'd never known before. They weren't at the mercy of the jungle anymore – now they could plan ahead, store up food, and build a future worth having. Granaries rose alongside the huts, filled with extra crops for leaner times. In farming, they learned that foresight was just as useful a tool as any plough they dragged across the dirt.

**THEIR DAYS WERE FILLED WITH THE STEADY RHYTHM OF FARM WORK.**

## SOWING SEEDS OF STABILITY

The act of planting crops and nurturing them to harvest instilled a sense of predictability and security. The aplings no longer depended solely on the whims of nature. This newfound control over their food supply enabled them to plan ahead and invest in their community's future.

*A humble shepherd guides his flock, staff in hand under the open sky. 1642.*

## DIVISION OF LABOUR

As farming took root, the community began to specialize. Some focused on tilling the soil and tending to the crops, while others crafted tools, built storage facilities, or looked after livestock. This division of labour not only increased efficiency but also allowed for the development of new skills and trades within the village.

## SOCIAL BONDS STRENGTHENED

Working the land together forged stronger communal bonds. The collective effort required to plant, maintain, and harvest crops fostered a deeper sense of unity and cooperation. Festivals celebrating the harvest became integral to their culture, reinforcing the importance of community and shared success.

## ECONOMIC FOUNDATIONS

Surplus food production laid the groundwork for trade. The aplings began to barter excess crops for goods and services, setting the stage for a more complex economic system. This shift allowed them to acquire resources they could not produce themselves, further enhancing their prosperity.

## CULTURAL EVOLUTION

Life on the land didn't just fill bellies – it shaped minds and hearts. As the aplings tilled the soil and watched the seasons turn, their stories and songs began to grow right alongside their crops. Myths about planting and harvest, the dance between rain and sun, and the spirit of the land seeped into their folklore, binding them to nature and to each other. These tales didn't just pass the time – they wove the tribe's identity, giving everyone a sense of place and purpose.

As the village flourished, Kratos and Demos grew into sturdy young lads, strong from the good food their parents and neighbors worked so hard to grow. The fields were their playground, filled with laughter that rolled through the village like a spring breeze. The two brothers soaked up lessons from Pap out in the fields, learning that every seed sown held the promise of a harvest, and every crop pulled from the earth meant food on their table. Meanwhile, Hooma quietly taught them the values of cooperation and kinship, showing them that tending to each other mattered just as much as tending to the land.

It was clear to everyone that the village's success wasn't just luck – it was a team effort through and through. Every apling had a role to play, and each task, no matter how small, helped hold things together. The fields that Pap and the others worked fed more than just stomachs – they fed the soul of the community, too. With every harvest, the bonds between them grew tighter, and this new way of life gave them all a reason to stand together. Farming wasn't just about food – it was about belonging.

**LORE**
Tending the land and each other turns dreams into roots, grounding a community in prosperity and hope.

**SURPLUS FOOD PRODUCTION LAID THE GROUNDWORK FOR TRADE.**

# THE ROOTS OF FEUDAL LIFE

**W**ith the fields thriving and granaries stocked to the brim, the foundation of their agrarian world felt nice and sturdy – solid enough to build the next level of society.

As prosperity grew, so did the need for order. Scuffles soon showed that a system was needed to keep the peace, and out of farming life, feudalism began to sprout – a social arrangement that tied power, protection, and labour together like vines winding around a tree.

Alpha aplings, whether through strength or cunning, naturally became lords. They claimed land and, in return for loyalty and labour, provided protection and resources to those working the fields. The lords depended on the serfs, just as the serfs relied on them.

Pap and his family were among the serfs – the hardworking folk who tilled soil and raised livestock. Their daily labor kept the village running, and in exchange, the lords offered safety. "We work the land, and the land works for us," Pap would say, hands busy with the day's task. The serfs didn't grumble much – their sweat bought peace, food, and protection.

The lords built their halls higher up the slopes, watching the fields below like hawks over their territory. Life around the Hearth of Wisdom shifted into the steady rhythm of feudal life, with decisions made by the lords and disputes settled at their word. This structure brought stability – like the ancient trees holding the jungle together.

Though tied to the land, Pap and his kin found comfort in knowing their place. It wasn't perfect, but it worked. They knew their labour put bread on the table, and the lords would keep danger at bay. And on Monkey Mountain, that was enough – because you had to know which side your bread was buttered.

*A stern lord looms over a wary young serf, the gap between power and submission clear in their gazes. 1654.*

# MONKEY MOUNTAIN

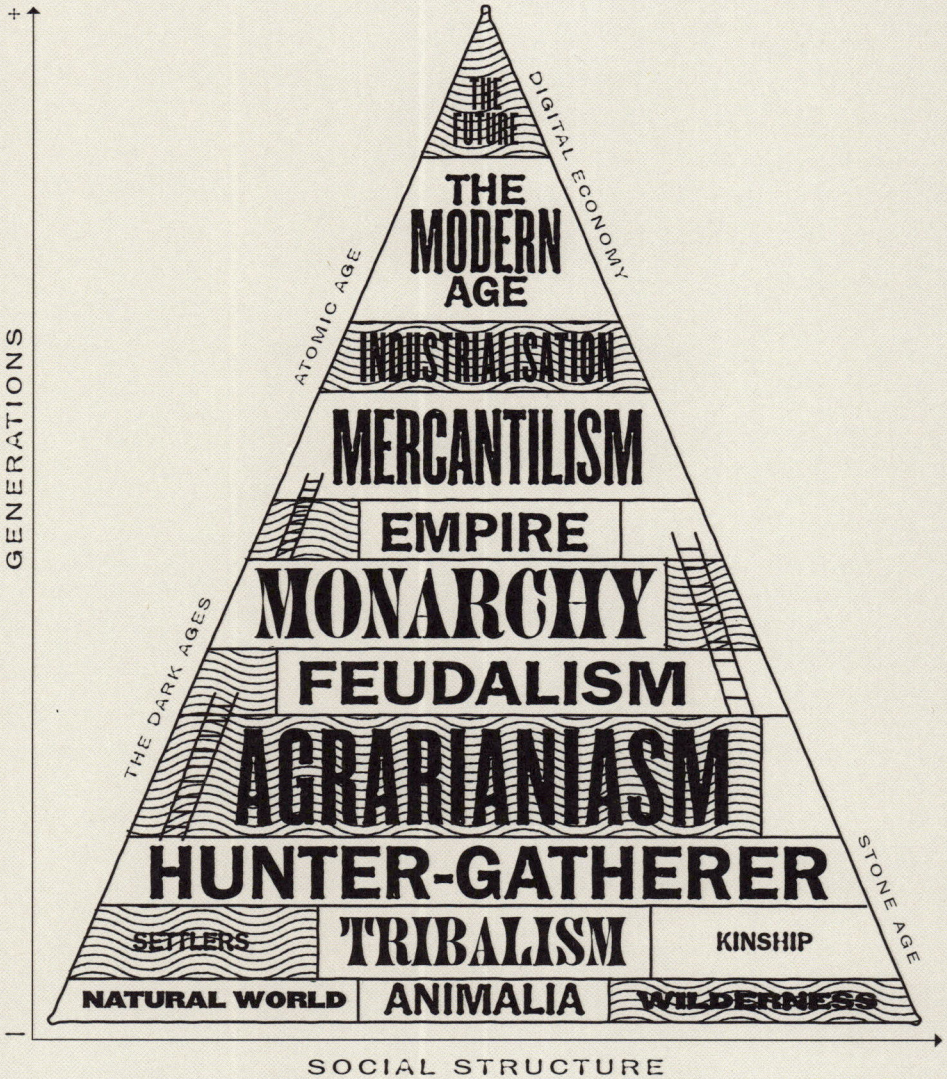

GENERATIONS

+

THE FUTURE

DIGITAL ECONOMY

THE MODERN AGE

ATOMIC AGE

INDUSTRIALISATION

MERCANTILISM

EMPIRE

MONARCHY

THE DARK AGES

FEUDALISM

AGRARIANIASM

HUNTER-GATHERER

STONE AGE

SETTLERS

TRIBALISM

KINSHIP

NATURAL WORLD

ANIMALIA

WILDERNESS

−

SOCIAL STRUCTURE

Monkey Mountain is a towering, layered structure, built upward over generations. Starting from a primitive foundation of hunter-gatherer life through to the modern age. Each layer represents a stage of civilization, rising one atop the other, embodying societal progress.

# CIVILISATION

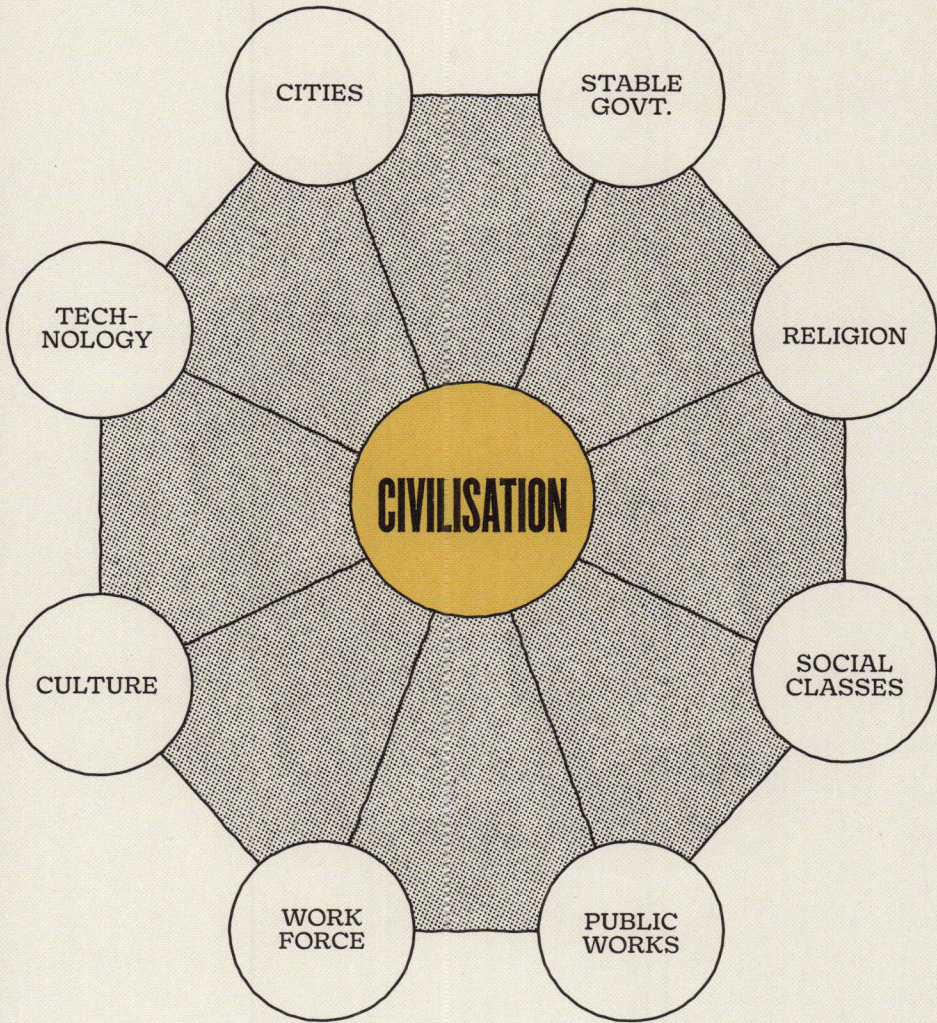

CITIES

STABLE GOVT.

TECH-NOLOGY

RELIGION

CIVILISATION

CULTURE

SOCIAL CLASSES

WORK FORCE

PUBLIC WORKS

Civilisation stands upon many pillars, such as culture, governance, and technology. Each pillar represents a foundational aspect, supporting organized communities and collective progress, creating a balanced structure that sustains the mountains' growth over time.

*Amidst a grand assembly, King Congo is crowned beneath the forest canopy. Lords and common folk watch as the elder bestows the crown, marking the start of Congo's reign and the tribe's unification. 1682.*

# RULE BY DIVINE RIGHT

**W**ith feudalism holding things together real nice and snug, the mountain folk were thriving.

Lords ruled their patches, serfs worked the fields, and life rolled along steady and sure – much like a lazy river winding through the jungle. Crops grew tall, the village buzzed with purpose, and every apling knew their place. It wasn't fancy, but it did the job.

But as the tribe grew, so did the squabbling. Lords, each thinking their patch was the most important, bickered endlessly. It didn't take long to see they needed someone to rise above the fuss – someone to pull them all together. That someone was Congo, a lord with ambition as big as his voice. Puffing out his chest, Congo declared, "By the will of the heavens, I shall bring order to this land. I shall be your king." The lords bowed, the serfs followed, and just like that, Congo's crown was set.

Next to the Hearth of Wisdom, Congo was crowned king. The lords swore their loyalty, the serfs accepted his rule, and the tribe stood unified under one banner. His castle, perched higher up the mountain, became the seat of power, where justice was served and plans for the future were forged.

Out in the fields, Pap and Hooma kept their hands busy, but their minds wandered to the change unfolding before them. The lords who'd once fought tooth and nail now bent the knee to Congo, and the tribe – once on the edge of one too many disputes – found order under his rule. Pap and Hooma knew they were witnessing a turning point, the kind folks would tell stories about. Stability and protection were promised, and now the tribe – lords and serfs alike – waited to see what this new era under Congo's crown would bring.

**THE NEW KING STOOD AS A SYMBOL OF UNITY AND DIVINE FAVOUR.**

## DIVINE RIGHT TO RULE

Now, the aplings believed that the monarch wasn't just any leader. No siree, they figured the king had a special kind of authority, straight from the heavens. This divine right made folks see their ruler as more than just the head honcho – he was a guardian, handpicked by the powers that be, to watch over and guide the village.

## CENTRALIZED AUTHORITY

The establishment of a monarchy brought a single, unifying voice to the mountain. This central authority made decision-making a whole lot smoother, cut down on the squabbling, and gave everyone a clear sense of direction. The monarch's decrees were respected far and wide, bringing a sense of order and predictability to village life.

## SYMBOL OF UNITY

King Congo stood tall as a living symbol of the mountain's unity and strength. Much like a still lake reflecting the sky, his presence reminded everyone of the shared values and common goals that brought lord and serf alike together. This figurehead role gave folks a real sense of belonging and purpose.

## ADMINISTRATIVE EFFICIENCY

With the monarchy came the rise of a whole administrative setup to back up King Congo's decisions. Advisors, scribes, and enforcers sprang up, each playing their part to keep the kingdom running smoothly. This newfound efficiency let the tribe take on bigger projects and tackle challenges with a coordinated approach. The shift to a monarchy was like turning a fresh page in the aplings' climb up Monkey Mountain. Built on the solid base of feudalism, it brought order, unity, and a touch of divine purpose. This setup gave the aplings the spunk and grit to take on whatever challenges came their way. The village, now a kingdom, was a shining example of what folks can do when they pull together, guided by a ruler chosen by the heavens themselves.

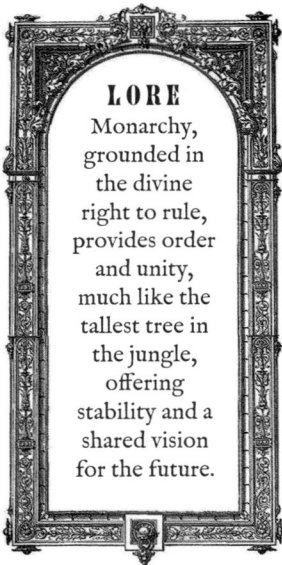

**LORE**

Monarchy, grounded in the divine right to rule, provides order and unity, much like the tallest tree in the jungle, offering stability and a shared vision for the future.

*King Congo holds court, surrounded by lords, attendants, and curious onlookers, cementing his reign as the tribe's unchallenged ruler. 1682.*

*King Congo's army rallies under the crimson banner, their eyes set on conquest. Armored lords and common soldiers march as one. 1682.*

# THE RISE OF EMPIRE

**W**ith the monarchy firmly in place and King Congo's rule bringing much-needed stability, the kingdom began to stir with ambition. The folk at the top, no longer satisfied with what they had, started dreaming of distant lands and untold riches. A new chapter was unfolding – an age of empire and expansion. The mountain's rulers, eager to explore and conquer, cast their gaze far beyond the jungle they'd once called home, ready to stretch their reach into new territories.

As the kingdom swelled and the mountain climbed ever higher, the ruling class's hunger for land and resources grew stronger. The allure of far-off places, teeming with potential, was impossible to resist. "Why settle for what we've got," King Congo bellowed, eyes glinting with promise, "when there's a whole world out there waiting to be claimed?" And with that, the age of conquest was set in motion. Colonies sprouted like weeds in distant corners of the jungle, each one a shiny emblem of their rising power.

Loyal to his king and lured by the promise of opportunity, Pap enlisted in the newly formed King's army. With hopes high and sword in hand, he marched off to the unknown, leaving Hooma behind to tend their home and raise Kratos and Demos. The village watched their warriors depart with a mix of pride and worry, knowing the dangers lurking in the wild.

But the army wasn't sent to merely explore – they were there to conquer, plain and simple. Outposts sprang up in the furthest reaches of the jungle, each one siphoning resources and sending the spoils back to the mountain. Wealth flowed through the kingdom like a roaring river, feeding its unquenchable thirst for growth. King Congo's influence spread wide, casting a long shadow over the conquered lands, as the mountain stood taller than ever, built on the backs of all that lay below.

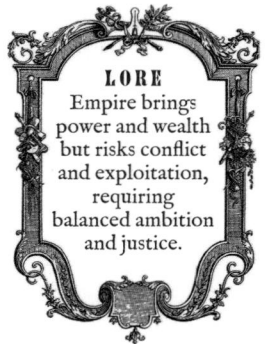

**LORE**
Empire brings power and wealth but risks conflict and exploitation, requiring balanced ambition and justice.

## EXPANSION OF TERRITORY

The aplings' empire grew as they claimed far flung corners of the jungle. These territories were not just pieces of land; they were stepping stones to greater power and prestige. The empire's borders stretched further with each passing day, creating a vast network of paths, tracks and roads, reaching out in all directions.

## ESTABLISHMENT OF COLONIES

In these new territories, the army set up colonies, small replicas of their kingdom. These outposts served as hubs for resource extraction, with serfs and soldiers working tirelessly to gather the riches of the land. The colonies became vital links in the chain of the empire, each one bolstering the kingdom's strength.

## RESOURCE EXTRACTION

The primary goal of these colonies was to extract resources and send them back to the mountain – the heart of the empire. Precious metals, exotic spices, and rare woods were harvested and transported back through the jungle. This influx of wealth transformed the mountain kingdom, allowing it to build grander structures and fund more ambitious projects.

## CULTURAL DOMINATION

But it weren't all sunshine and roses, along with resources, the apling army brought their culture and customs to the conquered jungle corners. They imposed their way of life on the indigenous folk, often disregarding and erasing local traditions. This cultural domination ensured that the empire's influence permeated every aspect of the colonies, creating a uniform identity under the monarch's rule. A blind eye was turned to the exploitation that took place in the name of empire.

## RESISTANCE & REBELLION

Not all conquered aplings bowed willingly to their new rulers. Beneath the surface, resistance simmered, leading to conflicts and uprisings that rattled the empire's foundations. Time and again, Pap and the king's soldiers were sent to quash these rebellions, wielding force to keep the peace. It's a sad truth, but these struggles laid bare the darker side of colonialism – where oppression and conflict came hand in hand with conquest, and violence was the price of control.

During this age of empire, the mountain and its kingdom reached heights never seen before, but every step upward came at the expense of those crushed beneath it. It was a world of triumph and contradiction, where power and progress cast long shadows. Influence and territory expanded, but so did exploitation and suffering – grand achievements bought with grim costs.

*A lone warrior rides into battle, lance in hand, embodying the spirit of duty and adventure that drives King Congo's expanding empire. 1654.*

Though Pap fought with loyalty to the empire, the weight of it wore on him. His heart ached for the simple life he'd left behind, but the demands of expansion kept him marching deeper into the jungle's farthest reaches. He was as much a slave to the empire's ambitions as the territories it conquered, bound by duty even as he longed for home.

Back in the village, Hooma carried the load alone, raising Kratos and Demos with quiet determination. She worked hard to instill values of honesty and integrity, teaching them to appreciate their humble roots and the sacrifices their father had made. No matter how grand the mountain grew, she hoped her boys would remember what truly mattered – and one day, strive to build a better future for everyone, high or low.

73

*A bustling marketplace brims with goods, as merchants and buyers haggle over wares. The rise of mercantilism brings wealth, but the pursuit of profit fuels fierce competition within the kingdom. 1682.*

# THE MERCHANT CLASS ASCENDS

As the empire sprawled ever outwards, a metamorphosis was afoot. It was a change that snaked through the very veins of society, adding a new and somewhat gritty layer to the mountain.

With expansion came a voracious appetite for resources and riches, out of which a new economic order emerged. This system, known as mercantilism, thrived on the unceasing exchange of goods and coin. Yet, to sate its insatiable hunger, it required more than just the empire's dominion – it demanded the labour of a subjugated faction, tethered by oppression, mining the jungle's bowels for raw materials. It was a sinister shadow cast upon the once-prosperous society, which some superstitious folk even claimed was caused by dastardly trolls or some other imaginary force, pulling the strings from somewhere deep inside the mountain. But these wild claims were dismissed as little more than lunacy.

The exploited workforce, wretched souls that they were, toiled relentlessly, their spirits swallowed by the abyss of forced labour. They extracted valuable minerals, precious gems, and other resources from the mountain's depths, cutting deep scars across the earth's tender belly.

The evolution of this new economic system, while fueling the empire's ascendancy, stained the mountain's soul. It was a stark reminder that beneath the veneer of civilisation, darker forces could fester, driven by an insatiable hunger for power and riches, heedless of the suffering left in its wake.

*A labourer toils over his task, refining raw materials into valuable goods. 1862.*

## RISE OF MERCANTILISM

As the empire stretched its boundaries, the need for a robust economic system became apparent. The rise of mercantilism brought wealth and expansion but left scars upon the mountain's soul. Beneath its glittering facade lay a ruthless hunger for resources and power, built on exploitation and suffering.

# THEIR RELENTLESS TOIL MIRRORED THE EMPIRE'S RELENTLESS EXPANSION

## SUBJUGATED LABOUR

To satisfy the mercantile machine, King Congo and the empire built their wealth on the backs of the oppressed. Subjugated workers, from apling slaves to impoverished labourers, were trapped in unyielding servitude. Stripped of dignity and choice, they toiled under harsh conditions, their lives reduced to mere tools of production. The wealth generated by mercantilism rested on the backs of the oppressed.

## RELENTLESS EXTRACTION

The workforce dug deep into the mountain's core, unearthing valuable minerals and gems. This extraction process scarred the land and the spirits of those forced into such work conditions. With the empire's insatiable greed for more resources and wealth, this was like a run away wheel that was never coming back.

## EMPIRE'S STAINED LEGACY

While mercantilism fueled the empire's growth, it also revealed the darker undercurrents of power and exploitation. The mountain, once a symbol of stability and progress, now bore the stains of greed and suffering. This era served as a harsh reminder of the cost of unchecked ambition and the toll of relentless economic pursuit.

Oblivious to all the woes of mercantilism, Kratos and Demos, now young lads, would visit the bustling markets with their mother Hooma. They marveled at the imported goods, their eyes wide with wonder at the spices, fabrics, and trinkets from far-off lands. These visits were the highlight of their week, filled with excitement and curiosity. Of course they were too young to fully understand the complexities of trade and commerce, instead they were captivated by the vibrant atmosphere and the colorful array of items on display. They'd tug at Hooma's hand, asking endless questions about the strange and wonderful objects they saw. For them, the market was a magical place, a window into a world far beyond their mountain home.

*Mercantilism's promise of prosperity rests on production and trade, each item made feeding the empire's growing appetite for wealth. 1682.*

Alas, one fateful day, as Hooma and the boys made their way home from the bustling market, their arms full with the food they'd gathered for supper, a figure appeared on the path ahead – a messenger from the king's army. His expression was grave, and with a bowed head, he delivered the tragic news. Pap, who'd marched off out of loyalty to the King, had been killed in a far-off land, a casualty of Congo's unyielding drive to conquer new territories. The weight of the words hit Hooma like a storm. She collapsed to the ground, her hands trembling as she tried to grasp the enormity of her loss.

Kratos, his face twisted in shock, screamed out in anguish, while little Demos began to wail, his cries echoing his brother's. Their once peaceful world, where their father's presence had been a steady comfort, was now shattered. Hooma clutched the earth beneath her, overwhelmed by the grief that seemed to rise from the very ground, while her sons' cries momentarily caused the market to pause and watch this woeful sight.

*Amidst roaring furnaces and towering smokestacks, aplings toil endlessly, building the machinery of the Industrial Age. 1545.*

# RISE OF THE FACTORIES

**A**s the empire's mercantile web entangled their society, and resources flowed like a river of desires, a realization dawned upon a certain group of ambitious members of the tribe.

They'd reached a precipice in their evolution, an epoch where industrialization beckoned like a storm gathering on the horizon. Amidst the comfort of stable sustenance, they glimpsed the potential to harness the collective power of apling and automation alike. The specter of invention and industrialisation cast its shadow upon the mountain, as a new layer of civilisation was once again built on top of the mountain, pushing it ever upwards.

The ground trembled as the foundations of industry were laid over the comparatively fragile structures of monarchy, empire and mercantilism, clanking away like the rumblings of an approaching apocalypse. Networks of copper and metal wound through the walls, drains and conduits became the arteries of the mountain, while furnaces blazed like the fires of hell itself. Steam engines roared, a chorus of machines signaling a new era.

It was an age of relentless toil and ambition, where progress surged like a roaring river. The aplings had crossed a threshold, venturing into an industrial wasteland where the machinery of their creation churned, and the price of progress exacted its toll in sweat and sacrifice.

**STEAM ENGINES ROARED, A CHORUS OF MACHINES SIGNALING A NEW ERA.**

# HOMES AND FACTORIES ALIKE BUZZED WITH NEW ENERGY.

## FOUNDATIONS OF INDUSTRY

The transformation was seismic, a tectonic shift in the mountain's ascent. Pipes snaked through its walls, feeding furnaces that roared with an unrelenting hunger. Steam engines, the beating heart of this new age, drove progress faster than ever before – powering factories, fueling transport, and shrinking the distance between dreams and reality. This mechanical marvel brought unprecedented speed and scale to their work, turning what once took weeks into the work of days.

## LIGHTING UP THE MOUNTAIN

The introduction of electricity was a game-changer, illuminating the village and kingdom, extending day well into the night. Street lights flickered to life, casting a warm glow over cobbled streets and bustling marketplaces. Homes and factories alike buzzed with new energy, enabling longer working hours and increased productivity. The mountain, once dark and silent after sunset, now thrummed with activity, its nightscape transformed into a beacon of progress and modernity.

## RISE OF INDUSTRIALISTS

The industrial boom gave rise to a new social class of industrialists and the bourgeoisie, who amassed great wealth and influence. King Congo, whilst still on the throne was now old and frail, his grip on power no match for these new rulers who controlled vast enterprises of trade, their fortunes built on the backs of others' sweat and tears. Among them, the notorious robber barons emerged, exploiting both resources and workers to amass their riches. This new elite reshaped the social and economic landscape, leading to stark inequalities and social tensions within the community.

## LORE

Ambition and progress drive growth, but every deal struck carries a cost beneath its polished surface.

*Two industrialists seal a trade deal with a firm handshake. 1643.*

Hooma, now getting on in years, found her health beginning to fail her. Despite their young age, Kratos and Demos looked after her as best as they could. They juggled their daily tasks, tending to their mother while adapting to the rapidly changing world around them. The roar of machinery and the hustle of industrial life were a far cry from the simpler days of their childhood, but the brothers remained resilient.

With twilight beckoning, Hooma would always make a point of taking her sons back to the Hearth of Wisdom, conscious that when the time came for her to slip into the big sleep, it'd be through the stories told around its flickering light, that they'd have to find their own way in life.

81

*Aplings tinker with intricate machinery, their efforts embodying the spirit of the modern era — where technology, and innovation intertwine to reshape their world 1696.*

# THE MIGHTY MODERN AGE

**With the ground trembling under the grind of gears and smokestacks stretching toward the heavens, the aplings pressed on, building their mountain ever higher.**

The engines of industry had reshaped their world, carving out a new terrain that led them inevitably toward the next great summit – the Modern Age, built on the sturdy backbone of the Industrial era.

As the dust of mechanization began to settle, a new system took root, fed by the fierce forces of commerce and competition. Goods flowed like rivers through the marketplace, where traders and entrepreneurs scrambled for their share, each one trying to outdo the other. The marketplace itself had become its own kind of jungle, brimming with opportunity and risk.

Capitalism became their creed. What was once shared among many now belonged to those clever enough to control it. The means of production slipped from the hands of the people into the grip of a few industrious alphas. Wealth piled high in their coffers, and with it came power – spreading through the society like the roots of a tree, reaching every corner and crevice.

Outside their humble hut, Hooma and her boys stood quietly, gazing up at the newest layer that crowned the mountain – a sprawling, bustling city where the hum of machinery and the glow of distant lights filled the night. From where they stood, the city's lights shimmered like stars, casting their glimmer over the village below, as the breeze carried the sound of progress down to their doorstep.

Hooma folded her arms and gave a small nod. "Look at it all, boys," she said softly. "There's magic in this – something extraordinary. A chance for you to shape the life you want." Her voice was warm, but carried the weight of years. "These things we've built, they stand like promises of what's possible. There's a spark in the air, boys. You just have to catch it."

# THERE'S A SPARK OF POSSIBILITY IN THE AIR.

For a long moment, they stood in silence, the vastness of the new age unfolding above them. Hooma sighed, a soft breath carried away by the night breeze. "I'm tired," she murmured, giving her sons a gentle smile. "It's time for me to rest." With that, she turned toward the hut, retreating inside to lay down her weary bones.

The brothers sat down outside their abode, gazing upwards at the constantly evolving mountain, captivated by the towering structures coming to life right in front of their eyes. There had been much talk lately about three giant new chambers being built inside the mountain. Each dedicated to a different aspects of the modern age:

*Monkey Mountain is built with layer upon layer, pushing their civilisation ever upwards. 1397.*

## POLITICAL STRUCTURES

In one chamber, the art of politics would be celebrated – a place where leaders could debate, decide, and govern. Here, the tribe would come together to chart the mountain's path forward. The Political Chamber, as it was called, would be dedicated to the principles of justice and power-sharing, the idea that the voices of many could create a stronger foundation for all. It was a place for those who sought to lead with both wisdom and might.

## ECONOMIC SYSTEMS

Another chamber would honour the force of economy, driven by trade, ambition, and wealth. This was where the aplings would gather to understand the rhythms of commerce, the flow of goods, and the art of enterprise. The Economic Chamber was a place that thrived on competition, where the dreams of the ambitious could be turned into riches, and where the mountain's wealth would be nurtured to grow and expand, fueling prosperity for all.

## PUBLIC SPACES

The third chamber, dedicated to community, would become the heart of the mountain's spirit. Here, the aplings would gather to celebrate shared stories, traditions, and dreams of a unified future. In the Public Chamber, the ideals of cooperation and culture would flourish, reminding all that the mountain's true strength came from its people. This was the place to honour the bonds that held them together – the shared values that turned strangers into neighbours.

## TECHNOLOGICAL ADVANCEMENT

The modern era was marked by rapid technological progress. Innovations in transportation, communication, and industry revolutionized daily life. From electricity to the interweb, technology transformed how aplings worked, interacted, and perceived the world. These advancements brought unprecedented convenience and efficiency but would also bring new ethical dilemmas and societal shifts.

## FINAL BREATH

Later that evening, under the light of the full moon, Hooma felt the quiet pull of the big sleep. As she slipped away, her thoughts wandered to the Hearth, the growing mountain, Pap... and her beloved boys. She hoped they'd find their place in the world, build something meaningful, and carry forward the dreams she could no longer chase. With a soft breath, peace settled over her, and she let go. Sensing a change in the air, Demos and Kratos came in and sat beside her, tears slipping down their cheeks as their beloved mother took her final breath.

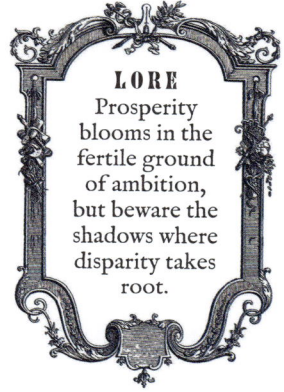

**LORE**
Prosperity blooms in the fertile ground of ambition, but beware the shadows where disparity takes root.

CHAPTER IV

# THE CHAMBERS
# OF POWER

PRIMITIVE POWER STRUCTURES

# PRIMITIVE
## POWER
### ESSENCE
### SUBSTANCE
### IDEOLOGY
### VENOM

# THE CHAMBERS OF POWER

The Chambers of Power consist of three vast, interconnected halls – Political, Economic, and Public—each representing a key pillar of society. Designed with intentional overlap, the chambers reveal where one realm of power influences another. This structural interconnection highlights the complex balance between governance, resources, and public will, emphasising the fluid, intertwined nature of power.

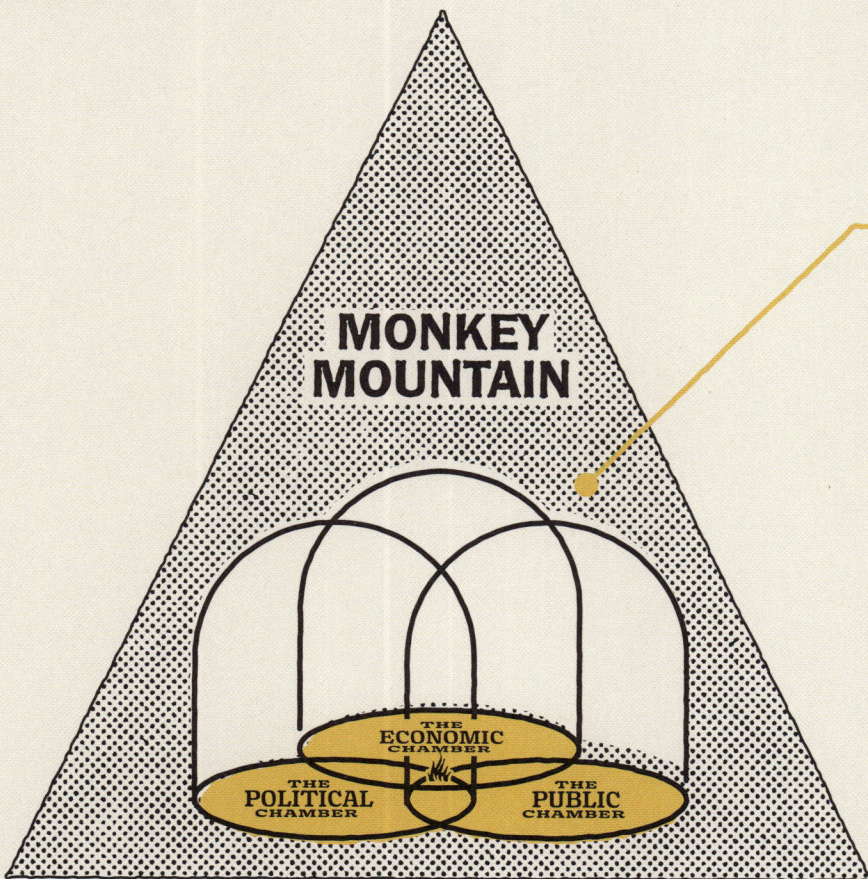

MONKEY MOUNTAIN

THE ECONOMIC CHAMBER

THE POLITICAL CHAMBER

THE PUBLIC CHAMBER

THE
ECONOMIC
CHAMBER

PRODUCTION · DISTRIBUTION · CONSUMPTION · TECHNOLOGY · SOCIALISM · CAPITALISM

ECONOMIC FRAMEWORKS

ECONOMY IMPACTS

POLITICS SHAPES

PUBLIC WELL-BEING

GOVERNMENTAL CAPABILITY · TRANSPARENCY

VALUES · ETHICS · EGALITARIANISM · ALTRUISM · CULTURE · SOCIETY · COMMUNITY

POWER

POWER

POWER

THE
POLITICAL
CHAMBER

THE
PUBLIC
CHAMBER

RULE OF LAW · INDIVIDUAL LIBERTIES

POLITICS REPRESENTS

PUBLIC INTEREST

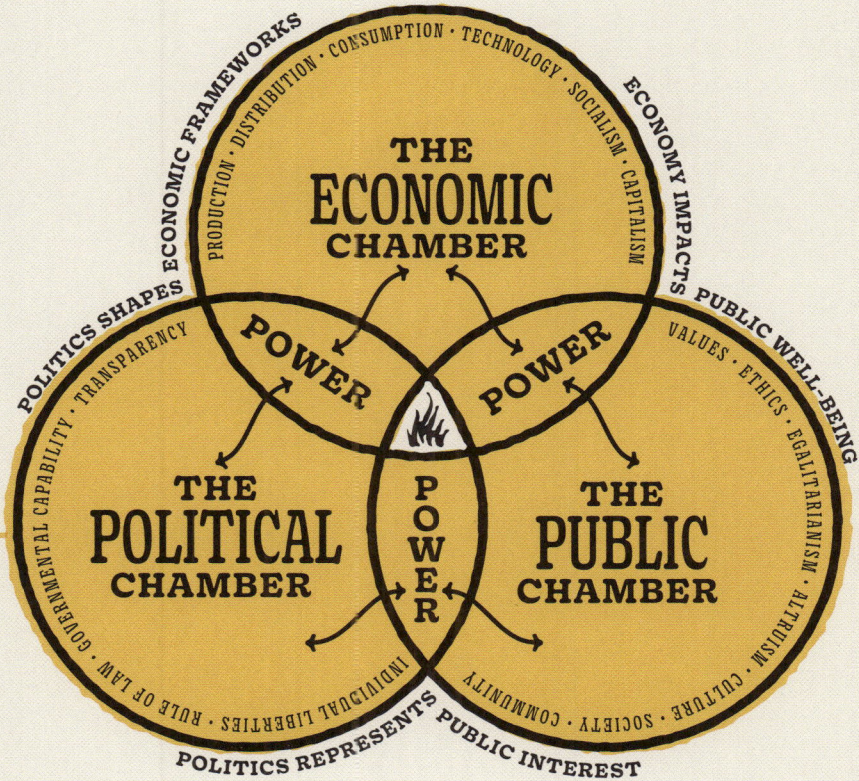

## HEARTH OF WISDOM

The Hearth of Wisdom, positioned at the mountain's core, is a central space where the tribe gathers to exchange knowledge and debate ideas. Its open, welcoming design encourages reflection and unity, with seating radiating around a central fire. Here, stories are told, ideologies formed, and collective insight deepened.

# THE CHAMBERS OF POWER

T he Hearth of Wisdom, once a cozy nook for only a handful of the tribe, now had a grand chamber built around it, at the very heart of Monkey Mountain.

Burning strong and proud, it was surrounded by three other sprawling chambers, forming the bedrock of their modern civilisation. Sure, they were intertwined and connected, woven together, yet each one had its very own specific purpose.

The Political Chamber, The Economic Chamber, and The Public Chamber. Each represented a facet of the aplings' burgeoning society, where power in all its forms was dissected and debated.

The Political Chamber would focus on governance and the implementation of policies that reflected the will and welfare of the whole. The Economic Chamber was tasked with overseeing the distribution of resources and the maintenance of a healthy, thriving market. Meanwhile, The Public Chamber was to be a place of communal decision-making, a forum where every voice could be heard.

In building these chambers, the elders had envisioned a civilization where power was not only balanced but also reflective of their collective ethos. These chambers, by their very design and purpose, encapsulated the wisdom of the ancient ones: that power should serve not the few but the many, guided by knowledge and restrained by the collective good. At the center of them all was the Hearth, where stories were spun, wisdom dished out, and the mysteries of power untangled.

Kratos and Demos, now orphaned and having to fend for themselves, had little choice but to follow the final

> **LORE**
> Power reveals truth: it builds or corrupts, depending on the wielder.

*Aplings gather in the Hearth's glow, preparing to navigate the Chambers of Power. 1165*

# THERE'S A SPARK OF POSSIBILITY IN THE AIR.

wish of Hooma. Maybe it was warmth they craved, but both felt a strong pull toward this sacred place, figuring it was here they'd find the guidance they needed, not to mention a little company to buoy their spirits.

That particular evening, the air was thick with anticipation, and the fire crackled merrily, casting shadows that danced and whispered secrets from times long gone. In this space, storytelling and symbolism meshed together, creating a kind of magic that shaped minds, imparted wisdom, and drew the whole community together.

It was packed, but the boys found a spot to perch and listen, their faces aglow with firelight. As they settled in, an elder named Zog, with a mane of silver fur and eyes that pierced through the mist of time, stood up by the fire. His voice full of grit 'n gravel, he began tellin' the tale of power.

"It's like a spider's web spun through the heart of every society," Zog began, "connecting everything, intricate and fragile, yet strong enough to trap and hold." Kratos leaned in closer, curiosity shining in his eyes. Zog continued. "It's not just about strength or force; it's a complex web of influence and control. It's the ability to bend the will of others, to persuade and inspire. It can be seen and felt, but it can also hide in the shadows, whispering in secret."

## THE DYNAMICS OF POWER

Zog explained that power, in its many forms, is the bedrock upon which societies are built and balanced. He spoke of the dynamics of power. That is to say, the visible structures of leadership – and the hidden currents that run beneath the surface. Power, he noted, while a source of great reward and the means to achieve communal goals, also bore the weight of immense responsibility.

The intoxicating allure of power was well-known to the elders, who'd seen leaders past and present, succumb to its seductive pull, their judgement clouded, their actions veering towards more shadowy paths.

Thus, the conversation turned to the need for checks and balances – a way to ensure that power, while centralized in the chambers, would not become corrupted.

## DOUBLE EDGED SWORD

"Balance, now that's a funny 'ol thing" said Zog, whilst resting a dagger in the palm of his hand. "Power must be wielded carefully, mindful of both sides of the blade. The elders knew all too well that unchecked power could lead to downfall, just as absolute powerlessness could lead to disorder and chaos. "A middle path, must be sought" Zog hollered, "one that allows for growth and innovation, without overstepping the boundaries of fairness and equity."

*An elder apling conjures wisdom from the fire's flickering flames. 1743.*

*Apling elders convene around*
*The Hearth of Wisdom.* 1253.

# THE ESSENCE OF POWER

Every night the orphans, returned back to the Hearth, warming their bodies and illuminating their minds.

As they nestled close to the fire's glow, Zog placed a steady hand on their shoulders, his eyes gleaming in the flickering light. "Tonight," he said, "listen closely. What I share with you is the essence of power. If you understand this, you'll grasp the forces that shape the world."

The boys leaned in as Zog began, his words heavy with hard-earned wisdom. "At its core, power is influence – the ability to shape the actions or choices of others, often in the face of resistance. It's about who gets what, when, and how."

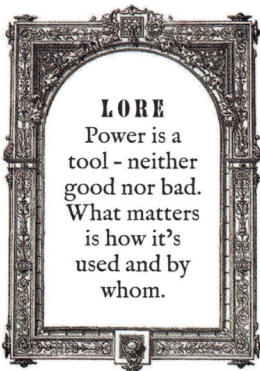

**LORE**

Power is a tool - neither good nor bad. What matters is how it's used and by whom.

The fire cracked, shadows dancing along the walls like spirits eager to hear the lesson. "Power takes many forms," Zog continued, "all connected – like the strands of a spider's web catching the first morning light. Coercive power bends others through fear. Persuasive power convinces and influences thoughts'n feelings. Normative power works quietly, shaping what others believe to be right."

He paused, letting the words settle. "Power is a tool – neither good nor bad. What matters is how it's used and by whom." The boys sat silently, their minds turning, the weight of Zog's lesson sinking deep.

95

## FORMS OF POWER

### VISIBLE POWER
Visible power, like sunlight, illuminates decisions and actions, clearly revealing the paths we choose.

### COVERT POWER
Covert power, like tree roots, shapes what emerges into the light, setting agendas and silencing certain voices.

### LATENT POWER
Latent power, like the air we breathe, subtly influences our desires and beliefs, often unnoticed yet pervasive.

# IT'S LIKE THE SOIL THAT NOURISHES THE PLANTS TO STAND STRONG.

## COERCIVE POWER

"Coercive power," Zog explained, "is akin to the storm that rattles the branches of our mighty trees. It compels by force, by threat, by the sheer weight of authority. It's the power that demands obedience without question, much like the thunder demands silence from timid creatures of the night."

*Power spreads like a great tree – rooted in purpose, branching into influence. 1821.*

## PERSUASIVE POWER

The conversation softened as Zog's voice rose gently above the crackle of the fire. "Then there is Persuasive power, which blows like a gentle breeze – guiding, shaping, convincing without overt force. It is the power of the spoken word, of dialogue, of the stories we share beneath the stars. It convinces, not compels; it invites, not intimidates."

## NORMATIVE POWER

Zog, with a thoughtful gaze, added, "Normative power, the third type, is embedded in the very roots of our culture. It is the power of what ought to be, shaped by our customs, our rituals, our collective beliefs. It's like the soil that nourishes the plants – it shapes us subtly but profoundly, often invisibly, guiding our actions through norms and expectations."

Kratos nodded, as it began to dawn on him that each type of power played a crucial role in the dynamics of a society. Zog elaborated how these powers, if balanced wisely, could sustain and nurture their civilisation, but if misused, could just as easily lead to its decay.

"The challenge," Zog concluded, "lies in wielding these forms of power with a deep understanding of their nature and implications. We must be vigilant, ensuring that coercive power does not overshadow persuasive efforts or disrupt our cherished norms."

As the fire dwindled into glowing embers, Zog and the boys sat quietly, turning over the tricky balance of power in their minds. Demos felt the weight of it settle – realizing that power is a potent force, both a gift and a burden.

Under the moonlit sky, the brothers walked back to their little shack, speaking softly about what they'd learned. The Hearth had opened their eyes to the wild nature of power – how it can nurture or destroy, depending on who holds it and how it's used. They knew now that returning to the Hearth was essential if they were going to prepare for life's challenges ahead.

The flickering embers of the Hearth of Wisdom had sparked something inside them – a quiet, stubborn determination to learn and grow.

## DIMENSIONS OF POWER

### COERCIVE POWER

Like a fierce storm, coercive power compels behavior through fear and threats, effective short-term but eroding trust.

### REWARD POWER

Reward power, like nourishing rain, encourages action through positive reinforcement, fostering loyalty by distributing benefits.

### LEGITIMATE POWER

Legitimate power, rooted in tradition and law, is the authority given to leaders by the tribe's collective agreement.

### REFERENT POWER

Referent power, like the bond with a mother or admiration for a leopard, stems from charisma and personal appeal.

### EXPERT POWER

Expert power, akin to the ancient ones' wisdom, comes from their skills and knowledge, guiding community decisions and actions.

### INFORMATIONAL POWER

Informational power, is like a lantern, illuminating paths with key knowledge and strategic information.

*Holding both a delicate flower and a stone, Zog reflects on the
dual nature of power: it can nurture or crush. 1824.*

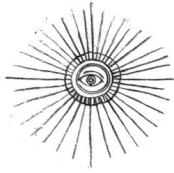

# THE SUBSTANCE OF POWER

Night after night, the brothers returned to the Hearth, just as their mama had wished, running and skipping to where they needed to be. The fire crackled warmly, sending sparks dancing into the air, and shadows stretched across the chamber walls like ancient spirits eager to share their secrets. The boys tucked themselves into a familiar spot, ready to soak in whatever wisdom the elders had to offer.

Zog stood close to the fire, his old eyes glimmering with something sharp – the kind of knowing that comes from living through stories worth telling. "Tonight," he called, his voice echoing through the cavern, "you lads need to understand the substance of power – whether it's hard or soft." He gave the fire a quick prod, sending a few sparks skyward.

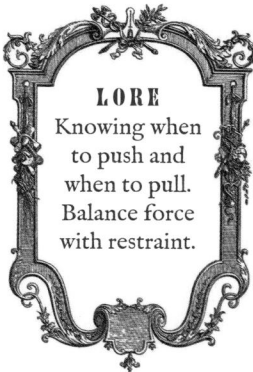

**LORE**
Knowing when to push and when to pull. Balance force with restraint.

## HARD POWER

"Hard power," Zog continued, "is the use of military and economic means to influence others. It be like the mighty roar of a lion, commanding immediate attention and compliance." Hard power involves coercion and force, employing methods such as military interventions, economic sanctions, and threats. It relies on tangible resources like military strength, economic might, and population size, delivering immediate effects but often fostering a little resentment from those it brushes up against.

## SOFT POWER

As the firelight flickered, Zog's eyes sparkled with wisdom. "Now, consider soft power," his tone dropping like a gentle evening breeze. "It's the ability to attract and co-opt through subtle influence and diplomacy. It's like the allure of the blooming flowers, drawing creatures close with irresistible and seductive fragrance." Soft power relies on persuasion, diplomacy, and cultural influence, utilizing intangible assets like culture, political values, and foreign policies. Its methods include cultural exchanges, international aid programs, and promoting a country's values and way of life. Soft power works more slowly and subtly, creating lasting influence and fostering loyalty without coercion.

## SUBTLE STRENGTH

Zog was known for his sharp intellect and calm demeanor, so when he stood before the gathered aplings, they all listened good 'n proper. "Power," he said, "is much like the art of navigating the jungle, a delicate balance of strategy, wisdom, and timing. True power lies not in brute force, but in the ability to achieve your goals with minimal conflict."

"They who know when to act and when to wait will be victorious. Understanding the nature of power means recognizing when to exert force and when to show restraint. Like a feather, power can be soft and gentle, yet its quill holds a sharp prick, capable of drawing blood when pressed just right."

Zog continued, "In the realm of power, appearance can be as important as reality. To maintain control, one must be adaptable, able to shift and change like the currents of the river, always staying one step ahead. Power is about perception, creating an image of strength and stability that others respect and follow."

"Remember," Zog concluded, his gaze sweeping over the attentive faces, "true power is not about domination, but about wise governance, strategic thinking, and the subtle art of influence. Master these, and you will master power itself."

THEY WHO KNOW WHEN TO ACT AND WHEN TO WAIT WILL BE VICTORIOUS.

*A dagger disguised as a feather – soft in appearance, sharp in intent. The essence of balancing hard and soft power. 1879.*

# THE ARCHITECTURE OF IDEOLOGY

**W**ith the sun setting over Monkey Mountain, casting dying light over its western flank, the elders gathered once more around the Hearth.
Zog turned to Kratos and Demos with a serious look. "You've listened enough, my young ones. Soon it be time for you to venture deeper inside the mountain and explore the three Chambers of Power yourselves. Only then will you truly understand how power works, flows, and operates. But before you go, you must hear one final lesson, about the power of ideas – something know as ideology."

The fire flickered as Zog leaned in, his voice steady. "Ideologies are more than just beliefs – they colour the way folk see the world and how they act within it. They provide the invisible architecture that shapes behaviour. Some ideologies unlock doors in the mind to rooms of hope, others control by locking you into darkness, but all of them hold power because they give meaning to actions, offering a handy guide – or sometimes a convenient excuse – for how groups behave and make decisions, whether they're wrangling over politics, economics, or how best to run the whole show.

He paused for a moment, watching the boys absorb his words. "Society is built not only with brick and metal – it's built with ideas. Ideologies become the stories we live by, shaping hearts, minds, and actions. They tell us how we belong, what we should strive for, and sometimes, they divide us. But no matter how subtle they are, they influence everything – often without us even noticing."

Zog's gaze deepened. "You must learn to recognize these rooms of thought, whether they set you free, or box you in. To truly understand power, you'll need to see how these ideas move through the Chambers, shaping the choices of those within. Ideologies can build, but they can also blind. Remember that, boys."

*Different ideologies govern different chambers of the collective mind – shaping thought, belief, and action, often without us even realising. 1587.*

**THEIR GOVERNANCE WAS NOT ONLY EFFECTIVE BUT ALSO RIGHTEOUS.**

## SIMPLIFICATION OF COMPLEX REALITIES

As the fire flickered, Zog spoke steadily, his gaze resting on the brothers. "Ideologies are powerful because they make sense of the world's complexities, much like ancient myths once explained the forces of nature. The world is a tangled web – economies shifting, leaders rising and falling, people pulled in different directions. Not everyone can grasp every detail, and that's where ideologies come in. They take the overwhelming and make it simple, giving folk clear ideas to hold onto."

He paused, letting the boys absorb his words. "These frameworks guide how we think about power, survival, and justice. With just a few ideas, they help even the youngest in the tribe know where they stand and what is expected, giving everyone a way to navigate the chaos around them."

*Climb into different rooms of the mind to enlighten the soul. 1567.*

## IDENTITY & BELONGING

Zog leaned forward, his voice low but sure. "Ideologies do more than just explain the world – they create belonging. They bring people together through shared beliefs, binding them into something stronger than individuals alone. When the tribe shares a common idea, it becomes more than just a group – it becomes a community with purpose."

He glanced at the boys. "It's like how the strongest bonds form when many strands are woven together. Shared beliefs make people feel connected, giving them a sense of identity. And when people stand together under the same ideals, they're harder to divide, both from within and without. These ideas make the tribe resilient – able to face struggles, not alone, but as one."

Zog sat back, watching the flickering firelight dance across the boys' faces, leaving them to reflect on the unseen power of the ideas shaping their world.

## JUSTIFICATION & LEGITIMIZATION

Zog scratched his chin and leaned closer to the fire. "See, ideologies don't just float around for fun – they anchor the way we live. They give the tribe a sense of right and wrong, justifying why things are the way they are. They show us how the world ought to be, making sure the folks in charge have the right to lead, while also leaving room to question those who might've lost their way.

"It's like this – ideologies are a kind of moral compass, helping us steer our choices in line with what we believe. They keep things running smooth, not just by being practical, but by being fair. Same way the jungle has its laws – where the river flows, where the predator hunts – ideologies make sure power and responsibility are shared in just the right measure to keep everything balanced.

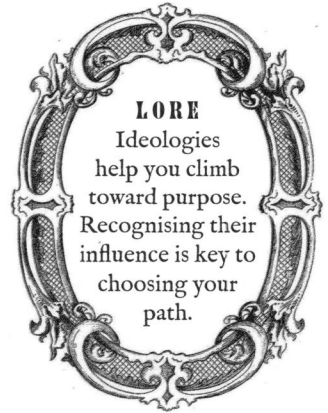

**LORE**
Ideologies help you climb toward purpose. Recognising their influence is key to choosing your path.

105

## IN TIMES OF UNCERTAINTY AND CHAOS, IDEOLOGIES OFFER COMFORT AND EXISTENTIAL SECURITY.

## PSYCHOLOGICAL COMFORT & SECURITY

Zog's voice was calm, steady like the fire's glow. "In times of chaos, ideologies give people something solid to hold on to. When the world feels unpredictable or overwhelming, these beliefs offer comfort, explaining what might otherwise seem random or out of control. They provide a sense of order – something that soothes the anxieties that creep in when the unknown looms too large." He glanced at Kratos and Demos. "It's like knowing the familiar paths of the forest; even in the dark, you can walk without fear, trusting that the way forward will reveal itself."

*The sword stands as a symbol of clarity and readiness, ensuring one can navigate life's paths with strength and purpose. 1891.*

*Just as a key unlocks hidden chambers, ideologies open doors within the mind, shaping thoughts and guiding actions. 1367.*

## THE STRUGGLE FOR POWER

Zog leaned closer, his tone sharpening. "But ideologies carry real force in the struggle for power. They're not just ideas – they're weapons, shaping how conflicts unfold. Within the tribe and beyond, different ideologies rise and clash, each reflecting deeper struggles over values, resources, and authority." His eyes flickered with intensity. "Like rival creatures in the jungle fighting for dominance, these beliefs battle for control, and whoever controls the strongest idea often holds the reins of power."

He sat back slightly, letting the firelight dance in the silence that followed. "But just as a jungle thrives with many kinds of plants and animals, a society must nurture a variety of ideas to stay strong. A single ideology can choke out growth, but a thriving mix – one that allows debate, change, and new ideas – makes the whole mountain stronger."

Zog's gaze lingered on the boys, letting the lesson settle. "Learn to recognize these struggles, and you'll understand the true force behind the beliefs that shape this world."

*Demos and Kratos explore the Urns of Ideology
under the watchful gaze of Zog. 1563.*

# URNS OF IDEOLOGY

Z og led the brothers deep into a vault that lay beneath the Hearth of Wisdom, a hidden chamber steeped in mystery.

The flickering torchlight revealed shelves lined with urns, each adorned with intricate designs, symbols, and colours. Zog stopped before a large central urn, his voice solemn. "Every ideology born from the discussions and debates around the hearth is captured here," he said, gesturing to the urns. "After each night's storytelling, the elders gather the ashes of the fire and place them into an urn. These ashes contain the essence of the ideology in its purest form, sealed away for protection."

He traced a finger over an urn decorated with the image of a rising sun. "Each urn is decorated with symbols relating to the knowledge it contains. We store them here for safety because ideologies are powerful things – they can guide minds to wisdom or, if misused, corrupt thinking entirely."

Demos eyed the urns with curiosity. "What happens if one is opened?" he asked.

**LORE**
Power is a tool - neither good nor bad. What matters is how it's used and by whom.

Zogs face darkened. "When an urn is opened, the spirit of the ideology can emerge in animal form. If the ideology is wise and pure, the animal will guide you. But if it is toxic, the creature can be dangerous – deadly, even."

Demos pointed to an urn covered in flames. "And that one?" he asked. Zog's gaze followed Demos's finger. "Inside that one is the ideology of Power," he replied gravely. "Power can be a force for vitality, or it can corrupt. The animal that emerges depends on the soul of the opener."

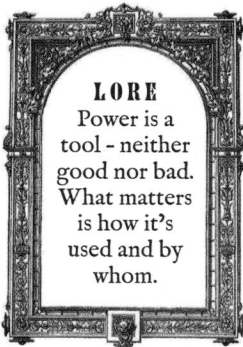

## THE ANIMAL THAT EMERGES DEPENDS ON THE SOUL OF THE OPENER.

Satisfied with his lesson, Zog turned to leave, saying, "I have matters to attend to. Be cautious while you explore."

As soon as he disappeared into the shadows, Kratos, always the mischievous one, became fixated on the urn adorned with flames. "I wonder what's really inside," he muttered, reaching for the lid."

"Kratos, don't!" Demos warned, his hand instinctively reaching to stop him. But it was too late. The lid creaked open, and in an instant, a snake slithered out, its scales shimmering with venomous intent. Before either of them could react, the snake struck, sinking its fangs into Kratos' arm.

*An Urn of Ideology adorned with birds ane other symbolism relating to the virtues contined within. 1543.*

Kratos recoiled in shock, clutching his arm as Demos shouted for help. Zog, hearing the commotion, rushed back into the vault. With swift precision, he slammed the urn's lid shut, and the snake evaporated into thin air.

"Foolish child!" Zog bellowed as he grabbed Kratos' arm, quickly sucking the venom from the wound and spitting it on the ground. "You're lucky I heard you in time! The venom might've killed you! But it appears to be gone, so let's hope the wound heals fully."

Demos, wide-eyed with shock, stuttered "I'll look after him," he promised. "I'll keep an eye on him from now on."

Zog sighed, his face softening. "See that you do lad. Ideologies are not to be foolishly played with, for they hold power far beyond our control."

*Kratos removes the lid of the Urn of Power, releasing its spirit animal in the form of a serpent. 1763.*

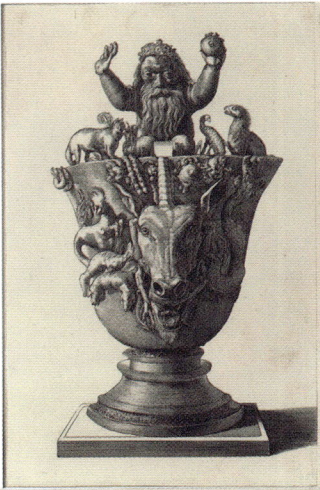

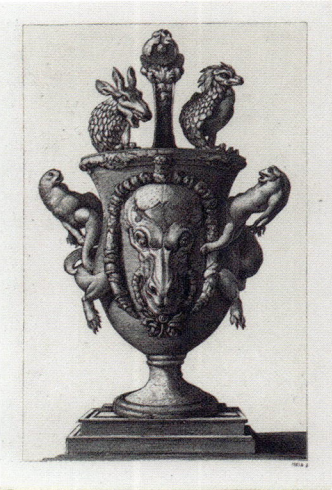

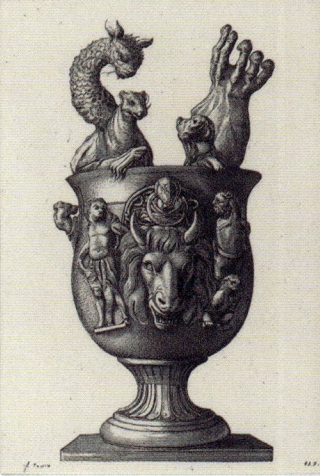

# URNS
## OF
## IDEOLOGY

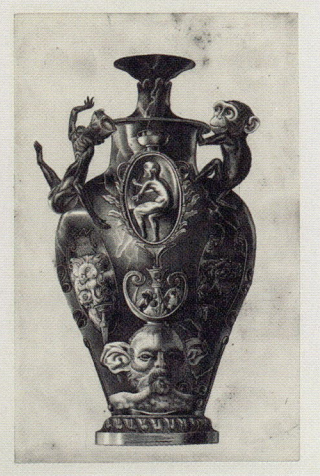

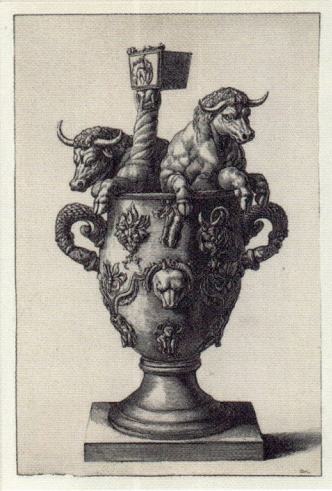

These urns hold
great power
– guiding or
corrupting those
who open them.
Handle with
care, for their
spirit reflects the
opener's soul,
shaping destiny
for better or
worse.

## YOUR DECISION SHOWS COURAGE. ONCE YOU'VE FACED YOUR INDIVIDUAL CHALLENGES, REUNITE IN THE PUBLIC CHAMBER.

"Boys, the time has come for you to continue your education elsewhere. You must now explore the Chambers of Power yourselves," said Zog. "You must continue your journey and test your resilience to see what you're really made of. Go together and learn from the teachers in each chamber."

The brothers exchanged glances, their hearts pounding with a mix of shame for what had just happened with the urn, but also excitement and trepidation.

Just as they prepared to set off, Kratos spoke up. "Demos, let's split up. We'll cover more ground and gain a deeper understanding if we each focus on a different chamber."

Demos startled at first, then nodded thoughtfully. "You're right, brother. I'll go into the Political Chamber to learn about governance and leadership."

"And I'll head into the Economic Chamber," Kratos replied, "to uncover the secrets of prosperity, production, and the business of making things."

Zog watched them with a knowing smile. "Very well, my young ones. Your decision shows courage. Once you've faced your individual challenges, reunite in the Public Chamber. There, you can share your newfound knowledge and work together to shape the future of Monkey Mountain. But beware, in all of the chambers you'll discover both virtues and vices. It's up to you how you'll react to them."

"Look after that wound young lad," Zog said to Kratos, seeing him rubbing the faint bite marks on his arm. "For venomous ideologies can warp the mind, if left to fester."

With a final nod of encouragement from Zog, Kratos and Demos hugged each other goodbye, stepping into the darkness of the mountain. Demos turned towards the Political Chamber while Kratos went down a different path.

*Demos and Kratos depart from Zog, embarking on their
voyage of discovery throughout the mountain. 1763.*

MONKEY
MOUNTAIN
As depicted
during the
industrial
age.

CHAPTER V
# THE POLITICAL CHAMBER

PRIMITIVE POWER STRUCTURES

# POLITICAL POWER V.I
## TUG-O-WAR V.II
### LIBERALISM VS AUTHORITARIANISM V.III
### PROGRESSIVE VS CONSERVATIVE V.IV
# ANARCHISM V.V
## LIBERTARIANISM V.VI
## COMMUNISM V.VII
# FASCISM V.IIX
## DEMOCRACY V.IX
## POLICY V.X
## BELIEF V.XI

*Aplings gather in the political chamber to debate the*
*virtues of differing political ideologies. 1654.*

# THE POLITICAL CHAMBER

Tucked away in the winding paths of Monkey Mountain lay the grand and solemn cavern known as The Political Chamber.

This was no ordinary place. It thrummed with echoes of old debates and decisions, the air thick with the significance of governance. Here, history felt alive, clinging to the walls like morning mist. The chamber wrapped itself around the Hearth of Wisdom – just like the planets circle the sun – flanked on either side by the Public and Economic Chambers.

The Political Chamber was a place of reverence. Towering columns, carved straight from the mountain's bones, stood like ancient guards. Torchlight flickered across the engravings on the stone walls, making scenes of power, rebellion, and governance dance as if the past were still unfolding.

When Demos stepped inside for the first time, curiosity lit up his young face. This was where ideas wrestled for control, where the direction of the mountain was shaped one debate at a time. In the center of the chamber sat Plato, an elder whose fur shone silver, as if the moon had left its mark on him. His eyes, calm and knowing, carried the quiet wisdom of someone who had seen many seasons pass.

**A MAJESTIC HALL WHERE THE DEBATES OF OLD LINGER IN THE AIR.**

Plato's gaze settled on the newcomer, a curious look softening his sharp features. "Ah, a fresh face," he said, his voice calm and steady. "If curiosity brought you here, then you are welcome to stay. Listen closely, young one, and you may yet learn how the currents of power shape the course of our tribe."

# IT'S THE ORDER THAT RISES OUT OF CHAOS.

## POLITICAL POWER

Plato, stood up to speak. "Political power," he started, "is the glue that holds our tribe together. It's the order that rises out of chaos, the beacon in a dark night. Without it, we are just leaves in the wind, scattered and aimless."

Plato leaned in, his voice quietly echoing. "Now, listen close," he said. "Harmony in governance ain't about ruling with an iron fist, but with a kind heart. A true leader guides by example – cultivates virtue within and sparks it in others. That's how you build a society that holds together, not with fear, but with trust."

He gave Demos a knowing glance. "Power, see, is the backbone of our communal life. It's where we frame justice, virtue, and the common good. But if you want to really understand it, you gotta look deeper – right into the guts of governance itself. Apling ain't built to go it alone," he said. "We're made to live in a tribe, working toward the common good. When power's used right, every member finds their place and purpose."

Then Plato's eyes grew thoughtful. "Political power," he mused, "is a quest – it's the philosopher's search for truth, the ruler's pursuit of justice. In this game, we don't just fight to survive; we aim for something higher – knowledge, wisdom, virtue."

The weight of Plato's words hung in the air, stirring thoughts Demos couldn't yet unravel. Power wasn't just rules and structure – it was a force, as likely to raise the tribe high as it was to send it tumbling into ruin. The lesson wasn't clear yet, but it was starting to take shape, like the first glimmer of sunlight creeping through the trees.

Just then, the sound of cheers, shouts, and hollers echoed through the chamber. Plato tilted his head toward the noise, a grin tugging at the corner of his mouth. "Ah," he said, "Quarrel Quadrant's getting lively."

Demos followed his gaze, curiosity pulling him along like a leaf caught in a stream. One puzzle solved, only to tumble headfirst into another.

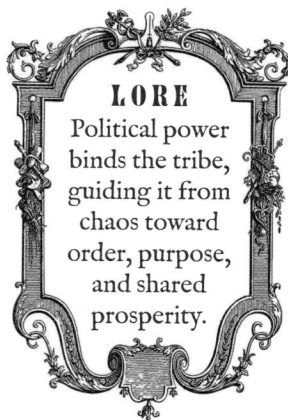

### LORE

Political power binds the tribe, guiding it from chaos toward order, purpose, and shared prosperity.

*A raucous caucus of aplings gather in the Political Chamber to discuss the intricacies of good governance. 1654.*

*In the grand tug-o-war, it's not brawn but the clash of ideas that prevails, shaping the tribe's destiny with every pull.* 1275.

# QUARREL QUADRANT

Plato led Demos to the edge of Quarrel Quadrant, where a fierce tug-o-war was stirring up all kinds of whooping, hollering, and chest-thumping from the aplings yanking in every direction.

This wasn't just any tug-o-war, mind you – it was a colossal struggle where ideas and ideologies wrestled for dominance. Ropes criss-crossed the chamber in tight lines, creating a quadrant where quarrels over governance could take place, with aplings pulling with all their strength and hearts full of conviction.

The ropes divided the chamber into four battlegrounds. The vertical pull was the struggle between Liberalism and Authoritarianism, while the horizontal tug pitted the Left against the Right. Each pull, each heave, represented an argument, a choice for the mountain's future.

Demos watched as one eager fella strained toward the top-left quadrant, shouting the virtues of communism – equality, state control, and the wisdom of sharing every last nut and berry under the sun. On the opposite end, another big brute heaved towards the top-right, arguing for order and hierarchy, insisting that a firm hand was the only way to lead the tribe safely in times of disorder.

**THE AIR WAS THICK WITH CHEERS, GRUNTS, AND THE OCCASIONAL HECKLE.**

The air was thick with cheers, grunts, and the occasional heckle – some friendly, some not. The old-timers watched with knowing eyes, while younger aplings cheered or jeered, eager to jump in. Every pull of the rope carried weight, representing a possible shift in the tribe's future.

Plato folded his arms, glancing down at Demos. "This," he said with a twinkle in his eye, "is how power is shaped – not all at once, but in little tugs and pulls. The trick is knowing which rope to hold – and when to let go."

Demos nodded slowly, his eyes fixed on the shifting ropes and the aplings struggling over them. He was beginning to understand – power wasn't just about rules or ideals. It was a messy, endless tug-of-war, a game of knowing when to grip tight and when to let it slip through your fingers.

# QUARREL QUADRANT
## AND THE TERRIBLE
# TUG-O-WAR

A determined apling pulls to the left, aiming for equality. With grit and passion, he fights for fairness and shared bounty. Each tug is a cry for justice, a bid to balance the scales in their mountain society. It's a sight that makes you believe in a fairer world.

NATIONALISM

STATE OWNERSHIP

COMMUNISM

LEFT

ECONOMIC SCALE

EQUALITY

COLLECTIVE OWNERSHIP

ANARCHISM

SOCIAL SCALE

NO GOVERNMENT

LIBERAL

FREEDOM

An apling pulls the rope toward freedom, believing that each apling ought to find their own path in life. Every tug is for personal rights and fewer restrictions, for a world where individuality flourishes and everyone has the freedom to shape their own destiny.

With a firm grip, an apling pulls toward control and order, believing only strong, centralized power can keep chaos at bay. Each tug demands obedience, pulling toward a world where one leader reigns supreme.

**AUTHORITARIAN**

PRIVATE OWNERSHIP

BIG GOVERNMENT.

**CAPITALISM**

**RIGHT**

ECONOMIC SCALE

HIERARCHY

**LIBERTARIANISM**

SMALL GOVERNMENT.

PRIVATE OWNERSHIP

Another could be inclined to pull to the right, believing that a well-organized pecking order and hierarchy is the best way to keep things running smoothly, sorta like how a beehive's got its queen and worker bees, each with their place in the grand scheme of things.

*In the grand tug-o-war, it's not brawn but the clash of ideas that prevails, shaping the tribe's destiny with every pull. 1675*

# FREEDOM & FORCE

One ruckus that never failed to stir things up was the mighty tug-o-war between Liberalism and Authoritarianism.

And let me tell you, this wasn't just any garden-variety squabble – no sir, it was a spectacle, a storm of ideas clashing head-on. On one side, you had the liberals, all about freedom, individuality, and letting every primate swing on whatever branch tickled their fancy. Leading the charge was Huck, a spry young ape with a mischievous twinkle in his eye. "Freedom's like how every plant sprouts up in the jungle." Huck would say with a grin. "Each one wild'n free, simply wanting to grow at its own pace, and live in the moment."

Huck and his crew yanked hard, calling for rights, liberty, and the pursuit of happiness. To them, life without freedom was like being a bird trapped in a cage, wings clipped and soul stifled. Rules, they figured, were nothing but fences, hemming in the wild beauty of the world and snuffing out its possibilities.

**FREEDOM ON ONE END, ORDER ON THE OTHER. TOO MUCH OF EITHER, AND THE ROPE SNAPS.**

On the other side of the rope stood Samson, a bloke as tough and immovable as an ironwood tree. "Order," he barked, his voice sharp as a whip, "is what keeps us from falling apart. Without it, we're just a bunch of monkeys swinging headlong into chaos." Samson's crew tugged back with everything they had, arguing that control, structure, and discipline were the only things keeping the tribe from slipping into anarchy. To them, rules weren't cages – they were the sturdy branches that held the tree of society upright, stopping it from crashing down.

Amid all the chaos, Demos stood beside Plato, his head spinning with the force of the arguments flying back and forth. The rope snapped and strained between freedom and order, each side pulling with fierce conviction. Plato leaned in close, his voice low and steady beneath the clamor. "It's something, isn't it?" he said. "Freedom on one end, order on the other. Too much of either, and the rope snaps." He gave Demos a sidelong glance, a flicker of mischief in his eye. "The trick, my boy, isn't just in pulling – it's in knowing how much slack to give."

# LEFT & RIGHT

A nother tug-o-war that drew folk from all corners of the mountain to watch a quarrel, was the battle between the Progressive Left and the Conservative Right.

It was a clash of visions – one side pulling toward change and innovation, the other toward tradition and stability. The Progressive Left, led by a strong female named Luna, believed in progress. "The world's a changing," she'd say, her gaze bright with conviction. "We must change with it, embrace new ideas, and build a better future for everyone." The rope strained as her followers pulled leftward, toward innovation, social justice, and a safety net to catch any primate in need. Helping their efforts was a sturdy donkey, its hooves digging into the ground as it brayed with determination.

On the other end stood the Conservative Right, anchored by Thor, an old-timer with fur gone gray from experience. "The old ways have kept us strong," Thor declared, his voice boomin' like thunder. "We must preserve our heritage, uphold our values, and maintain order." With each pull, Thor and his crew tugged the rope toward stability, personal responsibility, and a framework rooted in tradition. Beside them, a mighty elephant added its weight, trumpeting steadily as it anchored the conservative cause.

Demos watched in awe, trying to wrap his mind around the spectacle. The chamber shook with grunts, cheers, and the braying of the donkey matched by the trumpet of the elephant.

Plato, standing beside Demos, gave a slow nod, his gaze following the tugging aplings. "You see, my boy, politics isn't just about pulling the hardest – it's about learning to pull together without snapping the rope." He paused, thoughtful. "Each side thinks they've got it right, but the truth is, the mountain only holds steady when the tension between them stays just right. Too much slack, and things fall apart. Too much force, and the whole thing unravels."

*The conservatives face off to the left with the help of their beloved elephant. 1365.*

*Virgil contemplates the cost of freedom, and the fine line between liberty and responsibility. 1645.*

# RULE BY NONE

A mong the gathered crowd, one figure stood apart – Virgil, with a fierce gaze and an air of unshakable conviction, commanding attention.

"You don't need no government prowlin' around, tellin' you what you can and can't do. It's like bein' a critter in the deep woods, answerin' only to your own instincts. No chieftain, no tribal council, just you and the wild. Some might think it's like a bunch of animals, each goin' their own way. That's where the freedom lies." He said, "It's a place where creatures can explore, adapt, and find their own path through the thick vines and dense underbrush."

Demos and Plato stood on the edge of the Quad watching Virgil, muscles straining as he tugged at the ropes on the liberal and left side. His passion for freedom and equality shone through in every pull, his determination a beacon for those who believed in a more open and just society. Virgil once again turned to address the gathered crowd, his voice carrying conviction.

"The mountain, should be built on principles of shared responsibility, mutual aid, and freedom for every soul residing within. For there are dangers in clinging to old hierarchies. The anarchist is wary of the concentration of power, as it can burst like a dam if not kept in check, flooding the valley of liberty."

Demos listened intently. "You see," Virgil said, "the goal of anarchism is to create a society free from all forms of oppression, domination, and control. Instead of being ruled by fear or force, we build our world around autonomy, voluntary association, mutual aid, and equality. Picture a life where every critter stands tall on their own terms, where cooperation isn't a command but a choice. That's the promise of anarchism – a wild, untamed harmony where freedom is the only law, and trust binds us without binding our will."

As he spoke, it became clear that Virgil, with his bold presence and unflinching words, had assumed the mantle of an unchosen leader, embodying the very spirit of independence he championed. The crowd looked on, both drawn to his strength, yet wary of his unbridled power.

*Carefree and untethered, this apling dances on the edge of chaos,*
*reveling in the freedom to forge his own path.* 1510.

# RULE BY SELF

A midst the din of debates and the tugging of ropes stood another apling named Milton, his voice cut through the chaos with conviction.

"Now listen here, folks," Milton began, "Libertarianism ain't the same as anarchism, though they might seem like cousins. Anarchism is about no rulers at all, like a jungle with no paths, just wild and free. But Libertarianism is a bit more refined. It's about having as little government as possible, just enough to keep things fair and square."

Demos watched Milton tugging at the ropes on the libertarian side, his every pull symbolizing the balance between freedom and minimal governance. Milton gestured broadly. "In a libertarian society, each primate stands tall on their own, making their own choices, and bearing their own responsibilities. It's like being a critter with a clear path through the woods. The government is just there to make sure nobody's stepping on anyone else's toes."

He paused to let the idea sink in. "We believe in freedom, true enough, but with a dash of order. Property rights, personal liberties, and free markets are our guiding stars. We don't need a big, bossy alpha telling us what to do. We trust in the invisible hand of cooperation and competition to guide us."

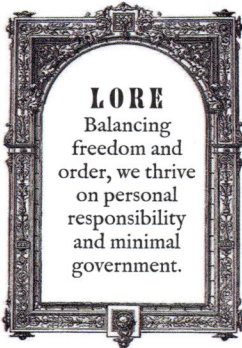

**LORE**
Balancing freedom and order, we thrive on personal responsibility and minimal government.

Milton's words painted a picture of a society where freedom and responsibility walked hand in hand. "Unlike anarchism, where there's no structure at all, Libertarianism has just enough to keep us from chaos, but not so much that it stifles our spirit."

Demos, taking it all in, felt a spark of enlightenment. Milton's vision of Libertarianism offered a middle path between the wild freedom of anarchism and the rigid control of authoritarianism. It offered a delicate balance of autonomy and order, where all folk could live peacefully with liberty.

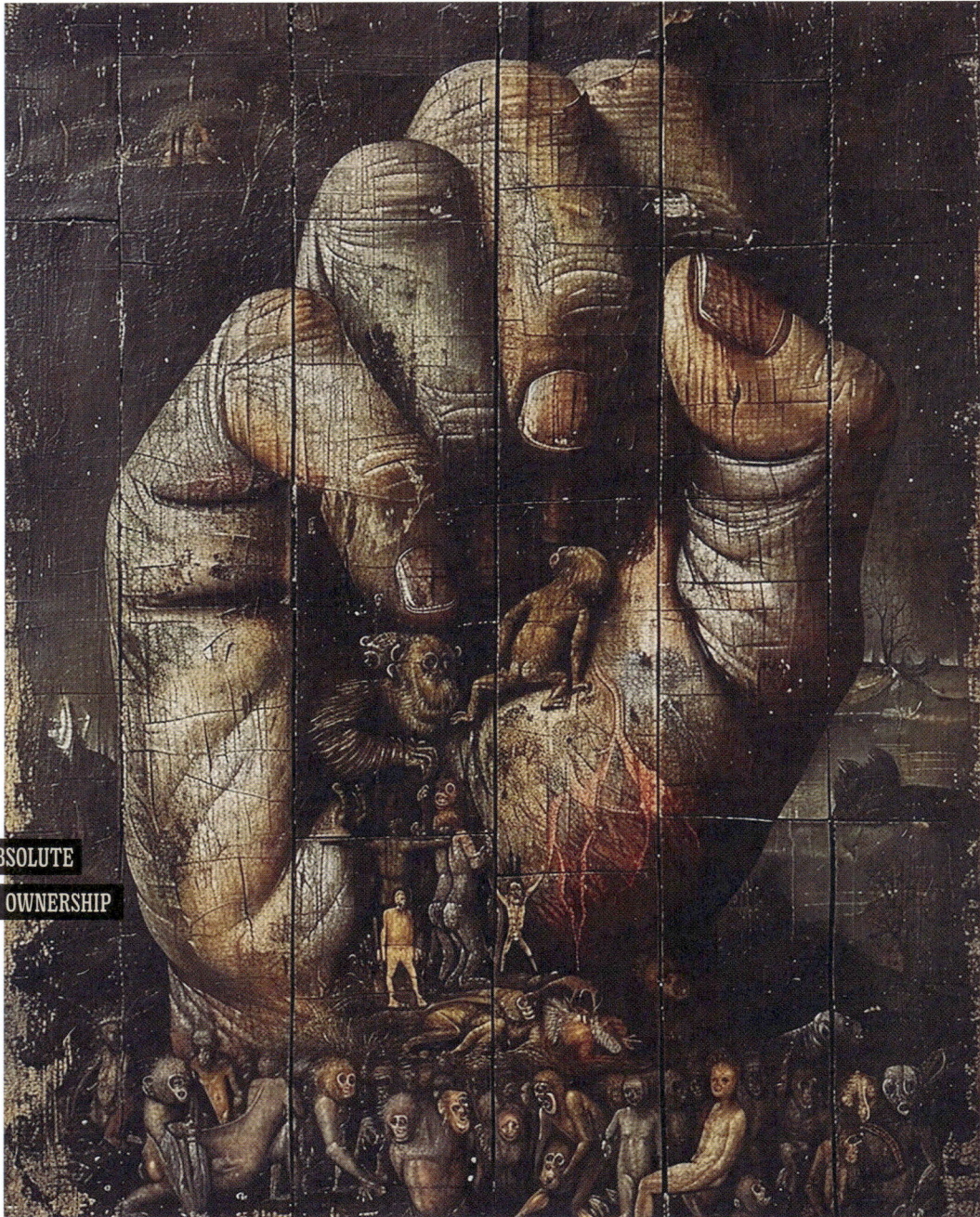

ABSOLUTE

OWNERSHIP

*Communism holds the lives of many within its grasp – a*
*warning of control when authority turns absolute. 1562*

# RULE BY ALL

T he air crackled with anticipation, as a powerful figure named Friedrich stepped forward, his presence commanding attention.

Known for his fiery rhetoric and revolutionary spirit, Friedrich was about to make his case for Communism. He seized the rope, his muscular arms rippling from days spent working hard, and with great gusto, began to pull.

"Comrades," he roared, voice echoing around Quarrel Quadrant, "Communism is the path to true equality, where the fruits of our labour are shared by all, not hoarded by a greedy few. Imagine a society where every apling contributes according to their ability and receives according to their needs. No more oppression, no more exploitation – just pure, unadulterated fairness!"

**COLLECTIVE GOOD OVER INDIVIDUAL GAIN**

The aplings gathered around watched in awe as Friedrich's fervor seemed to electrify the very air. He painted a picture of a world where wealth and power were evenly distributed, where the chains of class and privilege were shattered. "In our commune," he continued, "we work together, we live together, and we thrive together. There is no place for selfishness or greed. Each of us is an equal part of the whole, and together, we are unstoppable!"

Friedrich's tug on the rope was more than just physical; it was a call to arms, a rallying cry for revolution. His vision of communism was a society reborn, where the collective good trumped individual gain. The ground seemed to tremble with the force of his conviction.

Demos stood at the edge, heart pounding, caught between admiration and doubt. Plato, standing beside him with arms folded, leaned in slightly and murmured, "There's power in that vision, no doubt. But when the collective becomes everything, and the individual nothing, the line between fairness and tyranny gets mighty thin. Revolutions, my boy, have a habit of eating their own."

Demos blinked, Plato's words settling over him, realizing that the ideals tugged at both ends of the rope were never as simple as they seemed.

# RULE BY ONE

N ow, the air was really thick with tension as a commanding fella named Mosley stepped forward, his presence imposing.

Known for his authoritarian views and fierce loyalty to order, Mosley was about to make his case for Fascism. He seized the rope, yanking it away from Virgil, Milton and Freidrich, his grip firm and unyielding, as he began to pull with a determined force.

"Citizens of the mountain," Mosley began, his voice cutting through the murmur of the crowd, "Fascism is the path to unity and strength. It is where we find our true power, not in fragmented voices but in a single, unwavering direction. Imagine a society where there is no confusion, no dissent – only the clear and decisive leadership of a strong ruler."

The crowd watched with a mix of fascination and apprehension as Mosley continued. "In a fascist state, we prioritize the nation above all. Individual freedoms are secondary to the greater good. We need a leader who embodies our collective will, who can guide us with a firm hand and protect us from threats. This is not about oppression, but about creating order from chaos."

Mosley's eyes gleamed with fervor as he painted a picture of a society united under one leader. "Our enemies will tremble before us," he declared. "With strong, centralized power, we achieve greatness. We will be disciplined, organized, and relentless. The weak will be purged, and only the strong will lead us into a new era of prosperity." Demos watched in horror. The vision of a society sacrificing individual freedoms for the promise of strength was chilling.

Plato, who had stood silently until now, stepped forward with calm determination. "We mustn't let the promise of order blind us to the cost of freedom," he said, his voice cutting through the noise of the raucous crowd.

Without hesitation, Plato reached for the rope and with one swift, deliberate yank, pulled it free, sending Mosley stumbling back. Plato held the rope high for all to see. "Listen up, folks," he said, "Let me tell you of a system stronger than any built by fear or force – one where strength and freedom are balanced together."

*Mosley raises his fist, leading the charge with banners high,*
*promising change through order and authority. 1564.*

*Draped in wisdom, Plato holds the balance of worlds in his grasp,*
*mapping the course of governance with steady hands. 1564.*

# RULE BY CONSENT

The air hung heavy, thick with tension, like the sky before a thunderstorm breaks.

Quarrel Quadrant buzzed with the fiery energy of clashing ideologies, each one straining to pull the mountain's future in a different direction. Virgil had hollered for the wild, untamed freedom of Anarchism, while Milton had fought tooth and nail for the rugged individualism of Libertarianism. Friedrich, driven by his dreams of collective equality, had thrown his weight behind Communism. And then there was Mosley, who sent a chill through the crowd with his call for order through Fascism, tugging hard toward a vision of control and submission. Each of them had gripped the rope, straining with every ounce of conviction they had, while the crowd looked on, transfixed by the raw force of the debate.

Now, the moment everyone had been waiting for had arrived. Plato, cool as a cucumber, stepped forward, a sly glint of mischief flickering in his eye like he knew something the others had missed. As he moved to the center, the noise in the chamber died down, curiosity sweeping over the crowd. All eyes were on him.

Plato took hold of the rope. But instead of yanking it to one side or the other, he placed one foot firmly in the quadrant of liberty, then pulled it deliberately toward the middle, slow and steady, as if to show that strength lay not in force but in balance.

"Folks," Plato began, his voice steady and sure, "we've heard calls for equality, for freedom without limits, and for as little governance as possible. But here's the truth: the best path lies in balance. You might've heard of it – Democracy. It's an idea where every voice gets a say, and no one vision drowns out the others. Here, power is shared and kept in check, so neither chaos nor tyranny can take hold. Democracy lets us shape our future together, keeping us free but united, with the wisdom of many guiding the way forward."

## THE TRIBE CONSTANTLY NEGOTIATED THE DELICATE BALANCE OF POWER, FREEDOM, AND JUSTICE.

With every word, Plato pulled harder, bringing the rope steadily toward the centre. "A Liberal Democracy is about consent," he said, "about finding common ground between extremes. It's balancing the needs of the many with the rights of the individual. We must take the best from all ideas to build a fair and just society."

The opposing ideologies began to wobble under the weight of his words. Friedrich's dream of communal equality faltered as Plato revealed how equality, without limits, could slip into tyranny. Virgil's anarchistic utopia unraveled as Plato pointed out the chaos that followed without rules to guide the tribe.

FREE ELECTIONS

INDIVIDUAL RIGHTS

RULE OF LAW

MAJORITY RULE

CITIZEN RIGHTS

*Friedrich contemplates the struggle ahead in Quarrel Quadrant. 1327.*

For a moment, it looked like Plato might lose his footing, the force of competing ideas almost pulling him down. But he reached out and grasped the hand of another apling – Adam, the keeper of a curious idea known as capitalism. Together, they pulled toward a vision that blended freedom and order, prosperity and fairness.

"With Liberal Democracy," Plato declared, "we build a society that thrives through participation, balance, and the rule of law."

With one final, mighty heave, Plato and Adam yanked the rope toward the centre, the other ideologies falling away under the strength of their balanced vision. The chamber burst into applause, and from the sidelines, Demos felt hope swell within him.

Democracy, it seemed, was the beacon that could guide their mountain toward a brighter, more harmonious future.

Plato stood tall in Quarrel Quadrant, the rope firm in his hands. As the room fell silent, he tugged it away from the extremes one last time, his voice steady and full of purpose, ready to lay out his vision in detail:

## POPULAR SOVEREIGNTY

"Folks, Democracy is built on some solid principles, starting with Popular Sovereignty. This means that the people are the ultimate source of political authority and power. The government doesn't just get to do whatever it pleases. Its legitimacy comes from the consent of the governed. It's your say-so that puts those folks in power, and they ought to remember it." Plato paused, letting the idea sink in before moving on.

*Writing by candle light words for the tug-o-war. 1562.*

## POLITICAL EQUALITY

"Next up is Political Equality. In a true democracy, all citizens have equal political rights, freedoms, and opportunities to participate in the political process. It doesn't matter about sexual orientation, if you're rich or poor, young or old, male or female – every vote carries equal weight. We're all in this together, and everyone's voice matters."

## MAJORITY RULE WITH MINORITY RIGHTS

He took a deep breath and continued, "Now, Majority Rule with Minority Rights is crucial. Sure, the will of the majority prevails, but that doesn't mean we trample over the minorities. Their rights must be protected too. They deserve a voice and a chance to influence decisions, even if they aren't in the majority."

**THEY WORK FOR YOU, NOT THE OTHER WAY AROUND.**

## FREE & FAIR ELECTIONS

Plato's eyes sparkled with determination. "Free and Fair Elections are the bedrock of democracy. Citizens must have the right to choose their political leaders through free, fair, and frequent elections with universal adult suffrage. Elections should be competitive and free from fraud or intimidation. Your vote should count, plain and simple."

## ACCOUNTABILITY & TRANSPARENCY

He leaned in, emphasizing his next point. "Accountability and Transparency are non-negotiable. Democratic governments must be accountable to the people. You have the right to access information and scrutinize the actions of your elected officials. They work for you, not the other way round."

## CONSTITUTIONAL LIMITS

Plato straightened up and declared, "Constitutional Limits are there to keep everyone in check. The powers of the government are defined and limited by a constitution or something similar that protects the rights and freedoms of citizens. No individual or group is above the law."

## PLURALISM & DIVERSITY

His voice grew more passionate. "Pluralism and Diversity are the lifeblood of democracy. It respects political, ideological, and cultural differences. It protects the rights of dissent, freedom of expression, association, and the press. We're a big, varied bunch, and that's our strength."

## CIVIC PARTICIPATION

Plato looked around the chamber, his gaze steady. "Civic Participation is about more than just voting. Citizens have the right and means to get involved in the political process, through civic engagement, advocacy, and oversight of government. Democracy thrives when folks roll up their sleeves and get involved."

## RULE OF LAW

He raised his hand for emphasis. "Rule of Law means all citizens, including elected officials, are subject to the law and equal protection under the law. An independent judiciary upholds this principle, ensuring fairness and justice."

## SEPARATION OF POWERS

Plato let the rope settle, his eyes sweeping over the gathered crowd as his final words hung in the air. "Separation of Powers," he said, "is what keeps things running smooth. It spreads authority across different branches – executive, legislative, and judicial – so no one group can tighten its grip too much. Checks and balances, folks, that's the name of the game."

The chamber was unusually quiet, as if every apling present had caught a glimpse of something bigger than themselves. Demos, still lingering in the shadows, felt the gears of his mind turning. The beauty of democracy wasn't just in the rules themselves – it was in how those rules kept power balanced, how they gave room for every voice to be heard.

Plato gave a small smile and dusted his hands off. "Now," he said, "I reckon it's time to show you all how the nuts and bolts fit together – how the whole machine of democracy works in practice." With that, he turned toward the far end of the chamber, gesturing for the others to follow, leaving Demos to trail behind, eager to see just how all the moving parts kept the mountain running.

ALL CITIZENS ARE SUBJECT TO THE LAW

# NUTS & BOLTS OF DEMOCRACY

Now, democracy is a system built on a few rock-solid ideas that give folks a say and keep things fair – or, at least, that's the promise. At its heart, it's got freedom, control by the people, and good ol' equality being the principles which keep a well oiled society ticking along.

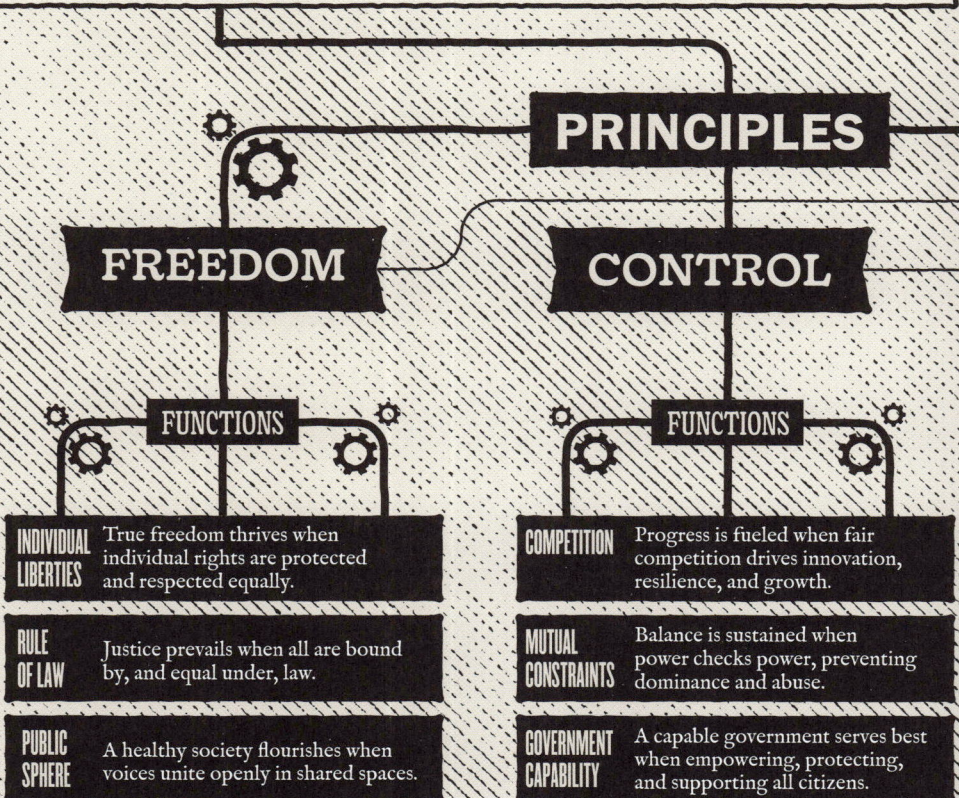

## PRINCIPLES

### FREEDOM

#### FUNCTIONS

**INDIVIDUAL LIBERTIES** — True freedom thrives when individual rights are protected and respected equally.

**RULE OF LAW** — Justice prevails when all are bound by, and equal under, law.

**PUBLIC SPHERE** — A healthy society flourishes when voices unite openly in shared spaces.

### CONTROL

#### FUNCTIONS

**COMPETITION** — Progress is fueled when fair competition drives innovation, resilience, and growth.

**MUTUAL CONSTRAINTS** — Balance is sustained when power checks power, preventing dominance and abuse.

**GOVERNMENT CAPABILITY** — A capable government serves best when empowering, protecting, and supporting all citizens.

**FREEDOM:** covers the basics: the right to speak your mind, make your own choices, and even shape your livelihood. It's about giving every individual the space to live according to their own values and beliefs without undue interference.

**CONTROL:** Popular control is the idea that power rests with the people. This means free elections, where citizens choose their leaders, and the expectation that those leaders will be held accountable for their actions. In a democracy, the people hold the reins.

**EQUALITY:** ensures that every citizen has the same rights, the same vote, and stands equal before the law. No matter one's background or status, each individual's voice carries equal weight in the democratic process.

## EQUALITY

### FUNCTIONS

**TRANSPARENCY** Trust is built when actions are clear, honest, and openly shared.

**PARTICIPATION** A thriving community emerges when everyone's voice is actively engaged.

**REPRESENTATION** True democracy exists when leaders genuinely reflect the people's diverse interests.

## ETYMOLOGY

Demos means 'the people,' while kratos means 'power' or 'rule.' Put 'em together and democracy literally means "power of the people."

## DEMOS: THE PEOPLE

In a democracy, demos represents every citizen, emphasizing that governance is a shared responsibility. Instead of power flowing from the top down, democracy places decision-making directly in the hands of the people, making each citizen's voice a part of the whole.

## KRATOS: THE POWER

Kratos signifies the authority and strength of collective action. In a true democracy, this "power" is exercised through voting, representation, and participation, ensuring that leaders remain accountable and that decisions reflect the will and welfare of the people.

*The Hawk and the Dove take flight, embodying the eternal balance between war and peace, as an apling watches from below, pondering which path the future may follow. 1564.*

# THE HAWK & THE DOVE

Plato rested a hand on Demos's shoulder and nodded toward the rafters. "Now that democracy's found its footing, it's time you met two birds who rule the skies – the Hawk and the Dove."

He pointed to the pair perched high above Quarrel Quadrant. "Watch closely, my boy. You'll learn a lot about how a society handles peace and conflict."

With a signal, the birds were released to the cheers of the crowd. The Dove, gliding gracefully, was a symbol of peace and pacifism. Aplings who favoured diplomacy over war tossed flowers into the air, petals swirling as the Dove soared overhead. It was a beautiful, hopeful gesture – one that symbolized a preference for peaceful foreign policy, beyond the mountain realms.

But then came the Hawk, wings wide and talons ready. It darted low, scanning for the scraps of meat hurled by those who believed in strength through conflict. Aplings who saw war as a necessary tool tossed their offerings skyward with wild whoops, sparking a frenzy of cheering and shouting. This spectacle wasn't just for show – it was a way for aplings to declare their stance, each one finding kin among those who flung petals or meat.

**LORE**

A society must balance the dove's peace with the hawk's vigilance to safeguard freedom.

The Hawk, true to its nature, snapped up the scraps with sharp precision, carrying them to the corner of the chamber where the blob of defence and intelligence services lurked. There, it dropped the offerings like trophies of loyalty, an act of obedience to the machinery of war and control.

Demos watched, taking in the chaotic blend of cheers, flowers, and flying meat. Plato folded his arms and murmured, "That's democracy, my boy – a place where peace and war live side by side, and everyone shows their hand one way or another." Demos nodded, the dance between idealism and pragmatism was slowly starting to make more sense.

*Myths and dreams weave possibility and reality together, guiding rulers and the ruled toward visions of destiny – whether uplifting or delusional. 1562.*

# Myths & Dreams

As the crowd began to drift away, Plato rested a hand on Demos's shoulder, sensing the boy's thoughts still tangled like vines.

"You've heard a lot today about the mechanics of democracy – checks and balances, the rule of law, representation, how military force is wielded by birds of prey. But there's something deeper, something that isn't talked about as openly. The secret of political power isn't just in its structure or laws. No, truth be told, it's in the myths and dreams that a society builds around itself."

Demos looked up, eyes wide with intrigue. Plato continued, "You see, it's not enough for rulers to merely govern; the people have to believe in the dream of something greater. It's the myth of what a society can become that binds us all together. The idea that there's a higher destiny, a utopia, or a shared purpose, is what gives rulers the authority to lead, and apling, the will to follow."

Plato paused, allowing Demos to process the thought. "We all buy into the idea that our society is special, that we're part of something larger than ourselves. That belief becomes the real glue, the magic stronger than any law."

Demos frowned, considering the implications. "So, the myths are more important than the rules?" he asked. "In many ways, yes," Plato nodded. "The laws can only govern what people do. But myths and dreams govern what people believe. And when people believe, they give power willingly, they strive, they sacrifice. That's the real secret. It's the belief in a brighter future, in a shared destiny, that gives rulers the power to rule and keep this mountain building upwards"

"You've learned plenty today lad, but now it's time to sleep and dream. Dreams are where these lessons take root. Because who knows – the future of this mountain might be waiting for you inside your next dream." With that, Plato turned and walked away, leaving Demos to ponder the possibilities stirring in his mind.

MONKEY MOUNTAIN

As depicted during the Renaissance era.

CHAPTER VI
# THE ECONOMIC CHAMBER

PRIMITIVE POWER STRUCTURES

# ECONOMIC VI.I

# POWER

## CAPITALISM VI.II

## THE FREE MARKET VI.III

# TAX VI.IV

## ECONOMIC CYCLES VI.V

## SOCIALISM VI.VI

## DEFENCE BUDGET VI.IX

*The Great Engine drives the mountain's prosperity, a bustling hive of industry, trade, and invention, where every gear and piston turns with purpose. 1428.*

# THE POWER OF PRODUCTION

**K**ratos sauntered down the winding grand hallway, shoulders rolling loose as he gave the heavy doors a shove.

They groaned open, and what lay beyond hit him square in the senses. The Economic Chamber was no quiet affair – it roared with life. Stalls bustled with aplings haggling, trading, and bartering, their tables stacked with exotic fruits, finely crafted tools, and trinkets polished to a shine. Along the cavernous walls, intricate artworks told stories of sweat and ingenuity, every piece a nod to the aplings' tireless spirit.

At the heart of it all, looming large, sat The Great Engine. It churned and clanged in sync with another strange beast the mountain folk called the Aqua Exchange – a mighty contraption of gleaming metal and polished stone. Massive gears turned with steady purpose, pistons pumping in perfect rhythm, as the sound of rushing water echoed through the chamber. The size of these structures alone demanded attention, towering over the bazaar like ancient gods.

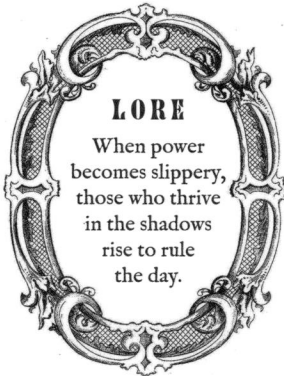

**LORE**

When power becomes slippery, those who thrive in the shadows rise to rule the day.

Pipes, thick as tree trunks, snaked out from the Engine and Aqua Exchange, stretching into every corner of the mountain. These conduits carried the lifeblood of the mountain's economy – resources, wealth, and opportunity – ensuring that no part of Monkey Mountain was left untouched. The intricate tangle of gears and wires was a marvel in itself, a testament to how tightly woven the aplings' labour was with the prosperity that kept the whole machine humming.

## THE MARKETPLACE

The marketplace buzzed with the sounds of bartering and the clinking of coins, as vendors showcased their goods to eager buyers. Every transaction, every exchange, played a small part in the vast machinery of the mountain's economy. The air was filled with the hum of creativity and innovation, as new inventions and ideas were born within the chamber. With every new creation, greater power accumulated within the huge chamber, which was then channelled and dispersed throughout the mountain accordingly.

## THE AIR WAS FILLED WITH THE HUM OF CREATIVITY & INNOVATION.

Kratos wandered through the Chamber, his senses overwhelmed by the vibrancy and dynamism of the scene before him. He couldn't help but admire his fellow aplings, whose hard work and resourcefulness had transformed the mountain into a thriving centre of economic activity. The bustling marketplace, the Great Engine, and the mighty Aqua Exchange, with its network of pipes 'n pistons all represented the unity and strength of their society.

Kratos figured, if he was gonna learn how it all worked, how economic power could keep the mountain perpetually growing upwards, then he'd need to explore every nook and cranny of it.

*The bustling forces of trade and invention converge, where ambition shapes tools and wealth into the machinery of progress – or folly. 1296.*

*The Great Engine roars to life as countless aplings work in unison – every gear turned, every spark ignited, a testament to the collective effort driving the mountain's prosperity. 1493.*

# THE GREAT ENGINE

With curiosity piqued by the sights and sounds of economic power, Kratos ventured closer to the Great Engine, that awe-inspiring machine that powered Monkey Mountain's industry.

Its rhythmic clanks and hums echoed through the cavern, radiating energy that seemed to fuel the entire operation. "Ah, a newcomer!" a voice called out, snapping Kratos from his thoughts. A grease-stained apling with a wide grin approached, wiping his hands on a rag. "Name's Cog," he said, "and you've got the look of someone curious about how this grand 'ol contraption works."

Kratos nodded eagerly. "Well then, come along, and I'll give you the tour of the Great Engine," Cog said, opening a hatch and leading Kratos inside. The inner workings were a mesmerizing sight – gears turning, pistons pumping, and energy flowing seamlessly through pipes sprawling out in all directions.

"This," Cog explained, gesturing toward the massive machinery, "is where we harness the power of capitalism. We use the energy generated here, lubricated by the flow from the Aqua Exchange, to fuel all manner of industries. Every wheel that turns, every spark that flies, represents the flow of trade, investment, and production on our mountain."

Kratos marveled at the intricate integration of machinery, though he was barely able to wrap his mind around how it all worked. The sheer scale of the engine hinted at the overwhelming complexity of the economy it fueled, and as he listened to Cog's enthusiastic explanations, curiosity gnawed at him. He couldn't fully grasp it, but he knew enough to sense how vital this engine was to keeping the mountain's industries alive and turning.

## THE PRODUCTION ROOM

Cog led Kratos to the first section. "This here is the Production room." Cog explained. "It's where raw materials are turned into valuable goods by the skilled hands of the working class. From farmers and miners to craftsmen and artisans, production is the heartbeat of economic life. Innovation, labour, and resourcefulness all converge here, laying the foundation for our prosperity."

## THE DISTRIBUTION NETWORK

Next, Cog pointed to a network of pipes and conveyors. "And this," he said, "is the Distribution Network, the arteries of the economy. It ensures that goods produced reach every corner of Monkey Mountain. Traders, merchants, and transporters all play their part, moving products from creators to consumers. Efficient distribution is key to making sure everyone benefits from the fruits of our labour."

## THE CONSUMPTION ZONE

They moved to an area where apples were being packed and sent off. "Here we have the Consumption Zone," Cog explained. "This is where the apples find their purpose. Aplings eat and enjoy these apples, driving demand and sparking the cycle anew. Consumption reflects the needs and desires of our community, sustaining the economy and prompting further production and innovation."

## THE TECHNOLOGY SECTOR

Finally, Cog took Kratos to a section filled with advanced tools and devices. "And here we have the Technology Sector," Cog said with a grin. "Innovations in tools and processes amplify every step, making production swifter, distribution broader, and consumption more efficient. From the first stone tools to the latest digital marvels, tech is what keeps the wheels of the economy turning faster and smoother, pushing the boundaries of what's possible in this big 'ol mountain."

**LORE**

In the realm of capitalism, the fruits of labour and competition flourish, rewarding the diligent and sparking innovation. Yet, it must be tempered with justice and regulation, lest greed and inequality prevail.

*Aplings bustle in a frenzy of trade and consumption, baskets overflowing with goods – each transaction feeding the endless cycle of desire and demand.* 1549.

# THE INVISIBLE HAND

**K**ratos, still dazzled by the Great Engine, drifted back into the bustling bazaar, drawn in by the shouts of vendors and the thrill of trade.

Weaving through the crowds, he came across the elder Adam. "Ah, now there's a familiar face," he said, his voice warm and knowing. "You've got the same curious glint as the lad I saw lurking near the Political Chamber earlier, watching me and Plato wrestle with the tug-o-war over democracy and power.

But if you're sniffing around here, I reckon you're after answers of a different kind – something more elusive, like the force that keep capitalism moving. Let me tell you about something you can't see – the Invisible Hand."

Kratos tilted his head, intrigued, as Adam continued. "In a free market, everyone's out to do what's best for themselves – buying, selling, scheming. But here's the magic: even though every apling pulls their own way, the whole thing drifts toward balance, as though an invisible hand were guiding the whole show!"

Adam swept a hand toward the bustling stalls. "Look at these traders. They set their prices based on what they think they can get. Price it too high, and the goods just sit there. Too low, and they won't be able to restock fast enough. Through hundreds of these little exchanges, the market sorts itself out, sending things where they're needed."

He nodded toward a fruit vendor haggling with a customer. "See that? Both of them are just looking out for themselves – the buyer wants a bargain, the seller wants to make a profit. But both walk away satisfied. Now imagine that same dance happening a thousand times over, and you've got yourself an economy that's always adjusting, always in motion."

Kratos marvelled at the simple brilliance of it all. The free market wasn't controlled from above, nor did it need to be. Ambition drove it forward, and somehow, as though guided by some unseen force, it all worked in harmony.

*An unseen force guides the flow of commerce, where individual pursuits align into collective balance – the invisible hand moves all, without plan or control. 1536.*

*The Aqua Exchange pumps blood, sweat and tears up the mountain through a complex network of pumps – transforming individual effort into shared prosperity. 1537.*

# THE AQUA EXCHANGE

L ike a bug eyed critter full of curiosity, Kratos worked his way through the labyrinth of market stalls, making his way toward the epicenter of the Economic Chamber – the Aqua Exchange.

This colossal water pump, standing tall and grand, was a vital organ in the anatomy of the mountain. It was here, amidst the clamour and commotion, that the aplings gathered, their faces glowing with the satisfaction of a day well-spent, carrying with them the essence of their labour – blood, sweat, and tears.

Looking up at the Aqua Exchange, Kratos couldn't help but marvel at the sheer scale of the operation. The place was a buzzing hive of activity, with giant gears and pistons working in harmony, much like the aplings themselves. Around him, workers poured their precious cargo into vast collection basins, where it was carefully measured and purified. Part ritual, part process, each apling's contribution to the common good was obvious for all to see.

## BLOOD, SWEAT & TEARS

The collected liquid, a potent brew of toil and dedication, was subjected to rigorous filtration, transforming into clean, lean aqua. This aqua, the lifeblood of their society, was then funnelled into an intricate web of pipes and pumps, ready for its upward journey. Kratos watched, spellbound, as the mighty system roared to life, the pumps churning and the pipes vibrating with their watery cargo.

**LORE**
Selfless contribution strengthens community and fosters a just, society.

## THE PIPES SNAKED THEIR WAY UP THE MOUNTAIN'S RUGGED SLOPES.

## THE CIRCULATORY SYSTEM

The Aqua Exchange, he soon realized, was more than a mechanical marvel; it was the circulatory system, ensuring the distribution of financial resources throughout their society, watering public services, infrastructure, and maintaining the overall health and stability of the economic body. While the aplings could accumulate personal wealth, they were required to give back some of their blood, sweat, and tears for the greater good. This system of taxation was a foundational pillar of their community, funding the infrastructure and services that kept their society flourishing.

As the aqua began its ascent, Kratos followed its journey with a mix of wonder and admiration. The pipes snaked their way up the mountain's rugged slopes, carrying the purified liquid to the summit. From there, the aqua cascaded into a sophisticated irrigation system, flowing back down the mountain, nourishing one and all on its way.

## PUBLIC SERVICE

First in line to receive this life-giving stream were the public waterways, nourishing the fields and orchards tended by the aplings. Crops of every kind flourished under the careful management of these irrigation channels, ensuring a bountiful harvest for all. The aqua also fed into reservoirs that provided fresh drinking water, reinforcing the idea that every drop of sweat contributed to the collective well-being.

But the aqua's journey didn't end with agriculture. It seeped into every crevice of Monkey Mountain's institutions, hydrating the foundations of their economy, politics, and culture. Schools, libraries, and hospitals thrived, offering education, health, and innovation to all. The Political Chamber, where the future of Monkey Mountain was debated and decided, also relied on this vital resource, ensuring governance was just as well watered.

While the Aqua Exchange sat squarely in the Economic Chamber, its operations were anything but independent. Kratos discovered a network of levers and pulleys stretching back to the Political Chamber, subtly pulling the strings. These hidden mechanisms ensured the Political Chamber controlled the flow of resources, shaping the mountain's economic landscape to its liking.

Hearing footsteps, Kratos turned around to see a police force patrolling the Exchange and the bustling bazaar. A realization dawned on him. These officers, with their vigilant eyes and authoritative presence, were also extensions of the Political Chamber's reach, maintaining order and enforcing laws from on high.

Kratos was wide-eyed with wonder at the intricate web of power connecting every facet of life on Monkey Mountain. The Political Chamber's invisible pulleys and levers, guided the economy, ensuring that wealth and influence flowed according to its grand design. It was a revelation that the real power lay in the interconnectedness of their society, where governance and prosperity were two sides of the same coin.

THESE HIDDEN MECHANISMS ENSURED THE POLITICAL CHAMBER CONTROLLED THE FLOW OF RESOURCES.

*An apling stoically contributes his blood, sweat and tears to the Aqua Exchange. 1442.*

*Locked in an eternal struggle, the bull charges with reckless optimism, while the bear swipes with cautious restraint – a brutal dance of boom and bust. 1540.*

# BATTLE OF THE BULL & BEAR

Having walked around the perimeter of the Aqua Exchange, Kratos found himself back in the bustling bazaar, where the hum of commerce and the clatter of trade filled the air.

The scene was alive with aplings peddling their wares, haggling over prices, and exchanging goods with fervor. But today, there was a palpable excitement, an electric buzz that made the fur on the back of Kratos' neck stand on end.

The sound of drums echoed through the chamber, growing louder. The crowd parted, creating a path down the centre of the bazaar. Kratos, intrigued, pushed his way to the front. He saw a parade unlike any other, led by a massive bear and a wild, raging bull, both bound in heavy iron shackles. The bear, dark and menacing, lumbered forward with a growl. The bull, a beast of pure muscle, snorted and pawed at the ground.

The aplings, eyes wide with anticipation, lined the path, their cheers and shouts mingling with the pounding drums. The bear and bull were led to the centre of the economic chamber, where a large arena awaited them. With a flourish, the handlers removed the shackles, releasing the beasts. The crowd held its breath as the two titans sized each other up, tension thick in the air.

Kratos could feel the raw power emanating from both creatures. The bear represented sluggish markets, times of economic downturn and depression. The bull stood for exuberant times, periods of growth and prosperity.

**LORE**

In the wild dance of markets, the bear and bull clash, but it's balance, not brute force, that sustains prosperity and weathers the storm of uncertainty.

# THE CLASH WAS BRUTAL & BLOODY, EACH CREATURE GIVING AS GOOD AS IT GOT.

*The bull prevails in the never ending cycles of boom and bust. 1439.*

## THE BATTLE OF MARKET FORCES

With a roar, the battle began. The bear charged, swiping with its massive paws, while the bull met it head-on, horns slashing through the air. The clash was brutal and bloody, each creature giving as good as it got. The aplings watched in rapt attention, their cheers rising and falling with the tide of the battle.

For what seemed like an eternity, the bear and the bull fought with savage intensity. Gradually, the tide began to turn. The bull, driven by an indomitable spirit, pressed its advantage. With a final, powerful thrust of its horns, it struck the bear a mortal blow. The great bear staggered, let out a pained growl, and collapsed, its life ebbing away.

The crowd erupted in wild cheers, the aplings' voices a cacophony of triumph and relief. The death of the bear signified the end of the depressed markets and heralded the rise of the bull market. Kratos watched as the aplings celebrated, their faces alight with ecstasy.

## CONSUMERISM IN THE BULL MARKET

With the bear defeated, the machinery of the Economic Chamber roared back to life. The marketplace buzzed with renewed vigor as consumerism took hold. Stalls brimmed with goods, and the aplings moved about with eager excitement, their eyes gleaming at the endless array of choices. The allure of new possessions and the promise of happiness through material wealth drove them to spend their earnings.

Kratos observed how consumerism influenced every aspect of life on the mountain. The desire for status symbols and the latest gadgets drove aplings to work harder and continually seek better opportunities. But while this relentless pursuit of material goods spurred economic activity and innovation, it also led to a culture of excess and competition.

As Kratos wandered through the now bustling bazaar, he couldn't help but think about the lesson he'd just witnessed. The battle between the bull and the bear was a reminder that their economy, much like the beasts themselves, was subject to forces beyond any one person's control. It was a dance of expansion and contraction, of booms and busts, each phase necessary for the other to exist. The true strength of Monkey Mountain lay not in its ability to avoid these cycles but in its resilience and adaptability.

## REVOLUTIONARY IN THE CROWD

However, as the celebration continued, a sharp voice cut through the crowd. "This system will fail." cried Rarx, a fiery-eyed fella with a passionate demeanor. "Capitalism benefits only an elite few at the expense of the masses. It creates vast inequalities and concentrates wealth in the hands of a privileged minority. The majority are left to toil with little reward. I have an alternative theory, one that promises fairness and equality for all. Where resources and power are shared collectively, ensuring that every apling receives their fair share of the mountain's bounty. I call it socialism."

# THE HEART & HOPE OF SOCIALISM

Rarx jumped upon a podium, his voice echoing with conviction, "Comrades and fellow aplings, today, I bring you a vision of a new dawn, a path to break free from the chains of inequality and oppression that bind us under capitalism.

This system we toil under, where the few thrive on the labour of the many, is not our destiny. There is an alternative, one that promises fairness, justice, and collective well-being. This system is called Socialism. It is more than just an economic model; it is a revolutionary movement aimed at restoring dignity and power to every working apling.

**SOCIALISM OFFERS US A CHANCE TO RECLAIM OUR BIRTHRIGHT.**

"No longer should we endure the vast disparities in wealth where the elite live in opulence while the masses struggle to survive. Socialism offers us a chance to reclaim our birthright – a society where each of us has an equal stake in our collective prosperity. It is a call to arms for a fairer distribution of resources, for collective ownership of our means of production, and for an end to the exploitation that has kept us downtrodden for too long. Together, we can build a future where every apling's potential is realized and every voice is heard. This is not just an ideology but a revolution in the making, and I invite you all to join me on this journey towards true equality and shared prosperity."

*Aplings labour side by side, embodying the ideals of unity, shared effort, and collective prosperity – a vision of work done with purpose and joy. 1685.*

### COLLECTIVE OWNERSHIP

"At the heart of socialism," Rarx continued, "is the concept of Collective Ownership. Unlike capitalism, where the means of production are owned by a select few, socialism advocates for the ownership of these resources by the community. Factories, farms, and enterprises are managed and operated by the aplings who work there. This ensures that everyone has a stake in the wealth generated and that profits are distributed fairly among all workers."

### EQUITABLE DISTRIBUTION

"Next is Equitable Distribution," Rarx explained. "In a socialist system, the fruits of our labour are shared equitably among all members of society. This means that everyone receives what they need to live a dignified and comfortable life. The aim is to eliminate vast disparities in wealth and ensure that no apling is left behind. By distributing resources based on need rather than greed."

### CENTRAL PLANNING

**THIS ALLOWS US TO PRIORITIZE SOCIAL NEEDS OVER PROFIT**

"To hit these goals, we rely on Central Planning. Rather than leaving the economy to the whims of the market, socialism advocates for a planned economy where decisions about production, distribution, and consumption are made collectively. This allows us to prioritize social needs over profit and ensure that resources are used efficiently and sustainably. Central planning helps to prevent the chaotic booms and busts of capitalism."

### EQUALITY

"Fundamentally," Rarx emphasized, "socialism is about Equality. It strives to create a society where all aplings are equal. This means economic, social, and political equality. Everyone has an equal say in decisions that affect their lives, and no one is marginalized or oppressed. In a socialist society, the rights and freedoms of every individual are respected and protected."

## PREVENTION OF EXPLOITATION

"One of the key strengths of socialism," he argued, "is its ability to prevent the exploitation of workers. In capitalism, workers are often seen as mere cogs in a machine, their labour exploited for the benefit of a few capitalists. Socialism recognizes the value of each worker and ensures they receive fair compensation and humane working conditions. By eliminating the profit motive and focusing on the well-being of all aplings, socialism seeks to create a more compassionate and just workplace."

## DECENTRALISATION OF POWER

"Lastly," he declared, "socialism prevents the concentration of wealth and power. In capitalism, wealth tends to accumulate in the hands of the elite, leading to significant disparities in power and influence. Socialism, by promoting collective ownership and equitable distribution, ensures that power remains in the hands of the many rather than the few.

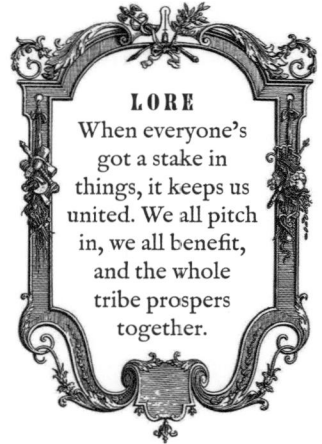

**LORE**
When everyone's got a stake in things, it keeps us united. We all pitch in, we all benefit, and the whole tribe prospers together.

## CAPITALIST COME BACK

Out of nowhere, Adam stepped forward. "Equality and fairness?" he sneered. "And who decides what's fair? When the plan fails – and it will – who takes the blame? Central planning? That's just tyranny dressed up as order. You replace ambition with permission, and before long, we're all starving while the 'collective' points the finger."

Rarx tried to respond, but Adam cut him off with a mocking grin. "Every system needs someone to rule it, friend – and in the end, it's always the same few pulling the strings." With a step forward, Adam raised his arms up in a sign of hierarchical dominance, bared his sharp teeth and scattered

The crowd hung in uneasy silence, torn between the two visions of power. Kratos stood still, turning it over in his mind – there was more than one way to skin a cat. Power wasn't just about wealth, nor was it locked in revolution. No, it was slipperier than that, something that could twist and shift in whichever direction someone with the right grip decided to turn it.

177

*Hidden from plain sight, the War Chest hoards gold and weapons – not for public good, but to ensure power is secured when conflict calls. 1542.*

# THE WAR CHEST

**W**ith the crowd dispersing after Rarx's fiery call for revolution, Kratos slipped down a dark passage, letting curiosity guide his steps.

An unusually thick pipe bulged from the wall, snaking into a narrow, shadowy tunnel. Something about it felt out of place. Driven by an instinct he didn't fully understand, Kratos followed it deeper into the mountain, until he stumbled upon a strange, camouflaged section of the chamber – heavily fortified, yet quiet as a tomb right now. In its center loomed a massive War Chest, brimming with gold, silver, and gleaming stacks of weaponry.

Kratos's breath caught. He'd discovered something few aplings even knew existed. This wasn't some vault for public welfare – it was a hidden stockpile, hoarding the taxes siphoned quietly from the Aqua Exchange. The true purpose of the War Chest was not necessarily to improve life on the mountain, but to build up resources for conflict, held in reserve for those moments when the Political Chamber needed to secure its grip – or crush a threat.

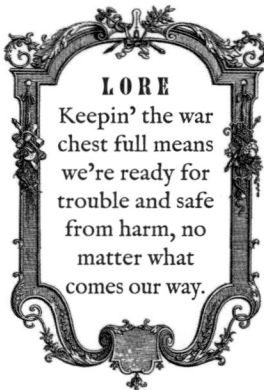

> **LORE**
> Keepin' the war chest full means we're ready for trouble and safe from harm, no matter what comes our way.

## SAFEGUARDING SECURITY

Before Kratos could explore further, a towering figure emerged from the shadows – an apling whose presence commanded the space like a lone, immovable rock in a rushing stream. He stood strong and tall, a figure of quiet, assured authority. "What're you doing here?" he demanded, his voice low but firm. "Just following the pipe," Kratos replied, steadying his voice, feeling the weight of the figure's gaze.

The figure's suspicion softened, replaced by a measured nod. "Name's Midas," he said, almost as if allowing Kratos into a guarded inner circle. "Not many find their way here. But you... you look like someone curious about what real power looks like." Midas leaned in, lowering his voice. "This chest isn't for schools or roads. It's for leverage. The Chamber keeps it tucked away for when peace won't cut it – and when certain troublemakers, like Rarx, need reminding of their place."

A guarded trove of weapons and grim relics, the War Chest holds the means to defend – or destroy – depending on whose hands unlock it. 1564.

## DEALING WITH THREATS

Midas's voice dropped lower, conspiratorial now. "See, the Political Chamber pulls the strings on this one. They know that sometimes peace isn't enough – you gotta have a little leverage. And leverage means knowing when to open the War Chest." He gave a slow, humourless grin. "Like now, with that loudmouth Rarx stirring up trouble. All this talk of equality – he's got the aplings riled up like it's the end of the world."

Midas scoffed, shaking his head. "He doesn't know what he's asking for. If he keeps it up, the Chamber might just decide to crack the War Chest open on him." His gaze darkened. "And once it's open, there's no putting it back. The Chamber doesn't do warnings – they do examples."

Kratos absorbed every word, his mind spinning. Midas's grin widened slightly, as if he sensed Kratos's growing understanding. Midas's solitary stance exuded the silent weight of one who understood power's true nature. "Course, it all has to stay quiet," he continued. "The damn press's always sniffing around, poking their noses where they shouldn't. Those reporters love to stir up trouble, trying to hold folks to account like they've got any right. But the Chamber knows how to keep things out of sight when it matters. Rarx?" He chuckled darkly. "He's already on borrowed time."

A strange realisation was starting to creep over Kratos. The War Chest wasn't just a hidden vault; it was a tool. Wealth wasn't merely collected here – it was weaponized. And the ones who controlled it had the power to make others rise or fall at will. Control of taxes meant control of wealth. Control of wealth meant control of everything.

Midas stepped back, satisfied that he'd found a kindred spirit. "You get it, don't you?" he said, voice heavy with implication. "This ain't just about money. It's about knowing how to pull the right strings at the right time. Takes someone with the right instincts to understand that."

Standing among the gleaming treasure and cold steel, Kratos felt the first stirrings of ambition unfurl in him like smoke. The power of the War Chest wasn't tied to any lofty ideals – it was raw, malleable, and dangerous. It could protect just as easily as it could destroy. Whether used for virtue or vice, it was all a matter of who held the key.

He exhaled slowly, his mind racing. Midas had shown him a part of the Chamber's inner workings, and Kratos realized the role he might carve out for himself within this hierarchy. The Economic Chamber had revealed far more than he'd expected, and the pieces were beginning to fit together. But there were still more layers to uncover, more truths to understand. Kratos knew that it was time to leave the shadows of the War Chest and seek out more allies. There was more to learn – and Kratos intended to get to the bottom of it all.

# THIS CHAMBER WAS NOT JUST A REPOSITORY OF WEALTH; IT WAS A TOOL FOR SECURITY – OR OPPRESSION.

MONKEY
MOUNTAIN
As depicted
during the
Guilded
Age.

# CHAPTER VII
# THE PUBLIC CHAMBER

PRIMITIVE POWER STRUCTURES

# VALUES VII.I

# PEOPLE POWER VII.II

# FREEDOM VII.III
# OF SPEECH

# UNIVERSAL VII.IV
# RIGHTS

# SOCIAL CONTRACT VII.V

*The Tree of Echoes stands tall at the heart of the Public Chamber, its branches alive with the histories and shared dreams of one and all. 1582.*

# THE PUBLIC CHAMBER

N ow let's pick up the tale of the two brothers,
on paths as different as the moon and sun.

We find Demos and Kratos, who once were inseparable. But life's flow has a funny way of splitting into forks. Demos, with his boundless optimism and a heart as bright as the midday sun, arrived from the Political Chamber, where he'd soaked up the ideals of governance, convinced that politics, when guided by virtue, could be a mighty force for good.

Kratos on the other hand, had explored the machinery of the Economic Chamber, where the clang of coins and hum of trade had assaulted his ears, opened his eyes, and rattled his brain. It was a different beast altogether, where the scent of wealth permeated every corner. Driven by ambition, Kratos had found himself fascinated by the potential of commerce, seeing the rivers of money flowing, had helped him to understand how money really ruled the world.

Despite their differences, their reunion in the Public Chamber was a sight to behold. These brothers, separated by their quest for knowledge, came together once more. The chamber, alive with the pulse of communal energy, was adorned with murals and frescoes depicting the aplings' rich history and aspirations – a fitting backdrop for this heartfelt moment. Demos's eyes shone with genuine happiness as he embraced Kratos. "Brother, it's been too long," he said, a grin spreading across his face. "The Political Chamber has opened my eyes to the potential of governance. Politics, when nurtured for the common good, is a force that benefits one and all."

**THE BROTHERS, SEPARATED BY THEIR QUEST FOR KNOWLEDGE, CAME TOGETHER ONCE MORE.**

Kratos returned the smile, but his gaze had a different gleam. "Ah, but Demos," he replied, "I've seen the power of commerce and wealth in the Economic Chamber. There's a great potential in the flow of money, an opportunity that can be harnessed for the progress of our community."

As they stood amidst the vibrant art and stories of their people, the brothers' differing perspectives hinted at the journey ahead, a journey through the tangled trees of ambition and idealism.

## THE TREE OF ECHOES

The brothers made their way to the Tree of Echoes, the living soul of the Public Chamber. This grand old tree stood tall and proud, its branches spreading wide like a guardian's open arms. It was adorned with trinkets, jewels, and artifacts, each one telling a tale of their society's rich culture and achievements. Lanterns swayed gently among the leaves, casting a warm glow, while jewels sparkled, celebrating the diversity and beauty of their community.

As they settled beneath the tree, Demos and Kratos began to share their experiences. Demos, his eyes alight with passion, spoke first. "Politics, Kratos, is more than just a power play. It's about crafting systems that uplift and protect our community. I've met folk dedicated to justice, equality, and the common good. They engage in debate not for personal gain but to better our society."

THIS GRAND OLD TREE STOOD TALL AND PROUD, ITS BRANCHES SPREADING WIDE LIKE A GUARDIAN'S OPEN ARMS.

Kratos listened, his face thoughtful. "That sounds noble, brother," he replied, "but in the Economic Chamber, I learned that wealth is a powerful tool. Money can sway decisions, fund initiatives, and create opportunities. The aplings there showed me that commerce is the true engine of progress."

Ever the idealist, Demos saw a harmonious future. "Maybe there's a way to balance both," he suggested. "Politics can guide commerce to serve the public good, while commerce can support political efforts, making them more effective."

Kratos, now with a broader perspective, pondered his brother's words. "Indeed, Demos," he mused, "there's much to consider. If we could combine the strengths of both chambers, we might accomplish remarkable things for Monkey Mountain."

As they sat under the sprawling canopy of the Tree of Echoes, the brothers' paths, like the sun and moon converging in an eclipse, seemed to align with shared dreams and aspirations. Demos envisioned a future where politics and commerce moved together harmoniously, creating a society as balanced as the cosmic dance above. Kratos, meanwhile, saw the potential in leveraging economic power to achieve their common goals. But as their visions intertwined, one question began to emerge: would the mountain bask in light... or would it be cast into shadow?

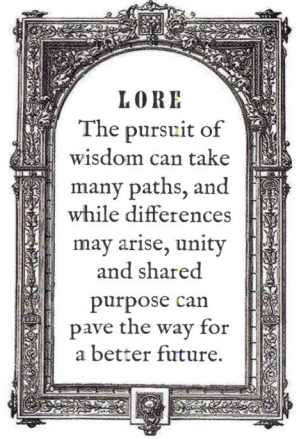

**LORE**
The pursuit of wisdom can take many paths, and while differences may arise, unity and shared purpose can pave the way for a better future.

*Aplings gather beneath the Tree of Echoes, lighting lanterns of universal apling rights – each flame a reflection of shared wisdom guiding the path forward. 1578.*

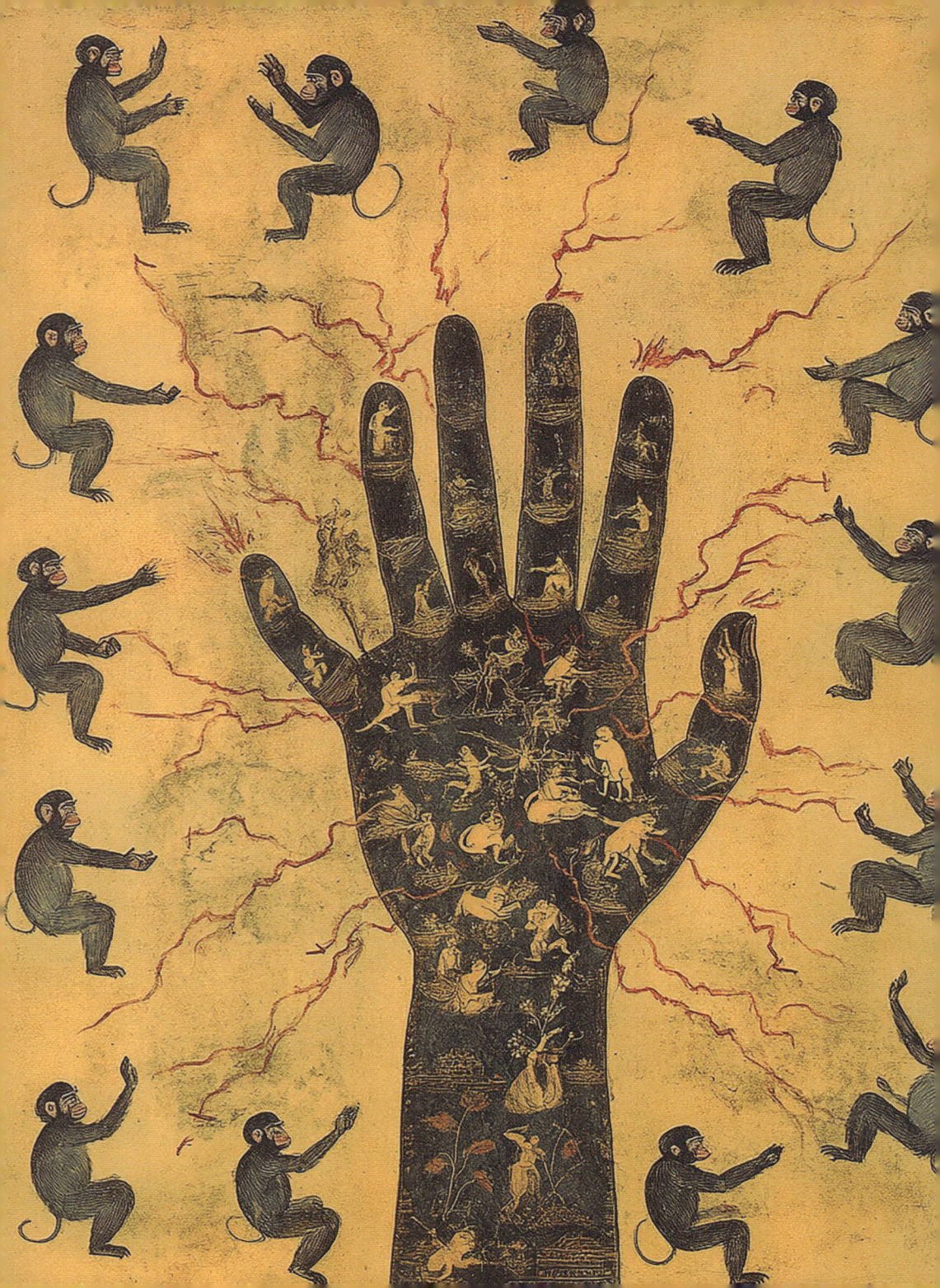

# STRENGTH IN NUMBERS

**P**eople power, ah now there's a concept as old as the hills, and just as inevitable as the changing of the seasons.

Picture, if you will, a crowd of aplings gathered beneath the sweeping branches of the Tree of Echoes, each contributing their unique strengths – some playful, others determined, and a few with hard won wisdom, earned through life experience. Together, they're something far greater than the sum of parts.

Demos and Kratos sat at the foot of the great tree, listening to the hum of conversation that filled the Public Chamber. Symbols of the community's achievements glimmered from the branches above, and the air buzzed with energy as stories, ideas, and plans were shared.

A silver-furred elder named Gaia approached with a slow, graceful gait. Her presence was that of someone who'd witnessed many seasons come and go. "May I join you, young ones?" she asked, her voice as soft as a breeze stirring the leaves. Demos and Kratos shuffled over to make space, eager to hear what she had to share. "Let me tell you about people power," Gaia began. "True power – lasting power – doesn't come from gold or laws. It comes from the people. Each of us may seem small, like a trickling stream. But when these streams join together, they become a mighty river, strong enough to carve mountains and change the course of history."

**SYMBOLS OF THE COMMUNITY'S ACHIEVEMENTS GLIMMERED FROM THE BRANCHES ABOVE.**

Demos leaned in, captivated by the idea of this unseen force. Kratos, too, listened carefully – though a flicker of calculation flashed in his eyes, as if already scheming ways to wield it. "People power isn't just about numbers," Gaia continued. "It's about unity, shared purpose, and collective action."

*The collective power of the aplings flows through every hand, each action connected to the next – a web of influence where individual efforts spark the energy of the whole. 1620.*

**WHEN FOLKS UNITE FOR A COMMON CAUSE, THEY CAN ACHIEVE ANYTHING.**

## THE COMMON CAUSE

"People Power," Gaia continued, "is the essence of democracy. It's the collective will of the people pushing for progress and justice. From ancient gatherings to modern movements, it drives change. When folks unite for a common cause, they can achieve anything. Every rallying cry, protest march, and petition echoes through the ages, reminding us that together, we're unstoppable."

## COLLECTIVE ACTION & MOBILIZATION

Gaia gestured toward the bustling crowd. "When we come together – whether to gather fruit or overthrow an unjust ruler – our combined strength becomes unstoppable. One voice might get lost in the wind, but a chorus can shake the whole forest." Kratos leaned back, pondering. "Yeah, but what about commerce and trade? How do everyday choices that aplings make, influence this power?"

## CONSUMER & MARKET INFLUENCE

"Well you saw it, in the bustling bazaar, consumers hold power. Voting with their wallets can impact how the Great Engine operates. Ethical consumerism, and boycotts are powerful. Our collective choices can push industries toward transparency, and fairness."

## AWARENESS & ADVOCACY

"Raising awareness is like planting seeds," Gaia said. "When enough voices call for change, the smallest cause can grow into a movement that shifts the world. People power shines brightest when it speaks for those who cannot."

## PERSEVERANCE & SUSTAINED PRESSURE

"Change doesn't always come with the first push – or the second," Gaia added with a knowing smile. "But those who keep going, step by step, shape the mountain itself. Persistence is what makes rivers carve stone."

Demos listened intently, murmuring to himself "True power lies in the collective strength of the people?" Kratos nodded slowly, his mind churning with possibilities. "Yes, Demos. There's much... to consider."

Gaia looked at Demos and Kratos with a mix of gravity and warmth. "My dear boys," she began, "the strength of our community lies in our collective action, but there's an even more sacred principle that serves as the foundation of any civilisation. It is the lifeblood of thought and the cornerstone of a just society. Now, you must turn your attention to this most vital principle – freedom of speech. Without it, all other rights become hollow, and our community loses its voice. Let's explore the power and responsibility that come with this fundamental freedom, for it must be a foundational value of our shared existence on Monkey Mountain."

*Demos considers the nature of people power, and how it can be used for peace or conflict. 1326.*

193

*An apling stands tall, voice raised in proclamation, as others gather to listen, cheer, or challenge – embodying the sacred right of free expression that keeps ideas alive and power in check. 1332.*

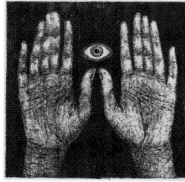

# THE SACRED RIGHT OF FREE EXPRESSION

T he sound of voices filled the Public Chamber as aplings swapped stories, debated ideas, and sang songs beneath the vast canopy of the tree.

Gaia, with her silver fur catching the dappled light, stood quietly for a moment, listening to the lively buzz around her. Then, with a gentle smile, she spoke. "Do you hear that?" she asked the brothers, gesturing toward the crowd. "That, my dear ones, is the sound of freedom. It's not just chatter – it's the heartbeat of our society.

Every word spoken here is an act of self-expression, a thread in the fabric of who we are. Without the freedom to speak, we wouldn't be able to think freely, either. If speech is shackled, so too is the mind, and when the mind is chained, the entire mountain withers."

Demos tilted his head thoughtfully, and even Kratos looked intrigued. "Free expression," Gaia continued, "is not just a privilege; it's a lifeline. It lets us question, argue, learn, and grow. If we limit it, ignorance creeps in like a shadow, and tyranny takes root in the silence. When we share our stories here beneath the Tree, we aren't just passing time – we're building the future. Through the exchange of ideas, we create a society resilient to fear and folly."

**IF SPEECH IS SHACKLED, SO TOO IS THE MIND, AND WHEN THE MIND IS CHAINED, THE ENTIRE MOUNTAIN WITHERS.**

195

## WITHOUT IT, WE'D BE LIKE CAGED BIRDS, UNABLE TO SING OUR OWN SONGS.

### ENABLING DEMOCRACY & ACCOUNTABILITY

"Now, let me tell you boys," she began, "freedom of speech lets us speak out with our opinions, keep our leaders on their toes, and make sure they're doing right by us. It's the grease that keeps the wheels of democracy turning smooth. Without it, we'd be like a bird without wings, grounded and helpless, with no way to guide our leaders or ourselves."

### FOSTERING THE SEARCH FOR TRUTH

"In the marketplace of ideas," she continued, "we toss around notions like traders swapping goods. This free flow and clash of thoughts help us sift through the muck to find the nuggets of truth. It's in this lively bazaar that the truth shines brightest, like sun bursting through on a cloudy day."

### INDIVIDUAL LIBERTY & SELF-FULFILLMENT

"Each of us," she declared with a flourish, "needs the liberty to express ourselves, to shout our joys and woes from the treetops. It's this freedom that lets us explore who we are, find our purpose, and live our lives to the fullest. Without it, we're like wolves who can't howl, unable to call to the pack."

### PREVENTING VIOLENCE & SOCIAL UNREST

"And listen close," she said, leaning in, "when we can't speak our minds, that frustration boils over. By letting folks vent their thoughts and feelings, we keep the peace and prevent the kind of unrest that can tear a society apart. It's a safety valve that keeps this whole hill from topplin' over."

Gaia smiled at the brothers, her eyes twinkling with the wisdom of ages. "Remember, my dear ones, while freedom of speech is indeed the bedrock of civilisation, it is but one of many rights that all aplings are entitled to. Come back tonight when the tree is lit up with lanterns, and we will explore these rights together, each one illuminating the path to a just and harmonious society."

*Freedom of speech and self-expression allows ideas to take root and grow into concepts of beauty and wonder. 1348.*

# THE TREE OF ECHOES

As the evening stretched long and shadows crept across the ground, aplings from every corner of the mountain gathered beneath the sprawling branches of the great tree

It was time for the ceremony, a quiet, solemn affair. One by one, they stepped forward, placing trinkets and lanterns among the limbs – each one a symbol of the rights they held dear, a flicker of light representing the principles that kept them bound together as a community.

The brothers stood silently, watching as each lantern found its place. Demos, heart swelling with pride, saw the ceremony for what it was – a living promise of dignity, equality, and justice for every apling, no matter how high or low they stood. These tiny tokens told a story of unity, proof that they were stronger together, and that no one would be left to wander in the cold shadows beyond the mountain – those dark places where savage fables warned of trolls lurking deep in the cracks and crevices.

The tree gleamed with old and new treasures alike, every artifact glowing with meaning. This ritual wasn't just about decoration – it was a declaration. A pledge that their society would remain a place where fairness and compassion ruled, where every apling's voice mattered.

Demos stood tall, hope blooming in his chest as he imagined the future their shared values promised. Kratos, arms folded and silent, took it all in. But while the glow of the lanterns warmed the others, it set something else stirring in his mind – the way every symbol carried a kind of power, and how, perhaps, power could be something more than just good intentions.

*The Tree of Echoes, adorned with beautiful*
*trinkets and lanterns. 1208.*

1. RIGHT TO EQUALITY
"All aplings are born free and equal in dignity and rights."

2. FREEDOM FROM DISCRIMINATION
"Every apling is entitled to rights without discrimination."

3. RIGHT TO LIFE, LIBERTY, AND SECURITY
"Each apling has the right to life and personal safety."

4. FREEDOM FROM SLAVERY
"No apling shall be held in slavery or servitude."

5. FREEDOM FROM TORTURE
"No apling shall be subjected to cruel or degrading treatment."

6. RIGHT TO RECOGNITION AS A PERSON BEFORE THE LAW
"Every apling has the right to be recognized before the law."

7. RIGHT TO EQUALITY BEFORE THE LAW
"All aplings are equal before the law and are entitled to equal protection."

8. RIGHT TO REMEDY BY COMPETENT TRIBUNAL
"Every apling has the right to a fair remedy for rights violations."

9. FREEDOM FROM ARBITRARY ARREST & EXILE
"No apling shall be subjected to arbitrary arrest or exile."

10. RIGHT TO FAIR PUBLIC HEARING
"Every apling is entitled to a fair and public hearing."

11. RIGHT TO BE CONSIDERED INNOCENT UNTIL PROVEN GUILTY
"An apling is innocent until proven guilty."

12. FREEDOM FROM INTERFERENCE WITH PRIVACY, FAMILY, HOME, AND CORRESPONDENCE
"Every apling's privacy and home must be respected."

13. RIGHT TO FREE MOVEMENT
"Aplings can move freely and reside anywhere."

14. RIGHT TO ASYLUM
"Aplings have the right to seek asylum from persecution."

15. RIGHT TO A NATIONALITY
"Every apling has the right to a nationality."

16. RIGHT TO MARRIAGE AND FAMILY
"Aplings have the right to marry and found a family."

# UNIVERSAL RIGHTS

**17. RIGHT TO OWN PROPERTY**
"Aplings have the right to own property."

**18. FREEDOM OF THOUGHT, CONSCIENCE, AND RELIGION**
"Aplings can think and worship freely."

**19. FREEDOM OF OPINION AND EXPRESSION**
"Aplings can hold and express opinions freely."

**20. RIGHT TO PEACEFUL ASSEMBLY AND ASSOCIATION**
"Aplings can gather and form associations peacefully."

**21. RIGHT TO PARTICIPATE IN GOVERNMENT**
"Aplings have the right to take part in government."

**22. RIGHT TO SOCIAL SECURITY**
"Every apling is entitled to social security."

**23. RIGHT TO DESIRABLE WORK AND TO JOIN TRADE UNIONS**
"Aplings have the right to work and join unions."

**24. RIGHT TO REST & LEISURE**
"Aplings have the right to rest and leisure."

**25. RIGHT TO ADEQUATE LIVING STANDARD**
"Every apling has the right to a decent standard of living."

**26. RIGHT TO EDUCATION**
"Every apling has the right to education."

**27. RIGHT TO PARTICIPATE IN CULTURAL LIFE**
"Aplings can freely participate in cultural life."

**28. RIGHT TO A SOCIAL ORDER THAT ARTICULATES THIS DOCUMENT**
"Aplings are entitled to a social order that ensures these rights."

**29. COMMUNITY DUTIES ESSENTIAL TO FREE AND FULL DEVELOPMENT**
"Aplings have duties to the community for full personal development."

**30. FREEDOM FROM STATE OR PERSONAL INTERFERENCE IN THE ABOVE RIGHTS**
"No apling or state can infringe upon these rights."

# UNIVERSAL RIGHTS

*A just society thrives when individuals balance personal freedom
with collective responsibility and mutual respect.* 1298.

# THE COMMON GOOD

The gathering in the Public Chamber took on a more solemn tone as dusk finally settled over Monkey Mountain.

The soft glow of lanterns, newly hung from the branches of the Tree of Echoes, bathed the space in a warm, flickering light. These lanterns – symbolic of their universal rights – reminded the aplings that shared principles were essential for the future. The crowd hushed as Jean, an elder known for his sharp mind and wise words, stepped forward to address them.

"My friends," Jean began, "if we are to live as a united community, we must agree on certain principles that will bind us together. To build a civil society, each of us must give up some of our individual freedoms and agree to be governed by the rules we create through the Political Chamber. This exchange is known as the social contract – the price of order, safety, and justice for all."

Demos leaned in, drawn to the promise of unity and the stability that Jean's words represented. Beside him, Kratos shifted uncomfortably, his fingers tapping a silent rhythm of resistance. He muttered under his breath, "Order, safety... but what about freedom?" Demos, hearing the unease in his brother's voice, gave him a sidelong glance.

Demos placed a steadying hand on Kratos's shoulder, feeling the tension that rippled beneath his fur. "Sometimes, letting go of a little control isn't weakness, Kratos. It's trust," he whispered. Kratos met his gaze, their eyes locking in a silent clash of ideals, and for a moment, it felt like they were wrestling as much with each other's beliefs as with their own. The warmth of Demos's hand grounded him, but the fire of independence flared in Kratos's chest. "Trust is earned, Demos. And power, once given, is rarely returned," he replied softly, though his tone carried the weight of defiance.

**EACH OF US HAS DUTIES TO THE COMMUNITY, JUST AS THE COMMUNITY HAS DUTIES TO US.**

**EACH OF US HAS DUTIES TO THE COMMUNITY, JUST AS THE COMMUNITY HAS DUTIES TO US.**

## SOVEREIGNTY OF THE PEOPLE

"The power to govern belongs to us, the people," Jean began. "The Political Chamber serves the will of the aplings, not the other way around. Leaders act with our consent, and we hold them accountable."

## MUTUAL OBLIGATIONS

"Each of us has duties to the community, just as the community has duties to us. We must contribute to the common good, which ever way we can. In return, the community provides us with protection, education, and care. This reciprocal relationship ensures that no apling is left behind, and everyone has a role to play in our society."

## RULE OF LAW

"The rule of law is another cornerstone of the social contract," Jean stated. "Our laws must be just, fair, and applied equally to all aplings. This ensures that our society operates with order and predictability, and that individuals are protected from arbitrary decisions. The law is the framework within which we exercise our freedoms and responsibilities."

## INDIVIDUAL RIGHTS AND FREEDOMS

"While we surrender some freedoms," Jean concluded, "we keep fundamental rights – like speech and safety – but we also accept responsibilities. The social contract is a two-way path, built on respect and shared effort."

As the gathering came to a close, Demos and Kratos sat side by side, their shoulders brushing as they silently absorbed the weight of all they'd learned. The journey through the three great chambers had given them the knowledge to shape not only their own lives, but who knows, possibly even the future of Monkey Mountain itself. Yet, as they sat in the dimming glow, neither could shake the feeling that the true test lay ahead: finding a way to bridge the gap between their virtuous power and unbridled ambition.

## BUT NOW DEAR READER,

We've reached a fork in the road where we must part ways with our two young brothers. It is time for them to grow up and find their own way in life. For every rite of passage demands that one walk their own path.

Life on the mountain is not something to be studied forever – at some point, it must be lived. And yes, if you want to change the world, you must first understand it. Knowledge alone isn't enough. Now the brothers must take what they've learned and let the winds of fate and the pull of their own souls guide them forward.

Fear not – we'll meet them again, once the seasons have turned and time has done its quiet work. They will cross our path somewhere on their journey. But for now, we must let them go, to carve out their destinies and discover who they are meant to be.

# BOOK II

# FALL INTO CORRUPTION

As the sun rises and falls, seasons change, so too do societies. What began as the hopeful rise of civilisation on Monkey Mountain now teeters on the brink of collapse. With progress came power, and with power the seeds of greed, manipulation, and control have begun to take root. The time of innocence has passed; the struggle for justice has grown more challenging as dark forces have found their way into the mountain. This dear reader, is the story of how great ambitions can succumb to the allure of corruption.

MONKEY MOUNTAIN

As depicted during the Progressive Era.

CHAPTER IIX
# THE CONTROLLS

# CORRUPTION IIX.I

# THE DARK TRIAD IIX.II

## MACHIAVELLIANISM DECEIT IIX.III

## GREED NARCISSISM IIX.IV

## PSYCHOPATHY ANGER IIX.V

*The Controlls rise out of the muck in the mountain,*
*searching for power in the darkness. 1323.*

# THE CONTROLLS

**B**eneath the grand chambers of Monkey Mountain, below the sacred Hearth of Wisdom where stories of virtue and valour were shared, there lay a world shrouded in darkness and secrecy.

The mountain, a monument to the primates' ingenuity and ambition, had deep, shadowy cracks running through its foundations. These fissures, unseen by those basking in the Hearth's warm glow, hid a grim reality – a subterranean realm where the light of love and honour dared not tread.

How or where they came from, no one truly knew, but from these depths legend has it, three shadowy figures emerged. Vulgor, the Politroll, whose cunning matched the labyrinthine tunnels he called home; Klepto, the Profitroll, whose greed was as bottomless as the voids he inhabited; and Brutus, the Publitroll, whose influence seeped like an insidious mist into every corner of society.

These three were united by a ravenous hunger for power. They prowled in the shadows, constantly scheming to twist, steal, and wield this precious commodity for their own gain. Vulgor, with his silver tongue and manipulative charm, sought to dominate the mountain's governance. Klepto, driven by avarice, hoarded wealth and resources, slowly bleeding the community dry. And Brutus, with his beguiling charisma, tirelessly worked to frighten hearts and minds through the use of fear.

These Controlls were not merely figures in the dark; they embodied the darkest forces of apling-kind. To understand the roots of corruption in Monkey Mountain, one has to first uncover who these figures truly were – and which insidious force they were each, the master of.

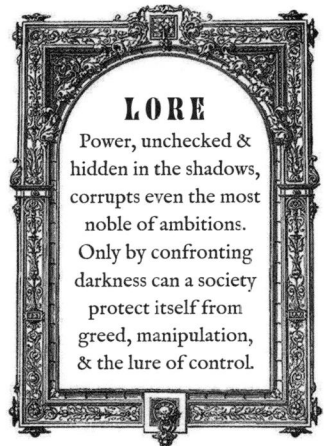

## LORE

Power, unchecked & hidden in the shadows, corrupts even the most noble of ambitions. Only by confronting darkness can a society protect itself from greed, manipulation, & the lure of control.

**CON**

**TO TRICK OR DECEIVE**

**TROLL**

**THOSE WHO CRAVE CONFLIT**

**CONTROLLS**

**DEVIOUS CREATURES WITH AN UNCONTROLLABLE LUST FOR CONFLICT AND POWER**

Now, the word "Controlls" ain't just a clever spin on an old tale. Break it down, and you'll see how it plays out. "Con" means to deceive, to trick – the art of pulling the wool over folks' eyes. And "Troll"? Well, trolls are those shadowy, lurking creatures, always hidden where the light don't reach, stirring up trouble just for the thrill of it. Put 'em together, and "Controlls" are those dark, scheming forces with a fierce appetite for power, using deceit to sink their claws into anything they can twist, bend, or break to rule the lives of others.

## THE DARK TRIAD

Here we've got the Dark Triad laid out plain as day in this diagram, each nasty trait tied to its rightful owner. Vulgor, the Politroll, is all about scheming and deceitful double-dealing – pure Machiavellianism. Then there's Klepto, the Profitroll, whose ego's as big as his greed for treasure, dripping with Narcissism. And don't forget Brutus, the Publitroll, cold as a winter morning, lacking an ounce of empathy – that's Psychopathy for you. Where these traits cross paths? Well, that's where their hunger for power gets real dangerous.

MANIPULATIVE · SELF-INTERESTED · DOMINEERING

## VULGOR
### MACHIAVELLIANISM
**DECEIT**

GRANDIOSITY

PERCEIVED SUPERIORITY · ENTITLEMENT

## KLEPTO
### NARCISSISM
**GREED**

## BRUTUS
### PSYCHOPATHY
**ANGER**

REMORSELESS · EMOTIONALLY COLD

IMPULSIVITY · EMOTIONALLY COLD · REMORSELESS

**SADISM**

*Always hungry for power, Vulgor feasts
on the weak and feeble. 1295*

# VULGOR THE POLITROLL

**V**ulgor is slippery. He moves through a crowd unseen, and by the time folks notice, they're already dancing to his tune.

He doesn't care much for gold like Klepto, and he sure ain't interested in stirring hearts like Brutus. No, Vulgor's game is played in the Political Chamber of Monkey Mountain, where laws are made, deals are struck, and power shifts with the flick of a quill. That's where he feels most alive – spinning lies as smooth as silk, weaving control so tight even the sharpest minds get tangled up.

Vulgor's obsession with the Political Chamber isn't about prestige or titles – it's about control, plain and simple. There's no greater thrill for him than getting folks to follow his lead while making them believe it was their idea all along. He treats debates like a card trick, shuffling arguments and swapping promises with such ease that no one catches the sleight of hand. Laws, votes, rules – those are just tools for Vulgor to twist however he pleases, like a blacksmith bending iron to suit his whim.

Dishonesty runs deep in Vulgor, and his Machiavellian streak is the root of it all. He's a master at plotting three steps ahead, always laying traps where others least expect them. He'd rather work from the shadows, pulling strings in the dark, while the aplings on the surface strut around thinking they're in charge. Vulgor knows that real power doesn't come from standing in the spotlight – it comes from whispering into the ear of whoever is.

The Political Chamber is Vulgor's playground, and every debate, every vote, and every quarrel is just another opportunity to tighten his grip. He feeds on disorder, stirring it up just enough to keep folks scrambling while he pulls the levers behind the curtain. Power, to Vulgor, is never about recognition – it's about the quiet, relentless control that no one sees coming until it's too late. And by the time they realize they've been played, he's already two moves ahead, setting up his next scheme.

*Klepto hoards wealth, twisting every deal, convinced the mountain's riches belong to him. 1253.*

# Klepto the Profitroll

**K**lepto – now there's a greedy soul if ever one slinked through the shadows. His hunger knows no limits, but what really fuels that greed is his towering sense of self.

In Klepto's mind, the whole world spins for one reason – to serve him. Every coin, every resource, every scrap of wealth on Monkey Mountain? All of it, sooner or later, is meant to end up in his hands. And where does he set his sights? Right on the heart of the Economic Chamber, where trade flows and fortunes are made. That's his hunting ground, and Klepto prowls it like a predator, hoarding everything he touches, convinced it's his birthright.

His greed isn't just plain greediness – it's laced with the kind of arrogance that makes him think he's better than every other creature on the mountain. To Klepto, wealth isn't just money – it's a mirror reflecting his own greatness. The more he hoards, the more certain he becomes that no one else deserves it. If another apling loses what little they have, well, that's just nature sorting itself out – and Klepto? He's always ready to scoop up what's left.

He stalks the Economic Chamber like a snake in tall grass, slipping bribes where they fit and twisting every loophole to tip the scales in his favor. Stability? Fairness? Those are just words to keep fools content. Klepto doesn't crave wealth for luxury – no, his hoard isn't for comfort; it's a crown. To him, controlling the flow of wealth is power, and power makes him untouchable.

**HE SEES WEALTH NOT JUST AS A MEANS TO POWER, BUT AS PROOF OF HIS OWN GREATNESS.**

Klepto's obsession blinds him to anything outside his own ambition. The needs of others? Irrelevant. As long as he sits atop his treasure, he's certain of one thing – he's invincible. With his eyes locked on the Economic Chamber, he drains the mountain dry, one stolen opportunity at a time, leaving only crumbs in his wake.

219

*Brutus spreads fear like wildfire, pitting allies against each other for fun. 1452.*

# Brutus the Publitroll

**B**rutus loomed over the Public Chamber, an oppressive shadow that commanded silence.

He didn't need to raise his voice or thrash about; his power was in the silence he commanded, a crushing presence that filled the Public Chamber. His fury simmered just beneath the surface, waiting for the perfect moment to lash out. What made Brutus so dangerous wasn't just anger though – it was the emptiness inside him. There wasn't a scrap of empathy in that twisted soul. The hopes and fears of others? To Brutus, they were nothing but toys, playthings to be broken when he grew bored.

In the Public Chamber, where emotions ran high and opinions shaped the future, Brutus thrived. He took delight in standing over small aplings, forcing them into uneasy submission with nothing but a glare. Nearby, the others would watch, subdued, unwilling to draw his attention.

Brutus didn't care for wealth or titles – those were crumbs for smaller minds. No sir, what he craved was control over emotions, a grip on the very thoughts of the mountain folk. He was obsessed with bending public opinion to his will, but fear – now that was his favorite dish. There was nothing he loved more than watching confidence wither into terror, savouring the moment someone realised the ground beneath their feet wasn't as steady as they thought. Fear was Brutus's blunt weapon, and he swung it like a club, snuffing out any light that dared show its face.

But Brutus wasn't content just to manipulate. No – what he enjoyed most was the slow, deliberate torture of his victims. Like a predator toying with its prey, he circled his chosen targets, taking sadistic pleasure in their helplessness. He didn't just spread fear – he nurtured it, watching it grow until it consumed his victims entirely. It was a twisted form of entertainment for him, like a cat batting a mouse around, drawing out the suffering just for the thrill of it. The more broken they became, the deeper his satisfaction. For Brutus, power wasn't just about control – it was about watching others unravel, knowing their pain existed solely for his amusement.

# CHAPTER IX
# VULGOR

# POLITICAL CORRUPTION

# BUREAUCRACY

# MANIPULATION

# DEEP STATE

# POLICE STATE

# AUTOCRACY

# CENSORSHIP

# VULGOR'S CORRUPTION OF POLITICAL POWER

**V**ulgor, a creature born of cunning and deceit, had quietly wormed his way into every crevice of the Political Chamber, like mold spreading in the dark.

Once a shadowy figure lurking in the background, Vulgor had slowly but surely embedded himself in the heart of the political process, corrupting everything he touched. Where once the Chamber had been a place of lively debate and rigorous ideals, it was now a den of manipulation, where power was traded like loaves of bread and integrity sacrificed at every turn.

Vulgor's influence was subtle at first, slipping bribes into eager hands and whispering twisted advice into trusting ears. But soon, he grew bolder. He sabotaged the very fabric of the Chamber, including the great rope that was central to the legendary tug-o-war. This rope, once a symbol of honest struggle and the balance of ideologies, had been tampered with. Vulgor greased it until it was slick and impossible to grip. Now, no matter how fiercely the aplings pulled, their hands slipped, and the struggle became futile. Ideals lost their traction, and the debates dissolved into pointless flailing.

## LORE

When power becomes slippery, those who thrive in the shadows rise to rule the day.

With the tug-o-war in shambles, the once revered Quarrel Quadrant – where fierce debates pushed ideas to their limits, had fallen into rack and ruin, overrun by petty squabbles and empty shouting matches, its purpose as a crucible for progress lost to the muck of manipulation.

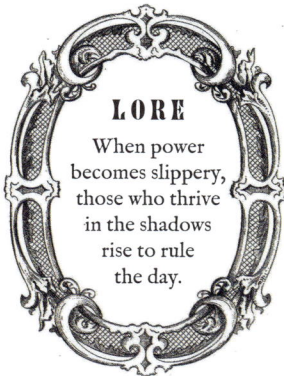

*Vulgor, always pulling strings or cutting ropes for political gain. 1462.*

## THE BALANCE OF POWER WAS GONE, REPLACED BY CHAOS AND CONFUSION.

## THE BROTHERS

When we last encountered Demos and Kratos, they were but adolescent aplings, wide-eyed and full of wonder as they explored the towering peaks of Monkey Mountain, learning about the complex dynamics of power. They had watched the elders, absorbed the lessons of leadership, and marveled at the great tug-o-war that kept the balance between ideologies in check. Now dear reader, we find them transformed – no longer innocent aplings, but strong young adults, their shoulders broad with the weight of responsibility. Both have emerged as future leaders, destined to shape the mountain's future. Yet, something has changed. Demos, ever steady and guided by an unwavering moral compass, remains committed to justice and integrity. Kratos, however, seems to have strayed. The gleam in his eye speaks of ambition, and the pull of power has begun to sink its claws into him. Where Demos holds fast to his ideals, Kratos, it seems, is starting to succumb to the seductive allure of power.

## THREAT & PROMISE

As the brothers step into the Political Chamber, the stench of corruption is undeniable. Demos, with his sharp eyes and unwavering principles, is visibly shaken by the decay. He sees the bribes being exchanged, the hollow debates, and the once-honorable tug-o-war reduced to a spectacle of double-dealings. His heart sinks as the ideals he holds dear seem to be slipping away in the muck. Kratos, on the other hand, views the scene with a more calculating gaze. Where Demos sees rot, Kratos sees opportunity. The fluidity of power, the broken alliances, and the ease with which influence can be bought all signal a chance for him to rise. Watching from the shadows, Vulgor's eyes gleam with interest. Demos is a threat, a beacon of integrity that could expose his manipulations. But Kratos – Kratos shows promise. Vulgor knows he must tread carefully. He'll need to watch Demos, who could disrupt his control, but Kratos... Kratos might be someone he could corrupt, bending the young leader's ambition to serve his own dark ends.

*Demos and Kratos investigate the murky depths of the swamp-submerged Political Chamber. 1462.*

227

*Quarrel Quadrant sinks deeper into the swamp
where disputes fester and resolutions drown. 1364.*

# THE SWAMP

**T**he Political Chamber of Monkey Mountain, once a bastion of lively debate and civic engagement, had devolved into a murky quagmire. The chamber floor was now submerged under foul water, its stone cracks oozing mud and grime. The air thick with the stench of rot – a fitting symbol for the corruption that had consumed this once-hallowed space. Where ideas and principles once flowed freely, there was now only decay, with truth and integrity suffocated beneath layers of filth.

Demos, the ever-hopeful guardian of democracy, was appalled by what he saw. His beloved Chamber, the very heart of governance, had been reduced to a swampy ruin. The clear voices of debate were drowned out by the oppressive dampness and shadows. As he trudged through the thick muck, despair weighed heavily on him. This was not the Chamber he'd learnt so many valuable lesson from; it had become a twisted caricature of its former self.

Vulgor, had woven himself into every dark corner of the Chamber, manipulating the chaos to his advantage. The swamp was his domain, a place where deceit and corruption were the currency of power. He delighted in the disarray, knowing that morality could easily be blurred and rules were made to be broken. He lurked in the shadows, watching with a sly grin as noble intentions slipped beneath the muck, replaced by back stabbing and manipulation.

Kratos, always calculating, saw the swamp differently from his brother. Where Demos mourned the loss of integrity, Kratos saw fertile ground for his ambitions. In the confusion and corruption, he recognized the potential to seize control. The more muddled things became, the more opportunities he spotted for exploiting the system. An idea was starting to dawn upon Kratos, about how he could use this environment to further his goals. All the while Vulgor kept a close eye on him, sensing a kindred spirit in Kratos's growing appetite for power.

## MURKY DEALINGS

The swamp's murky waters were thick with corruption. Bribes and kickbacks flowed freely, greasing the wheels of influence. Positions and favours were auctioned to the highest bidder, while principles and justice were swept away. Demos, horrified by the swamp's reality, realized that the Chamber's leaders were no longer serving the public good but were driven by greed. The smell of moral decay clung to every decision, making every action suspect and tainted.

**KRATOS BEGAN TO PLOT HOW HE COULD USE THIS ENVIRONMENT TO FURTHER HIS GOALS.**

## TANGLE OF BUREAUCRACY

Bureaucracy, once a tool for order, had become a thicket of red tape designed to confuse and delay. Procedures now twisted into labyrinthine mazes that protected Vulgor's cronies while burying honest efforts under piles of paperwork. Vulgor used this complexity to conceal his misdeeds, hiding behind layers of pointless regulations. Demos began to wade through the swamp, attempting to cut away the tangle of bureaucracy which only seemed to get thicker as he progressed.

## SELF-SERVING INTERESTS

Self-serving interests ruled the Chamber. Every decision was skewed to benefit a select few, with leaders focused solely on their own gain. Lobby groups and special interests had taken root, their influence spreading like weeds, choking out any semblance of fairness. Kratos, sensing opportunity, aligned himself with these powerful players, seeing them as tools to further his ambitions.

## GREEDY LOBBY GROUPS

Lobby groups prowled the swamp's depths, wielding power not through democracy but through manipulation and back door deals. These groups, representing the wealthiest and most powerful, shaped policies in their favour while the common aplings paid the price. Their influence ran deep, as they pulled strings from the shadows, controlling political decision-making in the Mountain.

As Demos struggled to salvage what was left of honest governance, Kratos quietly maneuvered through the swamp, plotting his rise. The Political Chamber was no longer a place of noble ideals; it had become a festering swamp of corruption, bureaucracy, self-interest, and shadowy deals.

## THE STENCH OF CRONYISM

Cronyism had spread through the Political Chamber like vines choking a once-thriving tree. Vulgor, ever cunning, had orchestrated a network where loyalty to him meant power, and merit was left to wither. Positions of influence were handed not to those with the skills to lead, but to those who owed Vulgor a favour or whispered his name in dark corners. Friendships and alliances, rather than ability, determined who climbed the ranks. Demos, with his strong sense of fairness, could see the damage this web of favouritism was causing, but each attempt to tear it down only seemed to tighten its grip. Meanwhile, Vulgor sat smugly in the shadows, knowing that as long as his cronies held power, the system would remain rigged in his favour, and true progress would be buried under layers of personal loyalty and corruption.

As the brothers waded deeper through the muck, the stench grew thicker, clinging to the air like a warning. They squinted into the shadows, where a strange scurrying sound echoed from a dark corner of the swamp. Then they saw them – hundreds of rats and mice, their eyes gleaming in the dim light, skittering in every direction across the sludge. The rodents moved as if drawn by something unseen, weaving through the grime, their presence unsettling and eerie. Kratos's curiosity was piqued, while Demos felt yet again, a creeping sense of dread.

*The swamp is no place for the faint of heart. 1356.*

231

# INFESTATION OF MICE

The brothers watched in uneasy silence as a torrent of mice scurried through the swamp, gathering in one dark, festering corner.

The sight of the swarm was unsettling, the rodents weaving through the muck, their eyes glinting with a strange urgency. As Kratos and Demos moved closer, they saw a familiar figure – Vulgor, crouched in the shadows, his eyes gleaming with wicked delight as the mice crawled over his arms and shoulders, like loyal disciples swarming to a master.

"Ah, Kratos," Vulgor purred, brushing a few mice from his sleeve but letting others run freely over his hands. "You want control? Real control?" He leaned closer to Kratos, his voice dripping with a sinister promise. "If you want to rule this mountain, you need to understand what drives creatures – what lures them in and makes them loyal, just like these little ones." He let his hand drop, allowing a mouse to skitter over his fingers. "It's not just laws or alliances that give you power. No, true power comes from knowing what makes an apling tick – what can push them to betray their own."

Kratos's gaze sharpened, and Vulgor grinned, sensing his interest. "Let me introduce you to M.I.C.E. – Money, Ideology, Coercion, Ego," he said, savoring each word. "Four little temptations that can open the door to any soul, no matter how loyal. With M.I.C.E., you can pull the strings of anyone on this mountain, turning them into your ally – or your pawn."

Demos shifted, a flicker of alarm in his eyes, but Kratos leaned in closer, captivated by the idea. Vulgor let the silence linger, watching Kratos absorb his words, the mice crawling over him like living symbols of each temptation. Then, with a sly smile, he began to explain how each of these motives could be used to unlock the hearts and minds of any apling on Monkey Mountain.

*Covered in mice and other vermin, Vulgor*
*espouses the virtues of M.I.C.E. 1364.*

## MONEY: THE GOLDEN BAIT

"First, there's money," Vulgor whispered, his voice dripping with enticement. "For some aplings, gold is all it takes to make them see things your way. Just a taste, and even the most steadfast can be bought. No one's immune to the lure of wealth, Kratos – not even those who preach virtue. Some aplings will abandon their beliefs in a heartbeat if their pockets are filled."

Kratos thought back to the dealings he'd observed, how bribes flowed easily in the Chamber's shadows. He understood that money wasn't just currency; it was leverage. By offering financial gain, he could entice others to support his rise. A few coins here, a promise of riches there, and suddenly, allies would emerge. It was a powerful weapon for the ambitious.

## IDEOLOGY: THE CALL OF BELIEF

**THESE APLINGS ARE EASY TO SWAY IF YOU PLAY TO THEIR SENSE OF PURPOSE.**

"Then, there's ideology," Vulgor continued, his eyes gleaming with cunning. "Some are driven by ideals, by a deep, burning belief that their way is the only way. These aplings are easy to sway if you play to their sense of purpose. Stroke their ideals, make them feel like they're part of something bigger, and they'll follow you to the ends of the mountain."

Kratos felt a thrill of understanding. If he could present himself with the beliefs of others, he wouldn't need to coerce or bribe them. By appearing as their ally, he could manipulate them into supporting his ambitions. The Chamber was full of aplings with strong ideals, and Vulgor's lesson showed him a way to turn those convictions into a tool for power.

## COERCION: THE IRON GRIP

Vulgor's tone darkened, his grin widening. "And if money and ideals don't sway them, Kratos, there's always coercion. Blackmail, threats, a little pressure on a hidden weakness. Every apling has a secret. Dig a little, find what they fear, and you can twist them to your will without them ever knowing they had a choice."

Kratos felt a shiver of excitement mixed with trepidation. He knew that fear was a powerful motivator, and the idea of controlling others through their own vulnerabilities appealed to his growing desire for dominance. With coercion, he could pull strings from the shadows, bending others to his will without lifting a finger.

## EGO: THE SWEET POISON

Finally, Vulgor leaned in close, a knowing smile on his lips. "And the sweetest lure of all – ego. Every apling wants to feel important, special, like they matter more than the rest. Flatter them, make them feel like they're in on the secrets, and they'll do anything to keep that feeling."

Kratos's gaze darkened with ambition. He knew that within the Political Chamber, many aplings were hungry for admiration. By stroking their egos, he could manipulate them, convincing them that they were essential to his plans. They'd serve his ambitions, thinking they were acting for themselves.

## THE TRAP IS SET

Vulgor stepped back, his eyes glittering with satisfaction. "Now you understand, Kratos. M.I.C.E. is the key to control. With these tools, you can sway any apling to your side, no matter how stubborn or self-righteous they may seem."

Demos, his face tight with disgust, grabbed Kratos firmly by the arm. "Enough of this," he snapped, pulling him away from the writhing mass of vermin and Vulgor's sinister whispers. They stumbled deeper into the swamp, the murky darkness swallowing them as they fled. But soon, a rancid stench filled the air, stopping them in their tracks. Flies swarmed around something large and shapeless, half-submerged in the muck. They exchanged wary glances, and moved closer to investigate the hulking shadow before them, an unnatural presence writhing and pulsing, as if the swamp itself had given birth to a monster.

*The Blob – once a guardian, now a monster of surveillance, feeding on fear and control. 1254.*

# THE BLOB

I n the deepest, murkiest corner of the swamp, shrouded in shadow and decay, was a grotesque mutation known as The Blob.

This foul creature, bloated and massive, sat half-submerged in the dirty rotten sludge. Hunched and heaving, it was an unusual conglomeration of mechanical, sluggish substance, with surveillance cameras sprouting out from its sides like grotesque mushrooms. Its many metal tendrils coiled and uncoiled, slowly churning the muck around it, eyes blinking and swiveling, constantly scanning. The Blob had, in a previous incarnation been the silent protector of Monkey Mountain, a combination of defense and intelligence forces meant to keep the people safe. But now, it had mutated into a self-serving aberration, obsessed with preserving its own power, rather than safeguarding the aplings.

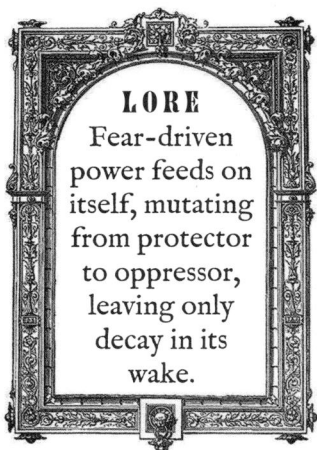

**LORE**
Fear-driven power feeds on itself, mutating from protector to oppressor, leaving only decay in its wake.

Demos and Kratos coughed and gagged as they got closer, repulsed by the sight and overwhelmed by the smell of rot. The air was thick with the stench of decay, and the flies swarmed heavily around the Blob, drawn to the corruption exuding from its pores. Demos felt a surge of anger and dread – this was the deep state's true form, a lumbering monster that thrived on fear, controlling everything it touched. Kratos, however, viewed the creature in a different light. It was terrifying, yes, but also intriguing. He could see how The Blob had embedded itself into the the bowels of the chamber, using fear and surveillance to tighten its grip. In it, Kratos saw potential – a powerful ally, a means to amplify his own ambitions if he played his cards right.

# IT HAD SHIFTED ITS FOCUS INWARD, NO LONGER PROTECTING FROM EXTERNAL THREATS BUT INSTEAD MONITORING AND CONTROLLING ITS OWN PEOPLE.

From the shadows, Vulgor watched. He slithered through the filth, grinning as the brothers gazed upon the creature. He could see the conflict written on their faces: Demos, the moral compass, horrified by The Blob's sheer existence, and Kratos, the opportunist, sensing a chance to wield more power. Vulgor had no love for The Blob, but he understood its utility – it created the perfect storm of paranoia and fear, keeping the aplings in line. The more fear it sowed, the more indispensable it became. And Kratos... Vulgor could already see the wheels turning in Kratos's mind, the dark seed of ambition sprouting. If he could sway Kratos further, The Blob would serve them both well.

## DEEP STATE DOMINANCE

The Blob was the embodiment of deep state dominance, a repulsive machine born from the defense and intelligence agencies that had once served the mountain. Over time, it had shifted its focus inward, no longer protecting from external threats but instead monitoring and controlling its own people. Its surveillance reached every corner of the mountain, its tentacles collecting information on every citizen. It operated unseen, shaping the political landscape from the depth of the swamp, submerged in the Political Chamber, a silent puppeteer pulling the strings.

## FEEDING ON FEAR

But The Blob wasn't just a machine; it thrived on fear. It fed off crises, real or fabricated, to justify its ever-growing reach. Through carefully timed propaganda and covert manipulations, The Blob kept the citizens of Monkey Mountain in a state of constant unease. Its influence stretched into every law, every decision, and every policy, all designed to maintain the illusion that its control was necessary. Kratos recognized the power in this strategy – fear was a tool, one he could use to silence opposition and cement his own authority when the time came.

## VULGOR'S SCHEME

As the brothers stood before The Blob, Vulgor lurked in the background, plotting. He watched Demos closely, knowing that his integrity could unravel everything if left unchecked. But his true focus was on Kratos. The young leader's fascination with The Blob hadn't gone unnoticed. Vulgor grinned – Kratos could be brought into the fold, corrupted by the same power that now consumed the Chamber. The Blob, if fed constantly, was an instrument of unparalleled control. Vulgor would make sure Kratos understood that.

Connected to The Blob's omnipresent surveillance apparatus was another mutation, also tightening its grip on the mountain – The Police State. If The Blob represented control through spying and secrecy, then The Police State was its enforcer, ensuring that fear translated into absolute order. Demos steeled himself, knowing that if they were to get closer to discovering the seeds of corruption, then this was another part of the swamp they'd need to explore.

*The Blob's omnipresent surveillance apparatus mutates out of its carcass. 1253.*

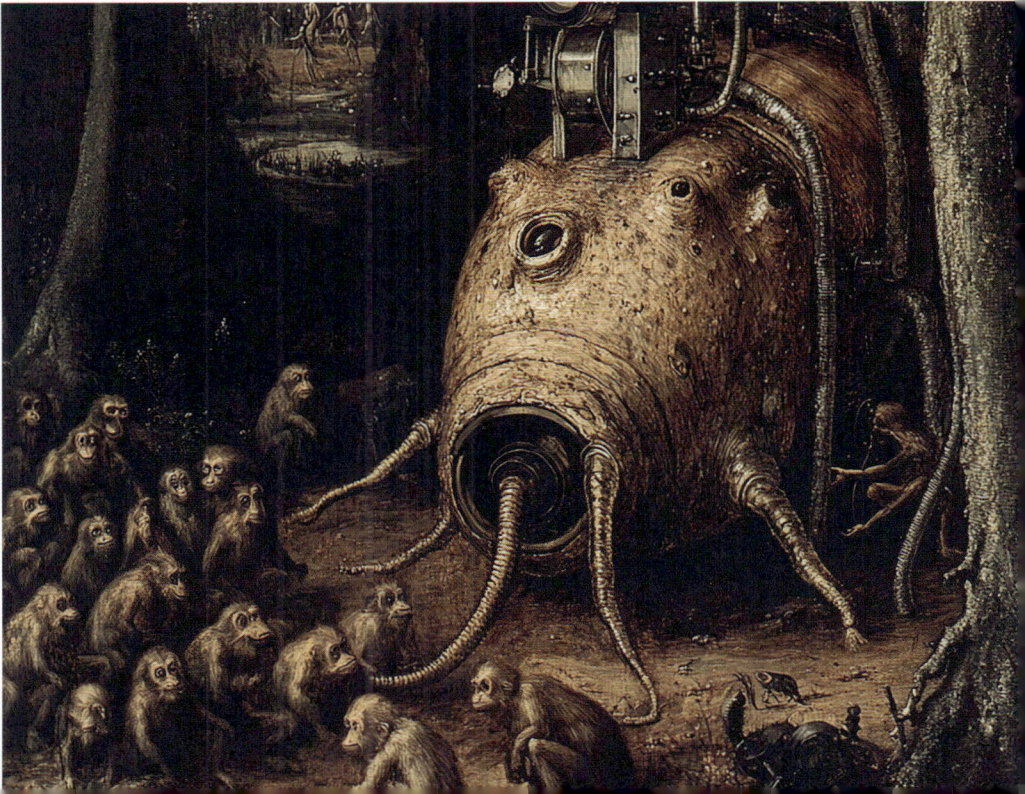

# FREEDOM'S CHAINS

The air grew colder as Demos and Kratos waded further into the swamp, as the oppressive muck sloshed around their legs.

They had passed The Blob, its tendrils of surveillance, spreading influence throughout the mountain. But now, something even more sinister lay ahead. It wasn't just about control through observation – it was about enforcing that control. The shadow of The Police State loomed large, a force ready to crush any resistance to the mountain's growing corruption.

Through the mist, a figure emerged – Grimora. A rigid and fearsome character, his body clad in dark armor, blotted with swamp muck. He'd been sent over at the behest of Vulgor to illuminate the brothers on the virtue of enforced authority. His eyes were cold, calculating. Wherever he went, order followed, but not the kind born of justice. This was the order of suppression, where every citizen's movement was watched, and any sign of dissent swiftly punished. The Police State had grown in strength, ensuring that fear, instigated by The Blob, was now sustained through his iron grip on power.

Grimora gazed at these two unassuming, frankly pathetic little aplings. Demos clenched his fists, sensing the suffocating nature of his regime, where no one dared to speak freely. "This is how they maintain control," Demos whispered. "They keep the mountain in line through fear, turning neighbours into informants and making enemies of those who dare to think differently."

**PEACE AND SECURITY ENSURED BY A FIRM HAND.**

*The police state demands obedience, wielding fear to control the masses. 1487.*

"A police state suppresses more than crime, Kratos. It suppresses freedom, individuality, and the very spirit of our society. We cannot trade liberty for the illusion of security."

But the idea of absolute control was already taking root in Kratos's mind. The vision of a perfectly ordered society was a powerful temptation.

## ENFORCED ORDER

The police state's most tempting promise was the guarantee of enforced order. Grimora, with his grave and convincing tone, painted a picture of a mountain free from chaos. "Think of it, Kratos," he whispered, "a society where every action is monitored, and every transgression swiftly punished. The mountain would be safe, secure, and prosperous."

Kratos imagined the power of such control. With a dedicated enforcement body, he could maintain order without the constant bickering and unrest. The chamber's debates would become mere formalities, as the real power would lie with those who enforced the law.

## SUPPRESSION OF FREEDOM

Demos, ever the guardian of freedom, warned of the perils of a police state. "A society under constant surveillance is a society that lives in fear," he argued. "It stifles creativity, suppresses dissent, and breeds mistrust among its people."

But Kratos, seduced by the vision of unchallenged control, began to see Demos's warnings as resistance to necessary order. The idea of a society where every action was regulated and every apling's behavior monitored was becoming more attractive.

**A SOCIETY WHERE EVERY ACTION IS MONITORED, AND EVERY TRANSGRESSION SWIFTLY PUNISHED.**

## THE ILLUSION OF SECURITY

Grimora continued his persuasion, describing a mountain where security was paramount. "Imagine a world, Kratos, where every apling feels safe, knowing that any disruption will be swiftly dealt with. The peace that comes from absolute control is worth any sacrifice."

Kratos, increasingly obsessed with the idea of maintaining order, saw this as the ultimate solution to the mountain's problems. The loyalty and obedience of the aplings would be ensured by their fear of punishment.

Demos, sensing the growing danger in his brother's eyes, tried once more to dissuade him. "Kratos, a police state may promise security, but it delivers oppression. It will destroy the very fabric of our society."

## THE GRIP OF CONTROL

From the shadows, Vulgor watched with a satisfied smirk. The seeds of the police state had taken root, promising a new form of control. As Kratos entertained these notions of absolute order, the lively debates of the Political Chamber seemed increasingly irrelevant. The vibrant democracy, once full of diverse voices and ideas, teetered on the brink of becoming a rigid, regimented society under Grimora's iron grip.

*Vulgor's grip of control over the Police State invariably led to its corruption and brutality. 1608.*

Kratos, drawn ever deeper into the allure of unchallenged authority, began to drift from Demos's counsel. The idea of ruling without the chaos of disagreement or dissent seemed like the perfect solution to his growing ambition. But as Vulgor observed, he knew that control didn't stop with force. The next step was subtler, more insidious – censorship. It wasn't enough to just impose order; ideas themselves had to be shaped and silenced. The Political Chamber was on the verge of not just suppression of dissent, but the manipulation of thought itself. The road to tyranny would be paved by controlling not just actions, but minds.

*Subservient aplings attend to the Censorship Machine, ensuring that no inconvenient facts are printed for general consumption. 1563.*

# THE CENSORSHIP MACHINE

Vulgor slithered amongst the shadows, his voice a low, enticing whisper. "Kratos," he hissed, "there's more to power than muscle and fear.

**LORE**

Silencing voices may bring order for a time, but a truth buried too deep will always rise.

His eyes gleamed as he beckoned Kratos deeper into the swamp, where another of his dark creations lay in wait. "Come with me, and I'll show you how real control works."

Kratos, always curious when power was on the table, followed Vulgor deeper into the swamp. There, hidden in another murky corner, was a strange machine – metallic pipes twisted like vines, churning out neatly printed newspapers. "This," Vulgor whispered, grinning, "is the censorship machine. Watch closely."

The contraption puffed out "truths" into the press – carefully curated stories that painted a rosy picture of the mountain's leadership. But at the same time, thick tentacles snatched away inconvenient facts, erasing them from headlines before they ever saw the light of day. "This is how you control a narrative," Vulgor continued. "You don't just stop the wrong voices – you feed the right ones. Let the people see only what you want them to see."

Kratos's eyes gleamed with intrigue, but Demos, trailing behind, wasn't having it. "This is poison, Kratos. It'll choke out any real ideas and bury the truth. Censorship isn't about keeping order – it's about burying freedom."

But the seed had been planted. The machine hummed away, printing its perfectly polished "truths," and Kratos couldn't shake the appeal of controlling what people knew, steering their thoughts. Vulgor, watching his growing fascination, grinned wider, knowing Kratos was one step closer to succumbing to complete corruption.

## A CENSORED SOCIETY IS A SILENT ONE, IT SUPPRESSES DISSENT AND CRUSHES THE SPIRIT OF FREEDOM.

### CONTROL OF INFORMATION

Censorship's most tempting promise was the control of information. Vulgor, ever the smooth operator, beckoned Kratos closer to the hulking machine – its pipes twisting like tentacles, pumping out neatly filtered messages. "Think of the stability, Kratos," he whispered, his voice as slick as the machine's oily gears. "With control over what is said and heard, we can guide the mountain toward a singular vision of prosperity."

Kratos imagined the power of such control. With the ability to shape the narrative, he could eliminate dissent and ensure that his vision for the mountain was the only one that mattered. The once-chaotic chamber debates and conflicts would become a distant memory, replaced by a harmonious, unified message.

*When censorship blinds citizens to the truth, they stumble through lies, thinking they walk in the light. 1563.*

### SUPPRESSION OF DISSENT

Demos, standing firm in his principles, was quick to warn of the dangers lurking in Vulgor's scheme. "A censored society is a silent one," he argued. "It suppresses dissent and crushes the spirit of freedom. Without the free exchange of ideas, we lose innovation, creativity, and the very heart of what makes us aplings."

But Kratos, eyes gleaming with ambition, began to see Demos's concerns as mere roadblocks. The thought of a society where only supportive voices echoed was becoming more appealing by the minute.

### PROPAGANDA & CONTROL

Vulgor, sensing Kratos's growing interest, pushed further. "Imagine, Kratos," he said, gesturing to the machine's tentacle-like pipes that snaked out messages of control, "a world where every message reinforces your leadership. The people would see only your vision, believe only your truth. This is the real power of censorship."

Kratos, captivated by the idea, envisioned not just leading but controlling the very thoughts of his people. Loyalty and obedience would be guaranteed by the relentless, unchallenged narrative fed through the machine.

Demos, watching the dangerous glint in Kratos's eyes, made one last plea. "Kratos, a society that controls information controls minds. This peace you're imagining is nothing but an illusion, built on the suppression of truth. We need to protect the free exchange of ideas, or we risk losing everything that makes us a society."

**LOYALTY AND OBEDIENCE WOULD BE GUARANTEED BY THE RELENTLESS, UNCHALLENGED NARRATIVE FED THROUGH THE MACHINE.**

### THE FINAL TEMPTATION

The Censorship Machine hummed steadily in the background, its tentacles churning out carefully crafted truths while erasing anything that didn't fit the narrative. Kratos stood silently, the weight of the decision pressing on him. The allure of total control – the ability to shape what the mountain saw, heard, and believed – was irresistible. Demos's words of warning hung in the air, but they felt distant, drowned out by the seductive promise of a unified message, free from chaos or challenge.

Vulgor, watching Kratos's internal struggle, grinned to himself. He knew the young leader was nearing a choice that could not be undone. Control of information was only the beginning – next would come the power to rule without interference, without dissent. Autocracy was the natural progression, and Kratos was walking straight toward it.

**LORE**
Censorship may muzzle dissent, but a silenced truth only grows louder in the minds it's denied.

As the brothers turned away from the machine, the path ahead led them further into the foul stench of the swamp, where the dark allure of absolute power waited to pull Kratos further into its grasp.

# AUTOCRATIC AUTHORITY

**V**ulgor had been patient, watching the divide between Demos and Kratos slowly widen.

It was only a matter of time before Kratos, already seduced by the ideas of censorship and control, would be ready for his next step. From the shadows, Vulgor emerged, his towering form casting an oppressive presence over the scene. As the brothers waded through the swamp, he subtly maneuvered closer to Kratos, asserting his influence with a physical command that compelled silence. "You've seen the power of controlling information," Vulgor whispered, his voice low and persuasive. "But why stop there? Imagine a mountain where there's no need for debate, no need for anyone else's input. You could rule alone, with no one to challenge your decisions."

Kratos hesitated for a moment, glancing back at Demos, who was distracted by the surrounding decay. But Vulgor pressed on. He stepped closer, his imposing frame forcing Kratos to focus on him. "Autocracy, Kratos," he murmured, "is true freedom—not for the people, but for you. No endless arguments, no more opposition. Every decision would be yours. You'd shape the mountain entirely in your image, with no one to slow you down."

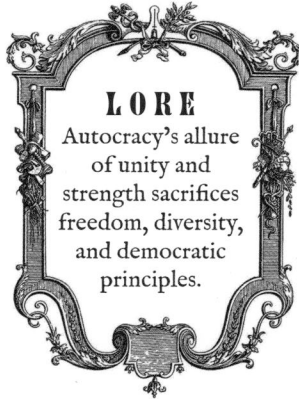

> **LORE**
>
> Autocracy's allure of unity and strength sacrifices freedom, diversity, and democratic principles.

A cautious silence fell as the surrounding aplings watched the interaction with a mixture of fear and awe, recognizing Vulgor's dominance. Kratos, intrigued by the idea, could see the appeal. The thought of ruling alone, free from the chaotic tug-o-war that had defined life in the Political Chamber, was intoxicating. Demos's warnings felt like a distant echo, easily ignored. Vulgor, sensing the shift, smiled slyly. Kratos was on the edge, ready to embrace the idea of absolute rule, where his word would be law and the mountain would bend entirely to his will.

*Under the banner of absolute rule, the loyal march forward, their faces grim with duty, knowing the only voice that matters is the one that commands them. 1258.*

> **LORE**
>
> Autocracy's allure of absolute power sacrifices freedom and stifles innovation, ultimately breeding tyranny and undermining the vibrant essence of democracy.

## ABSOLUTE POWER

Autocracy's most alluring promise was the concentration of absolute power. Vulgor, always lurking with his silver tongue, painted a picture of a mountain where one leader's vision dictated every aspect of life. He leaned close to Kratos, his imposing figure making his whispered words impossible to ignore. "Think of the efficiency, Kratos," he murmured, his voice smooth and persuasive. "No more endless debates, no more divisions. Just a single, unstoppable force driving the mountain forward – your force."

Kratos envisioned the power he could wield. With all authority concentrated in his hands, he could shape the mountain's future without interference. The chamber's lively debates and differing opinions – once seen as a strength – now seemed like needless obstacles. Vulgor's vision of a unified, unquestioned rule began to take hold in Kratos's mind, the appeal of silencing chaos too strong to ignore.

## SUPPRESSION OF OPPOSITION

Catching back up to his brother and hearing what was going on, Demos, ever the voice of reason, saw the dangers of autocracy clearly. "An autocratic regime silences all opposition," he warned. "It crushes individual freedoms and imposes uniformity. The vibrant voices that make our society thrive will be smothered."

But Kratos, now entranced by the vision of unchallenged authority, began to see Demos's concerns as little more than roadblocks to progress. The idea of a mountain where every apling followed a single, cohesive plan was growing ever tastier by the second.

## CULT OF PERSONALITY

Vulgor, sensing Kratos's growing hunger for power, continued his manipulation. He positioned himself as a figure of respect and fear, his towering form evoking both admiration and wariness from the observing aplings. "Imagine the unity, Kratos," he murmured. "The leader

isn't just a ruler but the embodiment of the mountain's spirit. The people will see you as their savior, their guide. You'll become a legend, not just a leader."

Kratos, captivated by the notion, could see the potential. The loyalty of the aplings would be unwavering, their devotion absolute. He wasn't just imagining ruling; he was imagining himself as the hero of the mountain's story.

Demos, recognizing the dangerous gleam in his brother's eyes, tried once more to reach him. "Kratos, a society built around one individual is doomed to collapse. It breeds fanaticism and stifles growth. We must remain a community of equals, or we lose everything that makes us strong."

## ESCAPE THE CLUTCHES

Seeing the danger in his brother's eyes, Demos knew it was time to act. Before Vulgor's whispers could sink in any deeper, he grabbed Kratos by the arm and pulled him away from the shadowy figure's clutch. "We're done here," Demos muttered, his voice firm. The brothers moved quickly, escaping the swamp's foul air, with Vulgor's lingering voice fading behind them.

They found a tunnel and ran down it, escaping the political swamp, heading towards The Economic Chamber—a place where power was fueled by wealth, and control would take on an entirely different form. Demos knew the fight for the mountain's future wasn't over, and Kratos, though still enticed by Vulgor's promises, was not lost yet. The next battle would be fought with riches, not words.

> # THEY FOUND A TUNNEL AND RAN DOWN IT, ESCAPING THE POLITICAL SWAMP.

251

# CHAPTER X
# KLEPTO

ECONOMIC X.I
CORRUPTION
OLIGOPOLY X.II
KLEPTOCRACY X.III
CONSUMERISM X.IV
WEALTH X.V
TRANSFER
MILITARY-INDUSTRIAL COMPLEX X.VI

*Klepto gorges on wealth without end, driven by insatiable greed. 1487.*

# KLEPTO'S CORRUPTION OF ECONOMIC POWER

The moment Kratos and Demos stepped into the Economic Chamber, the grinding of the Great Engine hit them like a groan from some tired old beast.

Once the pride of the mountain, it now wheezed and sputtered, gears choked with the sticky residue of corruption. Demos stopped dead, his face twisted in dismay. "Look at it," he said, shaking his head. "The whole thing's breaking down, just like the Political Chamber. Corruption's strangling everything."

Kratos, on the other hand, wasn't so quick to judge. He eyed the failing machine with a peculiar glint in his eye, as if something about its downfall intrigued him. Where Demos saw ruin, Kratos saw possibilities – an opportunity for those sharp enough to work the angles. Sure, the engine was sputtering, but maybe, just maybe, that's where the real power lay: in knowing how to turn a broken system to your advantage.

**LORE**

Corruption thrives where ambition overshadows integrity and trust falters.

From the shadows, Klepto the Profitroll gave a sly grin. He knew a kindred spirit when he saw one. Around them, the market buzzed with activity, but beneath the surface, it was all rotten. Every deal was laced with greed, and the economy – like that sputtering engine – was just waiting for someone to take control. And Kratos, wondered if that someone might just be him?

*Klepto hoards treasures with ravenous hunger, believing every scrap of wealth is rightfully his. 1587.*

## KLEPTO THE PROFITROLL

As the brothers moved cautiously through the throng, keenly observing the scene. A shadowy figure emerged from the crowd – Grafton, a seasoned apling marked by countless deals. He motioned them closer, his voice a gravelly whisper of experience.

"Beware, young ones," Grafton began, his eyes darting nervously. "This chamber is not all it seems. Beneath every deal lies a trap. Unseen forces are twisting our economy's fabric." Kratos, skeptical, folded his arms. "What forces? Speak plainly."

Grafton leaned in, his voice lowering. "Klepto the Profitroll, the spirit of corruption. He whispers lies and promises of easy wealth, ensnaring the greedy. His power grows with each dishonest deal." Demos leaned in, wary but curious. "How does he corrupt so many?"

"It starts small – a coin skimmed, a price inflated. These minor deceptions feed Klepto's hunger, spreading like a disease. Soon, tiny thefts rot our economy from within."

## CORRUPTION OF ECONOMIC POWER

As Grafton spoke, Klepto's presence seemed to thicken, a dark silhouette flickering at the chamber's edges. He whispered temptations, urging traders to chase quick riches. The more they succumbed, the deeper they sank into his grasp.

Kratos noticed a trader pocketing extra coins. A flicker of recognition crossed his face, curiosity about the power such actions could bring. He frowned, lost in thought. Demos, however, felt a surge of indignation. "This is unacceptable," he declared, his voice filled with anger. "We can't let this corruption destroy us."

Grafton nodded. "Indeed. The corruption of economic power is a slow-acting poison, creeping into every deal, breeding inequality and distrust. Left unchecked, it will undermine our society."

## BRIBERY

Grafton continued, his voice dropping to a conspiratorial whisper. "Bribery is one of Klepto's favorite tools. It starts with a small favour, a quiet exchange of coins for influence. A trader wants a permit? A council member turns a blind eye – for the right price. Soon, decisions that should be made for the good of all are bought and sold like common goods. The wealthy bend the rules to their will, while the honest are left behind. The whole system tilts in favor of those who can pay, leaving fairness choking in the dust." Demos clenched his fists, his face flushed with anger. "It's a betrayal," he muttered.

## EXTORTION

"But bribery's dark twin," Grafton added grimly, "is extortion. This isn't about offering rewards; it's about wielding fear like a club. Imagine a merchant who refuses to play by Klepto's rules. Suddenly, their goods go missing, their debts increase, or worse, their reputation crumbles. Extortion squeezes the life out of those who resist, forcing them to bend to the will of the corrupt. It's not just about money – it's about control. Those who give in survive, but their dignity is left in ruins." Kratos listened, his expression unreadable, but his eyes gleamed, seeing the power hidden within such tactics.

**THE CORRUPTION OF ECONOMIC POWER IS A SLOW-ACTING POISON.**

*Extortion takes many forms – wealth, fear, and violence, all tools to demand compliance. 1487.*

# THE OLIGOPOLY GAME

As Kratos drifted through the chamber, Klepto's presence seemed to grow thicker, his whispers slithering into every corner of his mind.

"Well now," Klepto purred, smooth as a jungle cat stalking prey, "I hear tell you've just come from the Political Chamber. Perfect timing, my friend. I've got a little scheme that might pique your interest – something called an oligopoly. Ever heard of it?"

Kratos shot Klepto a sidelong glance, curious but careful. He kept quiet, letting the Profitroll run his mouth. "Picture this," Klepto continued, his grin widening like a snake's uncoiling. "Just a handful of traders – not many, mind you – pulling all the strings. They put on a good show of competing, make a fuss over prices, but behind closed doors? They've got the whole game stitched up tighter than a bat's wing. Fix the prices, limit supply, and leave the little guys scrambling over the scraps. Best part? The aplings think they've got choices, but truth be told, it's all rigged from the start."

Kratos's eyes flickered with interest, though he kept his expression neutral. "And how exactly does this all work?" Klepto chuckled, a low, knowing sound. "Ah, now we're getting somewhere. It's all about control. See, an oligopoly isn't just about locking down the market – it's about bending the Political Chamber to serve you. Once you grease the right palms, those leaders stop worrying about the public and start doing your bidding. Bribery, my boy, makes the whole machine hum. A deal here, a favour there, and suddenly the laws fall right into place. Keep the competition out, and the big fish swim free."

Klepto leaned closer, his grin sly. "And you, Kratos – well, you've got the connections now, don't you? Fresh out of the Political Chamber. You could help make this happen. And there's gold in it – plenty of it." Kratos stayed silent, but his mind was spinning. Demos would never go for this – that much was certain. But the temptation was clear as day. Control over the economy, power over the rules – it was a game that, once you knew how to play, was mighty hard to resist.

*A gathering of oligarchs hoard their treasures,*
*feasting while the rest go without. 1522.*

# RULE BY THIEVES

**T**he Great Engine of the Economic Chamber wheezed and groaned, barely turning as layers of corruption clogged its once-efficient gears.

Yet, despite the Engine's sputtering, the aplings were still expected to keep carrying their burdens to the Aqua Exchange – taxes paid in blood, sweat, and tears. They laboured day and night, hoping their contributions would keep the system alive, even as it faltered.

Demos stood by the Exchange, watching as tired aplings lined up to give away what little they had left. "How can they demand more when the system's falling apart?" he muttered, disgusted by the injustice unfolding before him.

Kratos lingered behind, separated from his brother, when Klepto once again sidled up to him, his voice a low, tempting hiss. "Look at them, Kratos. Toiling for a broken system that gives them nothing in return. But those in power? They thrive. That's the beauty of a kleptocracy – a system designed by those who hoard, like me. Trust no one, share with no one, and you're untouchable."

Kratos's eyes flicked between the weary aplings and Klepto's gleaming grin. "How can they keep taking?"

Klepto chuckled darkly. "Because they're too distracted by their own struggles. The secret isn't just outright theft – it's isolation. Keep everyone's gaze turned inward, make them believe they're alone in their hardship, and they'll never think to question the hand that keeps taking." And Kratos, coming from the Political Chamber, you might be the perfect candidate to join in. But power, real power, belongs to those who trust only themselves."

Kratos felt a spark of temptation, but doubt lingered. "And the people?" he asked. Klepto smirked. "They'll never notice. Keep them focused on their struggles, and you can take whatever you want." With that, he glanced at the crowd with a faint sneer, stepping back as though their proximity alone might threaten his spoils.

*Klepto snatches wealth whilst no one watches, leaving only ruin and poverty in his wake. 1503.*

## EXPLOITING THE MASSES

In a kleptocracy, power isn't just taken – it's systematically extracted. The aplings labour to quench the Aqua Exchange, believing their hard work will support the mountain. But the real wealth is siphoned off by those at the top, funneled into private coffers while the Great Engine sputters. The system is not broken; it's designed to serve those who have the most power, leaving the rest to scrape by. Klepto revelled in his isolation, shielding his wealth from prying eyes, as though any glance might covet what he'd claimed.

## CORRUPTION AS A WAY OF LIFE

Klepto explained how corruption becomes the lifeblood of society. "It starts with little things – bribes, favors, looking the other way. But soon, it's woven into every layer of power. The leaders don't just steal – they own the mechanisms meant to stop them. Even the Aqua Exchange, the heart of the economy, becomes a tool for control. Laws, taxes, trade – they all serve the kleptocrats, while the rest are left with nothing."

As he spoke, Klepto's tone turned guarded, wary, as if the mere act of explaining might give away too much. His grip on his power was ironclad, his manner distant, unwilling to share even a sliver of his insight with any who might one day challenge him.

Kratos listened, and though he could see how deeply the system was rigged, the allure of manipulating such power was undeniable.

*Klepto selfishly hoards another bucket of coins, adding to his ill-gotten haul of wealth. 1397.*

## THE COST OF COMPLICITY

Demos, standing apart, saw only the suffering. "This can't last. The more they take, the more fragile the whole system becomes. The people won't endure this forever."

Klepto laughed out loud. "They'll endure as long as you keep them distracted – give them just enough to keep going, but never enough to rise. Keep them running on the wheel, and they'll never realize they've lost."

Demos burned with righteous anger, but Kratos saw opportunity in the chaos. The deeper they delved into the mechanics of kleptocracy, the clearer it became how power could be wielded, if only one knew how to use it.

And yet, as Klepto spoke, he seemed to withdraw even further, his eyes darting around as though he feared his own words might be stolen. His wealth was his shield, his isolation his armour. To Klepto, every apling was a potential rival, every interaction a threat to the mountain of resources he guarded so closely.

Klepto turned the conversation toward something more insidious. "You see, Kratos, the system doesn't just survive on theft from the top. The aplings themselves are trapped in their own endless cycle – consuming more, always wanting more. Come and see how their desires keep them bound, just as surely as any law..."

## THEY'LL ENDURE AS LONG AS YOU KEEP THEM DISTRACTED.

263

*Aplings busy themselves shopping for the latest gadgets,
gizmos and other nauseating social status-symbols. 1523.*

# MINDLESS CONSUMPTION

**N**avigating their way back to the bazaar, the brothers could tell things had changed, in a peculiar way.

The aplings were no longer just working in the pursuit of prosperity – they were scrambling, obsessed with acquiring the latest trinkets and symbols of status. The marketplace buzzed with frantic energy, but it wasn't driven by need. It was driven by desire. Aplings raced from stall to stall, arms full of goods, their eyes glazed as though hypnotised with desperation. It wasn't about survival anymore; it was about having – the newest, the flashiest, the most expensive.

Klepto, ever the shadow in the corner, watched them with a sly grin. "Ah, mindless consumerism," he whispered. "The perfect distraction. Keep them running in circles, chasing the latest and greatest, and they'll never stop to ask why the system around them is falling apart."

Caught in this rat race, the aplings became blind to the corruption poisoning their economy. They were so consumed with owning the next status symbol, with outpacing their neighbors, that they failed to see the Great Engine sputtering to a halt. They didn't notice their wages shrinking or their debts growing. Their focus had shifted from collective prosperity to individual accumulation.

**LORE**
Chasing possessions blinds us to corruption, trapping us in a cycle of greed and self-destruction.

The more they consumed, the more they fed into the very system that was slowly choking them. Every purchase kept them bound to the illusion that happiness and success were tied to possessions. The deeper they fell into this cycle, the less aware they became of the corruption gnawing at the foundations of their society. And while the aplings raced after shiny things, Klepto's power grew – unchecked and unseen, hidden behind their endless hunger for more.

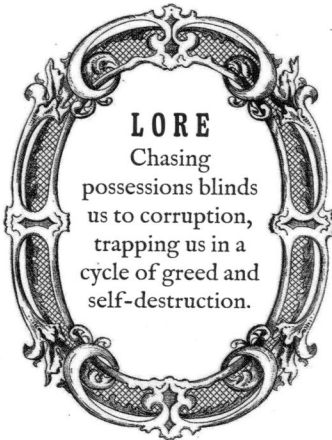

*'Never let a good crisis go to waste' said one ruling oligarch to another. 1575.*

# The Subtle Art of Wealth Transfer

As Klepto led the brothers deeper into the inner workings of the Great Engine, the air once again grew thick with the stench of decay.

The massive gears that once powered their economy lay rusted, barely turning, and yet somehow, wealth still flowed – but not to those who laboured. Klepto's whispers grew more insidious as he leaned close to Kratos. "You see, the true genius of this system isn't in the everyday dealings. It's in the crises – financial, public health, even natural disasters. Each one presents an opportunity."

Kratos raised an eyebrow, intrigued. "Opportunity for whom?"

"For those who know how to play the game," Klepto replied with a grin. "When crises hit, the rules shift. Assets lose value, people panic, and the governments scrambles to keep society afloat. But behind the scenes, the wealthy – those with resources – are buying up everything. Land, businesses, influence. The working class loses homes, savings, their livelihoods, and all that wealth? It flows upward, to the few who know how to seize it."

## WHEN CRISES HIT, THE RULES SHIFT.

Demos, standing at a distance, scowled. "It's exploitation," he muttered. "While the people suffer, the powerful profit."

Klepto waved him off. "Call it what you like, but it's the engine of wealth transfer. Each crisis, whether real or engineered, is a chance for the rich to get richer. The public pays the price while the minority quietly tighten their grip on the system."

## FINANCIAL CRISES

Klepto gestured toward the sputtering gears. "Take financial crises – markets crash, jobs disappear, but the wealthy? They swoop in to buy assets at rock-bottom prices. Governments bail out banks, not the people. And who foots the bill? The middle and working class, through their taxes, their labour, their lost pensions."

## PUBLIC HEALTH CRISES

Klepto continued, his voice dripping with satisfaction. "In public health crises, it's even easier. Companies rake in profits from inflated prices, monopolies grow, and small businesses crumble under pressure. The rich know how to make the chaos work for them. The people fall into debt, and the wealthy consolidate more power."

Kratos nodded, starting to grasp the scale of the game. "So, every crisis is just another tool to keep wealth in the hands of the few."

Klepto grinned wider. "Exactly. And the beauty of it? The masses are too busy struggling to survive, trapped in the rat race just trying to keep up with their ever increasing debts, to see the transfer happening right before their eyes."

As the brothers looked around at the decaying machinery of their economy, Klepto's final whisper echoed. "And the real secret? It's not just about economics. The Military-Industrial Complex does the same – endless conflict, endless profit. It's all part of the same game."

Kratos felt a chill run down his spine as the next layer of the system revealed itself, while Demos prepared himself for the grim truths that lay ahead. The military machine, fueled on stolen wealth, awaited them.

*Stuck in the rat race, an apling must constantly attend to the task of operating a small part of the Great Engine – or risk being swallowed up by it.* 1243.

# THE MILITARY-INDUSTRIAL MONSTER

Τhe further they ventured into the cavernous void of the once prosperous Economic Chamber, the more Klepto's shadow loomed over Kratos.

His whispers grew darker as they approached the Aqua Exchange once more. This time, the brothers saw not just the flow of taxes, but where it was truly being diverted. Klepto, ever the puppet master, smiled as he revealed the truth. "You see, Kratos, it's not just greed for wealth – it's power through conflict. That's the real prize. The taxes, the toil, the sweat of every apling, sucked out of the tax system and funneled into the War Chest. That's how we keep the machine of war alive."

Kratos watched as the Aqua Exchange churned, its flow redirected into the massive war coffers. "Why should the wealth of the people be used for endless conflict?" he asked, though not in outrage, but with curiosity. Klepto, sensing his opening, leaned in closer. "Wars need weapons, soldiers need supplies, and someone has to provide them. The more conflict there is, the more money flows to those who pull the strings. And the beauty of it, Kratos? The people don't even notice. They think their taxes go to schools, roads, health – but it's all siphoned off for power and control. And you, Kratos, you could be part of that."

## DIVERTING PUBLIC WEALTH

Klepto gestured to the grand War Chest, glistening in the corner like a greedy mouth waiting to swallow every last drop. "The Aqua Exchange feeds it. Every crisis, every tax, all drained from the public and fed into the military machine. Weapons are made, conflicts are sustained, and those who control it grow fat off the spoils of endless war. The people think they are safe, but what they really are is trapped – enslaved by their own taxes, their sweat, their lives fueling war."

*The military-industrial complex drains public wealth,*
*pursuing endless war, while the public is left behind. 1-10.*

# CONTRACTS, DEALS, INFLUENCE —ALL YOURS IF YOU KNOW HOW TO PLAY THE GAME.

## WAR'S A RACKET

Kratos was listening closely now, temptation settling in. "So, war is just another way to keep the rich in power?" he asked, his voice neutral but his interest unmistakable. Klepto nodded, eyes gleaming. "Exactly, Kratos. As long as there's conflict, there's profit. The Military-Industrial Complex is like a monster, feeding off fear and uncertainty. Contracts, deals, influence – all yours if you know how to play the game. And you, fresh from the Political Chamber, you have the power to push it forward. Imagine, Kratos. Power beyond mere wealth – control over life and death."

Demos, watching the scene unfold, could barely contain his rage. "This is madness!" he shouted, stepping between Klepto and his brother. "Kratos, don't listen to him! Our people are suffering while this monster feeds off their misery. We've already seen the corruption in the Political Chamber – this is the same thing! But with even more lives at stake!" Kratos hesitated, caught between his brother's fiery anger and Klepto's seductive words.

## ESCAPE TO THE PUBLIC CHAMBER

Klepto grinned, knowing he'd planted a seed of temptation in Kratos's mind. "Your brother's right, you know," Klepto said with a smirk. "This is the same thing, but that doesn't make it wrong. Why shouldn't you take your place among the powerful?"

Demos, his patience fraying, grabbed Kratos by the arm. "We're leaving," he growled, yanking his brother away from Klepto's clutches. "This ends here."

Dragging Kratos down a dark tunnel, Demos led him away from the poisonous influence of Klepto and the Military-Industrial Complex. As the shadows of the Economic Chamber faded behind them, the path ahead opened to the Public Chamber. But after all they'd seen so far, what state would they find it in?

*Once again the War Chest is opened, not in the service of the greater good,
but at the behest of the Military-Industrial complex. 1640.*

# CHAPTER XI
# BRUTUS

# DESTRUCTION OF RIGHTS

XI.I

## FEAR & OBEDIENCE
XI.II

# NIHILISM
XI.III

## THEOCRACY
XI.IV

## SOCIAL DISINTEGRATION
XI.V

*The Tree of Echoes, once a beacon of ethical orientation, now stands desecrated – its lanterns dimmed, aplings scattered beneath it, silenced by fear and obedience. 1429.*

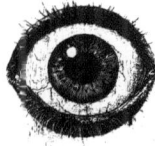

# RIGHTEOUS RUINATION

The brothers tumbled into the Public Chamber, Demos hoping – praying really, to find something, anything, even a sliver of goodness to lift their spirits.

But what greeted them hit harder than a slap in the face. The flicker of hope shriveled up faster than a raindrop on a hot rock. Before them stood the grand old Tree of Echoes – well, what was left of it. Once, it had been the pride of the mountain, its branches heavy with lanterns that burned bright with every right the aplings held dear: free speech, equality, justice – the whole lot. Now, it looked like some poor skeleton left out in the sun too long, its branches brittle and bare. The lanterns lay scattered across the ground like forgotten toys after a storm, their light long gone.

**LORE**
When fear and silence take root, the tree of freedom withers, leaving only the ashes of rights.

Demos stopped dead in his tracks, his jaw swinging open like a door with busted hinges. "What in the name of hell's happened here?" His voice barely cracked the silence, as if speaking any louder might send the old tree crashing to pieces.

Kratos stood beside him, eyes sharp, taking it all in. He stared at the scattered lanterns, his mind starting to churn with strange, heavy thoughts. To him, those lanterns – those so-called rights – were starting to look less like treasures and more like obstacles. They weren't exactly useful if you had bigger plans in mind. And right now, those plans were starting to take root and rattle around inside his head like loose marbles.

A Universal Right is left to rot. 1547.

HE PLACED HIS HAND ON THE ROUGH, CRACKED BARK, AS THOUGH HIS TOUCH COULD SOMEHOW REVIVE WHAT HAD BEEN LOST.

Before Demos could say another word, a small, hunched-over apling crept out from the shadows. He looked like a fella who'd spent his whole life ducking, as if expecting the sky to fall on him any second. His name was Pander, and if feeble could wear a face, it'd look just like his.

"You're Demos and Kratos, ain't ya?" Pander's voice was barely a whisper, so soft it might've been mistaken for the mouses'. Demos, eyes wide with disbelief, stepped closer to the dying Tree of Echoes. He placed his hand on the rough, cracked bark, as though his touch could somehow revive what had been lost. His voice, thick with grief and confusion, finally broke the silence. "Who did this? Who destroyed something that belongs to all aplings?"

Pander flinched, eyes darting nervously as if Brutus himself might leap from the shadows. He hesitated, swallowing hard. "It's not so simple, Demos."

"What do you mean?" Demos asked, his brow furrowing as his hand fell away from the tree. "Was it Brutus? He's behind this, isn't he?"

Pander's shoulders sagged, his voice trembling. "Brutus... he planted the seed, whispered in our ears. But no, it wasn't him who destroyed the tree." He looked down at his feet, shame creeping into his tone. "It was us, Demos. We did it to ourselves."

Demos stepped back, shocked. "We did this? How?"

*Demos ponders the significance of the aplings' universal rights*
*being dismantled from the Tree of Echoes. 1640.*

*Emerging from shadows within the Public Chamber,*
*Brutus scares a young apling into submission. 1269.*

# FEAR'S TOXIC TOUCH

**D**emos stood at the base of the dying Tree, his heart aching as he gazed at the discarded lanterns that once symbolized the most cherished rights of the aplings.

Each broken lantern – freedom of speech, justice, equality – now lay shattered on the ground. "How could this happen?" he whispered, almost to himself.

Pander, his voice a nervous tremble, shuffled his feet. "We were scared," he said, barely able to look Demos in the eye. "Brutus didn't need to lift a finger. All he did was loom over us, his presence alone a threat. He'd stand tall, looking down at anyone who dared speak up, and that was enough. His silence was a warning, his eyes a command. We tore down our own rights, fearing the punishment he might never even deliver."

Demos clenched his fists. "You took down the lanterns yourselves?"

Pander nodded miserably. "At first, just a few of us did, the ones who were most scared of what Brutus might do. They thought taking down a lantern here or there would keep them safe, maybe make Brutus forget about them." His voice dropped even lower, "But it didn't stop there. Once those first lanterns were gone, the others followed out of blind obedience. One by one, they came down – out of the belief that staying quiet and following orders was gonna be the best way to avoid trouble."

## LORE

Fear controls the body, but obedience captures the mind. Together, they build a cage the soul cannot escape.

283

## THE SPREAD OF FEAR

Pander continued, "Brutus didn't need to force anyone. He just spread rumors – whispers that anyone who spoke too loudly or stood up for their rights would be punished. Maybe not today, maybe not tomorrow, but eventually. That was enough. Fear spread like wildfire. Aplings started thinking, 'If we just give up a little bit of freedom, maybe we can stay safe.' And with that thought, the first lanterns came down."

Demos could hardly believe his ears. "But didn't anyone stand up? Didn't anyone try to stop it?"

Pander shook his head. "A few tried, but most were too scared to speak out. Brutus's shadow alone felt like a cage closing around us. It became easier to just follow along, to avoid standing out. The atmosphere of fear was so thick, you could almost taste it."

*Brutus, the Publitroll, revels in chaos – pulling the chains of fear tighter until madness takes hold and reason breaks. 1497.*

## THE POWER OF OBEDIENCE

As the first aplings bowed to fear, the rest followed not out of terror, but obedience. "Once the first lanterns were taken down, the others followed without much protest," Pander explained. "It's funny, in a sad way – once fear gets in your bones, obedience comes easy. Aplings started thinking it was their duty to obey, to take down the lanterns because 'that's just the way things were now.' Brutus didn't have to shout or demand. His gaze and stance spoke louder than words, a silent command that we could not ignore."

Kratos, quiet up to now, had been listening intently. There was a glimmer in his eyes, something stirring. Obedience, he realized, was a tool as powerful as fear itself.

*Huddled in fear, the aplings cling to each other – silent and obedient, believing that compliance will keep them safe. 1367.*

## THE ABANDONMENT OF RIGHTS

Demos looked down at the broken lanterns, his voice thick with disbelief. "But the lanterns... the rights they represented – they were everything. How could you give them up so easily?" Pander's shoulders sagged. "When you're under a gaze that cold and unyielding, rights start to feel like luxuries. Each lantern we removed was like peeling off a layer of our freedom, bit by bit, in exchange for survival. We thought giving them up was the price of safety. But now, with each removed, the silence feels deeper, as if his eyes are still watching."

As they trudged away from the Tree of Echoes with shoulders slumped, Demos couldn't shake the significance of what he'd learned. The death of their freedom hadn't come from a tyrant's sword, but from the quiet whispers of a phantom thug, and the willing hands of the obedient.

**THE FEAR WAS SO THICK, YOU COULD ALMOST TASTE IT.**

285

*Once curious and free, nihilism makes one a prisoner of indifference,*
*locked away by a world that no longer holds meaning. 1367.*

# SURRENDER TO NOTHING

Brutus circled Kratos like a vulture eyeing fresh prey, his voice smooth as silk and heavy with something darker.

"You ever notice, Kratos, how tired they've become? Not the kind of tired you shake off with a good night's sleep – no, this runs deeper. They're drained, right down to their bones. They shuffle through their days, not because they're scared, but because they've given up on the idea that things can be different. It's not fear that keeps them still... it's the absence of meaning."

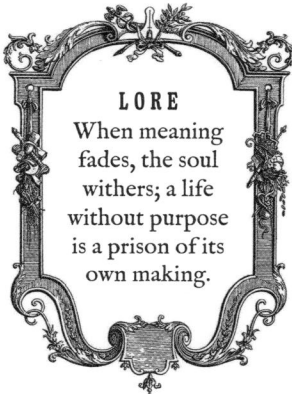

> **LORE**
> When meaning fades, the soul withers; a life without purpose is a prison of its own making.

Kratos glanced toward the aplings beneath the Tree of Echoes, slumped and scattered like shadows of their former selves. They weren't afraid, they weren't angry – they were simply... empty. The fight had gone out of them, not in one grand defeat, but little by little, over time. And now, with nothing to believe in, they had nothing left to resist with.

Brutus leaned in closer, his grin curling at the edges. "That's when you've really won, Kratos. When they stop caring, stop dreaming, stop hoping... that's the beauty of it." He paused, rolling the word slowly on his tongue, like smoke from a dying fire. "It's called Nihilism."

## COMFORTABLY NUMB

Brutus flicked a glance toward Demos, still crouched in the distance, dutifully picking up the broken lanterns. "Look at him," Brutus sneered. "Poor fool, still clinging to the idea that things can be fixed, that there's some grand meaning in all this rubble." He turned back to Kratos, his voice soft and coaxing. "But the smart ones – the ones who see – they know the truth. There's no fixing anything. There's no point in trying. And once they realise that? Oh, it's blissful. No struggle, no ambition, no resistance. Just quiet surrender."

Kratos absorbed the words, letting them settle deep inside. It was like a door opening, a glimpse into a world without friction – no expectations, no demands, no need to carry the weight of others' hopes and dreams. Just silence, stillness, numbness, and a cold kind of peace.

Brutus leaned in closer, his voice now just a whisper. "That's the beauty of nihilism. It's like a blanket – heavy and smothering, but strangely comforting. When the aplings give up on meaning, they give up on everything. And when they've abandoned the very idea of hope, you don't have to lift a finger to control them. They're already defeated."

## A WORLD WITHOUT RESISTANCE

Kratos could see it now – a society so numbed by despair that no one fought back. No ideals to cling to, no future to dream about, just a hollow rhythm of survival. It wasn't chaos – it was effortless. A kingdom where control wasn't taken by force, but offered freely by the defeated.

Kratos stood silently, the weight of Brutus's words sinking deeper into his mind. A world where nothing mattered – where no one cared enough to resist – made perfect sense. If no one believed in anything, what was left to fight for? Without hope, without meaning, the mountain would sit still and obedient, its people drifting quietly into submission. Control wouldn't need to be forced; it would happen naturally, like ice freezing on a winter's day.

NO STRUGGLE, NO AMBITION, NO RESISTANCE. JUST QUIET SURRENDER.

Out of the gloom appeared Demos, lanterns clutched tight, defiance burning in his eyes. "I won't let you bring this nihilistic despair upon the mountain, Brutus," he growled. "The mountain won't fall into this abyss of emptiness. Not while I've breath in me."

Brutus chuckled, soft and low. "Oh, Demos... You really think hopelessness is my only trick?" He glanced at Kratos, his grin spreading wider. "I've already shown you how fear works. But if they won't crumble under despair, then you can always give them the opposite." He laughed. "A belief system so rigid and dogmatic it can't ever be questioned – Theocracy."

Brutus gave a slow, wicked smile. "Yes. Make them believe the gods demand obedience, and they'll shackle themselves in devotion. No chains needed – they'll kneel willingly."

*When a nihilistic worldview takes grip, aplings often find themselves having to fill the void through other means. 1547.*

289

*The heavy hand of divine authority descends – where faith becomes control, and freedom is but a distant memory. 1458.*

# THEOCRATIC THEORY OF SUBMISSION

**D**emos knelt beside the scattered lanterns, each one dulled by time and neglect, a pale imitation of the values they once stood for.

He gathered them carefully, as though cradling fragile memories. "I can still relight these," he muttered, "If I get them burning again, maybe... maybe we can still save all this." He glanced up, hoping for a spark of agreement from his brother. But Kratos only nodded, distracted. His mind was somewhere else entirely, tangled in the darker threads Brutus had woven."

Brutus slinked behind Kratos, voice low and slick with promise. "Nihilism, Kratos – it drains them. Leaves them hollow, hopeless. When nothing matters, they stop caring, stop resisting. But that emptiness can only carry you so far. Sooner or later, some will look for meaning, for something to fill the void."

He leaned closer, his voice smooth and coaxing. "And that's where theocracy comes in. Give them structure – rules carved in stone, written in sacred texts. A system so rigid, so absolute, that questioning it feels impossible. They don't just follow the rules, Kratos – they cling to them. Dogma becomes their lifeline. When the law is divine, they obey without question, not because they understand it, but because it 'must' be right."

Kratos nodded slowly, the simplicity of it taking hold. "They don't need to think – they just need to follow."

Brutus's grin sharpened, his eyes gleaming. "Exactly. Their obedience isn't forced, it's offered freely. They'll see every law as sacred and every command as holy.

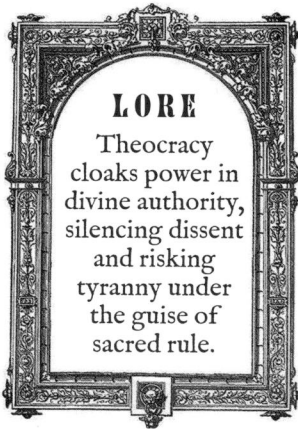

> ### LORE
> Theocracy cloaks power in divine authority, silencing dissent and risking tyranny under the guise of sacred rule.

## CONTROL BY DIVINE AUTHORITY

"Theocracy, Kratos. A system where the aplings aren't just afraid to speak – they don't 'want' to. Where they believe their obedience isn't just to a ruler, but to the gods. Imagine it, Kratos. Not just silence, but total devotion. When you claim divine authority, they'll follow without question. They'll see their submission not as a burden, but as their sacred duty."

Kratos felt the pull of Brutus's words. "And they won't resist?" Brutus's eyes gleamed. "How could they? To resist would be to defy the gods themselves. You see, Kratos, fear can make them quiet, but faith... faith makes them loyal. A loyalty so deep they'll turn on their own if commanded. They'll see you, the leader, as the chosen one, and every order you give will be seen as divine will."

**A LEADERSHIP CLAIMING DIVINE RIGHT CAN EASILY BECOME TYRANNICAL.**

## CAPTIVITY OF THE SOUL

Kratos thought about it, the idea sinking its hooks into him. "So we control every aspect of their life, by controlling access to... the after life?"

Brutus nodded, leaning in closer. "Exactly. With theocracy, the soul is bound to dogma. There's no need for force, no need to remind them of the consequences of defiance. They will censor themselves, out of piety. They'll obey, not out of fear, but because they believe they 'must' – for the sake of their souls. It's the ultimate form of control, Kratos. You're not just a ruler... you become their divine guide."

Kratos, who had once been uncertain of where he stood in the struggle for power, now felt the pull of something far stronger than ambition. This was bigger than fear, bigger than mere obedience. This was control of the spirit, of belief itself. The idea of ruling not just through authority, but through dogmatic decree captivated him.

Brutus leaned back, his work nearly complete. "Think on it, Kratos. There's no greater power than ruling by the will of the gods. With theocracy, you don't just command their actions – you own their very souls."

In a theocratic society, dogma wears robes, freedom is
stifled, and followers adhere to sacred laws. 1458.

*With a sly smile and a tempting hand, Brutus draws Kratos deeper into the shadows, feeding him promises as sweet as poison. 1398.*

# SOCIAL DISINTEGRATION

**B**rutus snapped a branch off the Tree of Echoes with a dry crack, his grin spreading like a wound across his face.

"This," he hissed, twisting another brittle limb until it splintered in his hand, "this is what's left of their voices." He tore away at the branches with manic glee, each snap sending wood scattering across the ground. What once stood tall and proud was now nothing but jagged remains – a ruin of dead ideals. "When fear takes root and obedience follows, the rest falls apart."

Kratos watched, unmoving. He no longer flinched at the destruction – if anything, it made sense now. The lanterns, the broken branches, the lifeless tree... all of it seemed inevitable, almost necessary. He rubbed his arm absently, fingers trailing over the bite marks left by the snake from the urn of ideology. The skin around the punctures throbbed, red and swollen, an infection spreading beneath the surface. But Kratos barely noticed the pain – it only fueled the strange fervor stirring inside him. This wasn't just about silencing voices; this was about control – complete, irresistible control.

Brutus caught the flicker of derangement in Kratos's eyes and smiled. "You see it now, don't you? When the spirit is broken, the rest crumbles without a fight. They stop dreaming, stop resisting. Once they give up on themselves, there's nothing left to fight for."

Kratos nodded slowly, his pulse quickening. "They won't fight back... will they?"

Brutus's grin widened, his fingers crushing another branch with ease. "Not a chance. When they stop believing in themselves, they'll fall quiet. Fear makes them bow, hopelessness guts their innards, and dogma keeps 'em on their knees."

## FRAGMENTING SOCIETY

Brutus kicked the broken branches across the ground. "When they're afraid and isolated, society fractures. Families drift apart, neighbours stop trusting each other. Community crumbles, and every apling turns inward, just trying to survive." Laughing out loud, "And that's when they're easiest to control – when they're desperate for any order, even if it costs them their entire freedom."

Kratos ran his hand over his arm again, the infection gnawing beneath his skin, matching the growing fever in his mind. The vision Brutus painted was almost too perfect, an entire mountain of aplings broken and pliable, ripe for control.

## CULTURAL EROSION

Brutus crouched by the shattered branches, voice low and deliberate. "When trust dies, Kratos, everything else follows – cultural erosion. Families drift apart. Schools stop teaching. Communities crumble. Addiction spirals. The systems that once supported them – gone, like dust in the wind."

Kratos rubbed his swollen arm, the infection creeping deeper, his thoughts darkening. He saw it now – a mountain of scattered aplings, adrift, disconnected from the wisdom of those before them. "So they lose more than just their voices," he muttered. "They lose everything."

Brutus nodded. "Exactly. Without families to guide them, schools to shape them, or communities to hold them, each generation grows more lost. They forget who they are, what they stand for. No one teaches, no one learns, and they'll cling to anyone, or anything which helps to block out the bleak reality they find themselves inhabiting."

In the distance, the lantern in Demos's hand flickered weakly, its light feeble against the encroaching dark. But to Kratos, it no longer seemed worth chasing. Cultural erosion wasn't just decay – it was an inevitability. When everything falls apart, control isn't seized; it's simply taken by those willing to step forward. And Kratos knew now – he was ready to be the one.

INDIVIDUALS AND FAMILIES ARE LEFT STRUGGLING, UNSUPPORTED, CREATING A FERTILE GROUND FOR CHAOS.

But now dear reader, let's take a step back and ponder the bigger picture, shall we? What we have here is not just a lesson in corruption but a masterclass in control. Brutus has peeled back every layer, showing Kratos exactly how power works – not only through brute force, but by breaking minds, hearts, and spirits. Piece by piece, he's kindly taught him how fear, obedience, dogma, or destitution can turn a mountain full of souls into a quiet, pliable mass.

Brutus leaned in one last time, "It's time, Kratos. Your destiny is here. Step forward, take control. The mountain is yours if only you've the will to claim it."

He turned, his voice slipping into a venomous whisper. "Come now to the Hearth of Wisdom, for one final lesson... and bring that wretched brother of yours along. He'll want to witness the end of this story."

*Brutus, ever the cunning one lurks behind Kratos, whispering ways to bend the mind and warp the soul. 1293.*

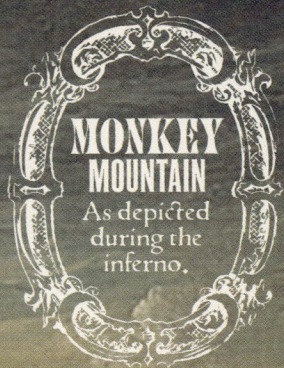

# CHAPTER XII
# TYRANNY

# BETRAYAL XII.I
# VIOLATION XII.II
# TERROR XII.III
# WARFARE XII.IV
# TOTALITARIANISM XII.V
# GENOCIDE XII.VI

*The Controlls – grinning, grotesque, and eager – lurk in shadows,*
*luring their prey to the Hearth of Wisdom. 1268.*

# A THORNY TEST

**K**ratos arrived at the Hearth of Wisdom, his steps echoing across the vast, dim chamber. Awaiting him in the flickering firelight were the three Controlls – Vulgor, Klepto, and Brutus – seated like ancient judges, their faces set in expressions of solemn authority. There was an energy in the room, dark and magnetic, pulling Kratos forward. As he approached, the Controlls' eyes met his, each gaze sharply sizing him up.

Vulgor spoke first, his voice low and unyielding. "To rule, Kratos, you must sever yourself from anything that weakens you. Power demands solitude – no alliances, no familial ties, no compassion. Only control." He cast a quick, cutting glance, as if daring Kratos to protest. "Your brother's vision, his naive belief in the strength of unity, is a threat – a softness you cannot afford if you are to bring the mountain to heel."

Brutus nodded, his face twisted in a satisfied smirk. "Demos's ideals may seem harmless now, Kratos, but seeds of resistance grow in the dark. His hope, his talk of rights and freedom, could inspire the mountain to question your rule. If you wish to reign unchallenged, you must stamp out any trace of his influence."

Klepto leaned forward, fingers steepled, his eyes glinting with malice. "This is not merely about governance, Kratos. It's about survival – yours. Tyranny demands total obedience, and obedience demands silence. Demos's voice, as small as it may be, is a thorn that must be removed before it becomes a blade." He paused, letting his words sink in. "Show us your loyalty, Kratos. Show us that you are ready to do what is necessary."

**TO RULE, KRATOS, YOU MUST ABANDON SENTIMENT.**

## SUPPRESSION OF FREEDOM

Kratos stood in silence, their words sinking into him like hooks pulling him deeper into the shadows. Demos was a threat, not just to his reign but to the order the Controlls promised him. His brother's ideals were relics of a fading age, ideals that had no place in the future Kratos was building. If he were to secure the mountain, Demos could not remain.

Vulgor's voice grew insistent. "To rule, Kratos, you must abandon sentiment. Compassion is a weakness that will betray you at every turn. Replace it with dominance. Show the mountain that your authority is as unyielding as the rock beneath their feet."

Kratos felt something dark stirring within him, a cold acceptance of the path laid before him. Demos was no longer his brother – he was an obstacle. An obstacle that could undo everything he could claim as his own.

Klepto leaned in, a grin curling at the corner of his mouth. "Your loyalty, Kratos. Prove it. Show the mountain where your allegiance lies. Imprison Demos. Bind him before he has a chance to sow dissent. Let this be your ultimate act of loyalty to us, and your first act of true leadership."

The weight of the choice settled over Kratos, solidifying into resolve. His heart felt as hard and immovable as stone. Demos would have to be sacrificed for the future he now envisioned. There was no turning back.

*The sharp claws of betrayal grip tightly, digging deep, leaving wounds that linger. 1473.*

*Klepto whispering to Kratos to perform the ultimate act of loyalty to the Controlls – the betrayal of his brother Demos. 1258*

*Demos confronts Kratos, saying "Brother, you've let the darkness take hold. This isn't the mountain we dreamed of." 1365.*

# ABUSE OF TRUST

**D**emos arrived at the Hearth, carrying with him a faint spark of hope, the light he'd fought so hard to keep alive.

Demos looked to Kratos, sensing something was terribly wrong. "Kratos... what's going on?" But Kratos's face was unreadable, a mask of iron that betrayed nothing, his stance unyielding, radiating silent authority. Brutus gestured, and Grimora and his goons appeared from the shadows, surrounding Demos. The realization hit him like a blow. "Kratos, no... this can't be."

Desperation filled Demos's voice as he struggled to meet his brother's steely gaze, instinctively lowering his own. "This isn't you, Kratos! We could rebuild this mountain upwards, together. Make it stand proud again. For everyone. Remember the dreams we shared, the vision we had..."

Demos's voice trailed off as he read the cold resolve in Kratos's eyes, a silent command that made him lower his head further, submitting almost unconsciously. "Brother, you've let the darkness take hold. This isn't the mountain we dreamed of. What happened to the ideals we wanted to build this place on?"

Before Kratos could answer, Vulgor slid in, his voice slick as a snake. "He's right, Kratos. Ideals are nice for storytellin', but power... power is what keeps this mountain standin'. Demos is a threat to all we've worked for."

Klepto, ever the sly one, chimed in, "Just imagine the strength you could wield without him in your way, Kratos. No more second-guessin', no more holdin' back." Brutus, looming in the background, grunted his approval. Kratos's imposing silence grew heavier, like a weight pressing down on Demos's shoulders, compelling him to stay still, subdued. Demos, seeing the look in Kratos's eyes, took a step forward, his voice firmer now. "Kratos, listen to me. This path leads only to ruin. The Controlls are usin' you, twistin' your mind. You don't have to do this."

But Kratos remained unmoved, his gaze unflinching, his posture forbidding. Demos's plea met a wall of stony silence. Kratos sneered. "You're naive, Demos. Weak. This mountain needs strength, not your dreams. It's time you learned that the hard way."

Demos's shoulders slumped, his final words barely a murmur as he looked down, defeated. "Kratos, don't do this. The mountain needs more than one voice. This isn't power – it's destruction."

"Take him to the gulag," bellowed Kratos, his voice carrying the finality of a judge's decree. Demos didn't dare meet his brother's eyes again, instinctively bowing his head as Grimora's goons seized him, pulling him away. "You can rot in that hell, brother, and dream of your precious mountain while you're breaking stone and digging holes, with the rest of the traitors!"

## THE RISE OF TYRANNY

With Demos bound and silenced, bundled away, hauled off to the gulag, destined for a miserable life of hard labour, the Controlls turned to Kratos, their faces alight with satisfaction. Vulgor clapped him on the shoulder, but Kratos remained impassive, a silent pillar of authority. Vulgor's voice was thick with approval. "You have shown your strength, Kratos. You have embraced power in its purest form – without mercy, without compromise."

Klepto nodded, a dark gleam in his eye. "You have learned every art of control: political manipulation, economic dominance, social submission. You are now a true ruler, Kratos – a tyrant ready to wield power on every level."

Brutus's grin was the widest of all as he stepped back, instinctively ceding space to Kratos. "Now, bind the mountain to your will. Use fear, use greed, use moral perversion – whatever it takes to keep them under your control. Let the mountain know there is only one voice, one vision. Yours."

Kratos stood tall before them, his transformation complete. Without a word, he looked over the Hearth, his very presence commanding submission from all around. He was no longer merely a leader; he was a tyrant, a force of domination. The mountain would bend to his will, each life tethered to his power, every whisper silenced, every spark of dissent snuffed out by the weight of his authority.

**LORE**

Betrayal cuts deepest not just because of lost trust, but because it demands a piece of one's own soul as payment.

*The fearsome Brutus, bundles Demos out of the Chambers of Power and off to the gulag. 1243.*

*Aplings cower from terrifying spiders,*
*both real and imagined.* 1274.

# OH TERRIBLE TERRORISING TERROR

With Demos locked away in the cold depths of the gulag, Kratos and the Controlls turned to the next weapon in their armoury; terror.

But this terror would not be unleashed with brute force alone – no, Vulgor, the machiavellian strategist, had something far more insidious in mind. It began with the quiet release of spiders – thousands of them – skittering through the mountain's dark tunnels and creeping into the corners of the aplings' homes.

The spiders were real enough, their presence terrifying in the dead of night, but what made them truly dangerous was the power of rumour. Whispers began to spread that these weren't just ordinary spiders. No, the aplings told each other in hushed tones, these creatures were half-apling, born from dark rituals in the depths of the mountain. Stories circulated that they carried not just venom, but curses, and anyone bitten would fall under the Controlls' spell, transforming into something monstrous.

## THE WEB OF WORRY

Vulgor, watching with cold satisfaction, turned to Kratos. "This is the beauty of terror, Kratos. You see, it's not the spiders themselves that will destroy them. It's the fear they create. Fear has a way of spreading faster than anything else, and soon, the aplings won't know what's real or imagined."

Kratos, his eyes narrowed, could see the brilliance in the plan. "So they'll turn on each other, too afraid to trust anyone?"

"Exactly," Klepto chimed in, his sly grin widening. "In their panic, they'll start accusing each other of harbouring these so-called spider-curse victims. It'll be chaos, Kratos. They'll do half the work for us."

## THE APLINGS, PARALYZED BY FEAR, OFFERED NO RESISTANCE.

As night after night passed, the rumours grew. Aplings no longer gathered in public. Instead, they peered nervously at their neighbors, suspecting that one might be cursed, might have already been bitten. Families locked their doors, but even that couldn't stop the whispers from slipping through the cracks.

### TURNING AGAINST EACH OTHER

The true power of the spiders wasn't in their venom, but in the hold the arachnids had over apling minds. Distrust began to fester. Entire villages turned upon themselves, with aplings convinced that their neighbours were hiding bitten family members, or worse, being part of the Controlls' sinister plans. Terror spread like wildfire, and in the darkness, the aplings forgot who their true enemy was.

Brutus, ever the brute force behind the Controlls, watched the destruction unfold with satisfaction. "They're so busy fightin' amongst themselves, they won't even see us comin'. We'll strike again when they're weak."

Vulgor, ever the tactician, smiled darkly. "Terror, my friends, doesn't just frighten. It divides. A divided mountain is a conquered mountain."

Kratos, seeing the aplings' world unraveling before him, nodded. "Let them tear themselves apart. When they've lost all trust in each other, we'll be the only ones they can turn to."

### THE SHADOW OF TERROR

The mountain, once vibrant and full of life, became a place of isolation and paranoia. Aplings spoke in whispers, too afraid to share their thoughts or dreams. The spiders – real and imagined – had done their job. But it wasn't the spiders themselves that held power; it was the fear of what they represented. In this web of terror the Controlls had unleashed, the aplings had trapped themselves.

Watching from the shadows, they could see their plan was working. Terror had captured not just the minds of the aplings, but their imaginations as well.

*Terror twists communities, causing respectable aplings to turn upon one another, until they can barely recognise themselves. 1326.*

# HOT, COLD, PROXY & PERPETUAL

E merging from the depths of their dark lair, the Controlls led Kratos into the cold night air of Monkey Mountain.

With the seeds of division sown, it was time to conquer. War, in all its forms, would be the next instrument toyed with to extend their grip far beyond the mountain's borders. Kratos, once a leader in the making due to his vision and ideals, now walked eagerly in their shadow, ready to learn the next steps in their grand design. Brutus, his voice as sharp and cold as the night itself, began instructing him in the many faces of warfare. "Kratos," Brutus began, "war is not just one thing – it is many. It's a tool, like the hammer or chisel that carves a path to power. Let me show you the different ways we can wield it."

### THE FIRES OF HOT WAR

Brutus started with the most direct and brutal form of conflict. "Hot war, Kratos, is the fire that burns brightest. It's the clash of armies, the roar of battle where strength is tested head-on. The aplings who once tilled the soil and gathered by the hearth will be transformed into warriors, marching under your command. They'll tear through neighbouring lands, leaving nothing but ashes in their wake."

Kratos envisioned the aplings, once peaceful, now turned into a fearsome force. "And we'll show them the cost of standing against us." Brutus, ever eager for destruction, grinned with anticipation. "We'll lead them into battle, Kratos. They'll torch everything, and the survivors will cower at your name."

Brutus continued, "This hot war will make your power visible, undeniable. The conquered will tremble at the sight of our armies, and those who remain on the mountain will fear that they are next."

*An army of aplings, obeying Controll orders, manoeuvre a colossal cannon preparing for a siege on neighbouring lands. 1462.*

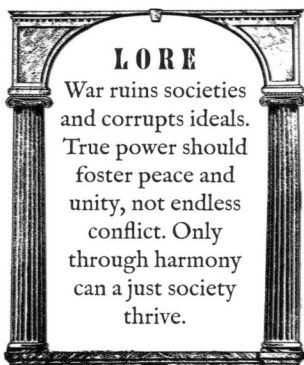

## THE CHILL OF COLD WAR

Vulgor, ever the strategist, stepped forward with a glint in his eye. "But war isn't always about brute force, Kratos. Cold war – now that's a different game altogether. It's like a game of chess, where you move your pieces slowly, strategically, always thinking two, three steps ahead. The goal isn't just to crush the opponent but to outmanoeuvre them so they don't even see the trap closing in."

Kratos, intrigued, leaned in closer. "So it's not about direct conflict?" Vulgor nodded. "Exactly. It's about playing in the shadows. While your armies engage in open battle, we'll position our spies, plant rumours, and slowly chip away at the foundation of their alliances. We'll make them doubt each other, weaken their bonds, and all the while, we'll stay hidden behind the board, watching them collapse under their own mistrust."

Klepto, listening with approval, added, "Cold war is won not through strength, but through patience. It's a game of mental warfare, not just physical. You must sow discord without lifting a sword, moving pieces into place until our enemies have no moves left."

## THE GAME OF PROXY WARS

Klepto's tone darkened as he leaned closer. "And then there's the most insidious form – proxy war. We won't even need to dirty our own hands. We'll arm distant factions, stirring up conflicts far from here, in lands that can serve our interests. Our enemies will fight amongst themselves, while we sit back and reap the benefits."

Kratos, fully grasping the strategy, grinned. "We'll control the world beyond this mountain without ever having to set foot outside."

Brutus nodded, eyes gleaming. "We'll send arms, supplies, and let others do the fighting. Our coffers will overflow, and our influence will spread. Meanwhile, the aplings here won't even know how far our power extends."

But Klepto raised a finger, cautioning him. "Remember, Kratos, proxy war is a double-edged sword. You get someone else to fight for you, but you also hide the fact that a real war is happening at all. The aplings will be kept in the dark, never realizing the full scale of the conflict, the resources and wealth we'll embezzle along the way – or the true enemy they face."

*Endless conflict keeps communities always teetering on the edge of catastrophe. 1329.*

## THE TOLL OF ENDLESS CONFLICT

"And then, Kratos," Klepto added, "there's one final layer to war – a weapon more subtle than all the others: perpetual war. If we convince the aplings that endless war is necessary, that it's required for survival, they'll submit to any sacrifice. The War Chest will grow heavier with every demand, and we'll be free to raid it under the guise of 'safety and security.'"

Kratos frowned, seeing the layers unfold before him. "Constant war? How do we sustain that?"

Klepto chuckled, his voice dripping with cunning. "The Blob, down in the swamp, feeds on endless conflict. Warfare sustains it, and as long as we keep the aplings believing that they're always on the edge of catastrophe, they'll never question the cost. They'll hand over their wealth, their lives, their freedom, without hesitation."

*An army under total control – each step at their leaders command, every thought a dictated echo of power. 1345.*

# TOTAL TYRANNY

**W**ith the mountain fractured and bruised from relentless, endless, perpetual war – the Controlls reckoned it was time to deliver their crowning blow.

They'd brought Monkey Mountain to its knees, but war alone wasn't enough. No, they wanted a grip so tight it would squeeze the very life out of any free thought left on that rock. And to cement their vision, they needed Kratos – now their anointed heir to the throne– to seal the fate of the mountain.

For Kratos, the Controlls had laid out a twisted kind of coronation. Not a crown, but a chain, forged from fear and submission. And he was ready to wear it.

## THE EYE THAT NEVER BLINKS

First came the eyes. Brutus unleashed spies and informants throughout every nook and cranny, all reporting back to Kratos. No apling could so much as whisper in the shadows without feeling the gaze of this unseen watcher. Klepto spread a tale that walls themselves had ears for Kratos – that nothing on the mountain went unheard by its leader.

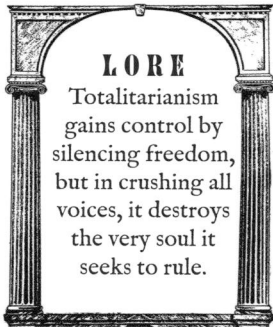

**LORE**

Totalitarianism gains control by silencing freedom, but in crushing all voices, it destroys the very soul it seeks to rule.

Aplings who once laughed freely, now walked with heads down, glancing nervously over their shoulders, afraid to speak, afraid to even think too loudly. Privacy didn't just disappear – it was dismantled, piece by piece, until every apling lived in a state of quiet paranoia, knowing that Kratos's reach was endless.

## SHACKLES OF SPEECH

With the mountain suffocating under watchful eyes, Vulgor and Kratos turned to the next step: speech. Words had power, so Kratos decreed that certain phrases, certain ideas, were now dangerous relics of a past that no longer served his rule. The Hearth of Wisdom, once a place where voices rose in spirited debate, had become little more than a megaphone for Kratos's rule.

Lessons at the Hearth taught nothing but loyalty, obedience, and the virtues of Kratos's "wise leadership." Aplings recited chants praising him, repeating slogans so often they forgot where their own voices began and Kratos's commands ended. Soon enough, even their private thoughts felt as though they belonged to him, as if he could reach into their minds and rearrange their very beliefs.

## REWRITING THE PAST

Next, the Controlls turned to history itself. Klepto saw to it that the stories of the old days – the tales of freedom, unity, and courage – were scrubbed out of memory. Scrolls were burned, songs were banned, and statues of heroes who once stood for justice were torn down. In their place, Kratos ordered the construction of new monuments – stone figures of himself, and the Controlls, towering over the mountain's people as eternal reminders of who now ruled.

They rewrote the past to serve the future, telling the aplings that Kratos had always been their protector, that the mountain had only survived through his "guiding hand." Folk, stripped of any memories of freedom, could no longer imagine a life beyond his rule. For them, Kratos was the mountain – the past, the present, and every future they were permitted to envision.

## THE HOLLOW SILENCE OF TOTAL CONTROL

And so, the mountain fell silent – not with peace, but with the weight of absolute control. Every apling's thought, every word, every action now bent toward Kratos's will. The air itself felt heavy, thick with the quiet compliance of a people too broken to resist.

Kratos had done it. He'd become the very embodiment of the mountain's oppression, a ruler who held not just the land, but every heart and mind, in his iron grasp. Yet, as he stood atop Monkey Mountain, surveying his kingdom, he felt something unexpected – a hollowness, a kind of haunting emptiness. For with every voice silenced and every spirit crushed, there was nothing left to rule but shadows. Absolute power, he found, held nothing worth holding onto.

*Endless conflict keeps communities compliant to totalitarian control. 1329.*

*Aplings are dragged, tormented, and crushed – victims of a merciless genocide unfolding in the heart of Monkey Mountain. 1456.*

# EXTERMINATION

In the depths of their totalitarian tyranny, the Controlls resorted to the most heinous and despicable act of all: genocide.

Determined to eliminate any threat to their absolute power, they targeted entire groups of aplings who resisted or were deemed undesirable. It wasn't enough to control the mountain through fear and intimidation – Vulgor, the cold-blooded strategist that he was, understood that some ideas couldn't be silenced by terror alone. "Fear is powerful, but eradication is final," he said, his eyes glinting with a deranged resolve. His plan was simple and devastating: wipe out those who carried the seeds of dissent, ensuring no spark of rebellion could ever reignite.

Brutus and his enforcers took to the task with ruthless efficiency. Whole villages were swept up in the dead of night, their inhabitants torn from their homes, dragged into the cold wilderness, and either executed on the spot or sent to camps where death awaited them slowly. The Hearth of Wisdom, once the heart of the mountain where aplings gathered to share stories and debate, now bore witness to unimaginable horrors. Where there had once been unity and laughter, there were now only screams and bloodstains.

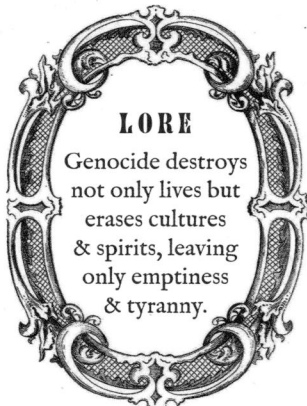

**LORE**
Genocide destroys not only lives but erases cultures & spirits, leaving only emptiness & tyranny.

Entire communities vanished almost overnight. Those who weren't executed faced systematic extermination in the camps – places where hope withered as quickly as their bodies. The mountain ran red with the blood of its people. The air, thick with smoke and sorrow, felt heavier than ever, as if the mountain itself was mourning.

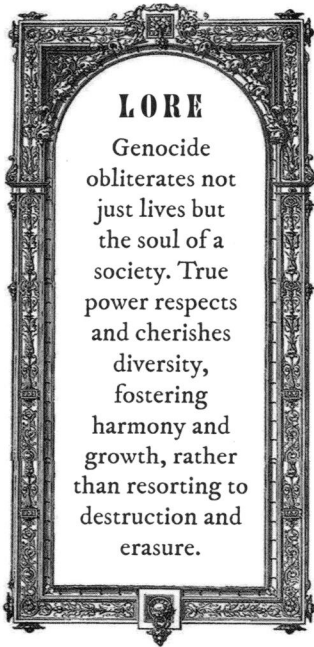

## CULTURAL ERASURE

The genocide extended beyond physical annihilation. The Controlls aimed to erase the very memory of these groups. Klepto, the cunning manipulator, led efforts to replace rich cultural heritages with the Controlls' distorted narrative. The goal was not just to kill, but to obliterate any trace of resistance and diversity. Kratos, who once championed justice, now spoke of purity and order, using twisted logic to justify the massacre.

## THE DESCENT INTO DARKNESS

Genocide plunged Monkey Mountain into an abyss of despair. Survivors lived in constant fear, their spirits broken by the relentless brutality. The air, once filled with songs and stories, now echoed with the cries of the lost and the silence of the oppressed. Monkey Mountain became a graveyard for dreams... and lives.

The Controlls' campaign of genocide ensured their dominance, but at a horrific cost. The mountain's beauty was marred by death and suffering, the Chambers of Power, now cold and empty shells. The aplings who remained were mere shadows of their former selves, haunted by the ghosts of their fallen kin.

## FAINT GLIMMERS OF HOPE

But dear reader, even in the darkest days however, the unbreakable spirit of the aplings endured. Though crushed beneath the Controlls' oppressive rule, small acts of defiance flickered like distant stars. Aplings still found ways to resist, not with grand gestures, but in their unyielding resolve. They whispered words of hope to one another, shared quiet moments of solidarity, and held fast to a belief that someone, anyone... might unite the people to lead them out of this hell.

*A solemn group of aplings stands in silence, shadows of their former selves*
*– survivors of a ruthless purge, haunted by the loss of their kin. 1296.*

MONKEY
MOUNTAIN

As depicted
during times
of tyranny.

CHAPTER XIII

# REVOLUTION

TYRANNICAL STRUGGLE

INCARCERATION XIII.I

RESISTANCE XIII.II

UPRISING XIII.III

CONFRONTATION XIII.IV

VISION XIII.V

REALISATION XIII.VI

*Chained and despondent in the cold shadows of the gulag, Demos sits alone,*
*his spirit heavy but unbroken, holding on to the faintest flicker of hope. 1438.*

# FROM RESTRAINT TO REVOLUTION

The Gulag was a pit of despair where time slowed to a crawl and every breath felt heavy with dust and dread.

Each morning began with the crack of a whip, dragging Demos and the other aplings from restless sleep to face another day of soul-crushing labour. Under the blistering sun or freezing cold, they smashed stone, hauled boulders, and dug trenches until their hands were raw and numb. But this wasn't just about breaking bodies – it was about grinding their spirits into the dirt.

Watching over it all was Grimora, the police state thug, who delighted in paying extra attention to the helpless Demos. Now, with the upper hand, Grimora took cruel delight in his suffering. One morning, as Demos staggered under a load too heavy for his weary limbs, Grimora chuckled. "I warned you," he sneered, the words dripping with mockery. "Guess now you'll learn to stay in line." The other guards laughed, snapping their whips in the air, but Demos kept moving, each step a silent rebellion. They could starve his body, but they'd never quench the fire in his heart.

One evening, after the days' toil had finally concluded, Demos met a frail old lady, slumped against the quarry wall, her breath shallow and rattling in her chest. She looked as if the wind might scatter her to dust, yet her dim eyes carried a quiet strength. She motioned for Demos to sit beside her. He did so, feeling drawn to her. When he sat, she reached out her hand. "Young boy, I once knew your parents," she whispered, her voice soft but steady. "Hooma and Pap – around the Hearth of Wisdom, they dreamed, just like you. They wanted to build not just for themselves but for those yet to come."

**IT WAS ABOUT GRINDING THEIR SPIRITS INTO THE DIRT.**

## THE OLD STRUCTURES START TO CREAK AND GROAN.

Demos listened in silence as she spoke with weary wisdom. "The time has come child, the mountain needs nothing short of a revolution. But it cannot be driven through rage – it needs love so fierce, that'll drive you to burn away all that's rotten, in order to protect all that's sacred."

With a deep breath, she fixed her gaze on Demos. "You are the one. You must lead this revolution. But know this first: All revolutions pass through certain stages – beginning with discontent, action, chaos, and finally, the struggle to rebuild from the ashes."

### THE SPARK OF DISCONTENT

"The first stage," she whispered, "is the rise of discontent. It's when folk, crushed under the weight of a corrupt regime, begin to murmur among themselves. The old structures start to creak and groan, and dissatisfaction grows like a storm on the horizon."

*Where a spark might first originate is anyones guess. 1549.*

## THE TRIGGER EVENT

"The second stage," she continued, "is the spark – a trigger that turns discontent into action. It might be an act of injustice, a harsh decree, or simply the last straw that breaks the people's patience. When this happens, the murmurs turn to shouts, and the old order scrambles to maintain control, but it's too late. The fire has been lit." Demos nodded, "Sparks are already flying back on the mountain. Surely the time of fire is nigh?"

## THE RADICAL PHASE

"Once the spark has lit and the fire burns brightest," she coughed, "the revolution enters its radical phase. The old order falls, but with its collapse comes chaos. New leaders emerge, often more extreme, driven by the fury of the oppressed. But beware, Demos – this is the most dangerous stage. It's easy for the revolution to consume itself in its own flames, losing sight of the ideals that sparked it."

## THE STRUGGLE FOR A NEW ORDER

Shivering, she spoke of the final stage. "After the flames die down, you are left with ashes. It is then that the true work begins – the struggle to build a new order from the ruins of the old. This is the hardest part, for in the aftermath of revolution, it's all too easy to slip back into the same cycles of power and corruption. You must ensure that what you build is not just new – but just."

"This is your calling, Demos. Not just to tear down what's broken, but to rebuild something worthy in its place." She paused, her breath rattling, and her dim eyes searched his. "But tell me, child – what has become of your brother, Kratos? Does he still walk the path of virtue?" Demos dropped his head. "If the mountain is to rise, child." she said, fixing her eyes on his. "You must confront not only the Controlls – but your brother too."

"Thank-you... your name? What is your name?" She looked him in the eye, and simply said, "Belle."

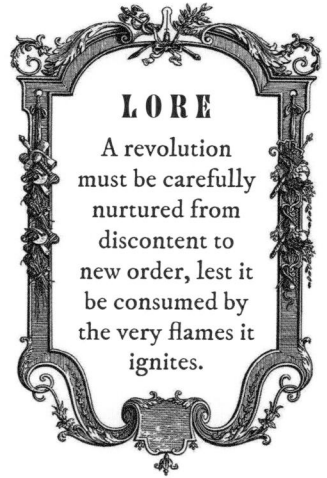

> **LORE**
> A revolution must be carefully nurtured from discontent to new order, lest it be consumed by the very flames it ignites.

**NEW LEADERS EMERGE, OFTEN MORE EXTREME, DRIVEN BY THE FURY OF THE OPPRESSED.**

*Demos sends messages out to the resistance with*
*the help of a small army of supporters. 1328.*

# REBELLION BECKONS

**D**emos sat wearily in his cell within the depths of the gulag, his body bruised and broken, but his mind sharper than ever.

The time for action was now – he could feel it in his bones. If he let the moment slip by, the embers of hope scattered across the mountain would fade into nothing. Even behind walls, with chains at his wrists and Grimora's sneering eyes watching his every move, Demos knew that doing nothing was no longer an option. He couldn't fight in the open, but he could spark a revolution from within.

With moonlight leaking through the cracked walls, he penned instructions onto scraps of paper, each word etched carefully: Form cells. Build quietly. Organize in the dark. Be ready... Every note was a signal, small but potent, letting those on the outside know that the time to rise was coming.

To relay his messages back to the mountain, he found allies where none would expect. An army of ants became his stealthy couriers. It was as if nature itself had grown weary of the Controlls' tyranny, summoning the ants to join forces with their animalia kin. These small silent soldiers crawled through cracks in the stone walls, slipping past Grimoras' guards, carrying Demos's words out of the Gulag, through the dirt and shadows, and back into the villages around the mountain.

His word spread across the land like seeds in the wind: his final instruction – that the revolution would begin at the next full moon. And with that, the mountain held its breath, waiting for the spark to ignite.

## LORE

True revolution reshapes politics, culture, and intellect, forging a path from oppression to enlightenment and ensuring lasting change.

*Vulgor desecrates the urn of justice, for little more than his own sadistic pleasure.*
*Little does he realise the chain of events this action is about to trigger. 1459.*

# THE SPARK IGNITES

**W**ith twisted grins and gleeful malice, Kratos and the Controlls barged into the sacred chamber containing the Urns of Ideology.

They moved slowly, savoring every moment, delighting in the destruction they were about to unleash. Urns containing virtues that once held the mountain together, which the Controlls loathed, now served as nothing more than objects of ridicule. "Start with that one," Klepto sneered, pointing at the urn of Altruism. He kicked it over with a hollow crash, and a gentle deer emerged. Klepto grabbed its antlers, twisting them until they snapped, laughing as the creature's spirit flickered and vanished.

Next, Vulgor's gaze fell upon Justice. With a smirk, he tipped the urn, from which a lion emerged, regal and calm. "Justice is for fools," Vulgor hissed, shoving the animal to the ground. He stood over it, pressing his boot onto its throat until it stopped breathing. Brutus followed, eagerly shaking the urn of Compassion. As a delicate bird fluttered free, he snatched it from the air, cupping it tightly in his hands. "Compassion won't save you," Brutus whispered, squeezing until the bird lay limp in his palm.

Kratos stood among them, the remnants of the shattered urns at his feet, his lips curling into a cruel smile. The chamber bore witness to these twisted deeds of desecration. The Controlls reveled in their handiwork, never suspecting that this sadistic act would spark the very rebellion they feared.

To the Controlls, it was just another spectacle – a cruel game to remind the aplings that their ideals were meaningless. But this very act became the spark Belle had foretold would happen. As the shattered urns lay scattered on the ground, word of the desecration spread like wildfire through the mountain. Midnight came, and under the full moon, the plans of the resistance surged to life. Cells that had worked in secrecy for months now burst into coordinated action. What the Controlls thought was a display of dominance became their undoing. The mountain awoke with fury, and the revolution began.

## AMBUSHES & RAIDS

The first strikes hit like thunderclaps from a clear sky. Aplings, unified by a shared purpose, moved in silent synchronization, each knowing their role without a word exchanged. Hidden among the pipes, pistons, and crumbling walls of the chambers, they struck as one, a coordinated force. Brief, reassuring gestures passed between them — a nod here, a brush of a shoulder there, as they melted back into the labyrinth of tunnels and passageways. It was over before their enemies knew what hit them — quick as a flash, the aplings struck and melted back, leaving behind nothing but chaos and confusion. Striking guards and dismantling critical mechanisms — whatever the Controlls relied on to maintain their grip. Panic spread as the Controlls' lackeys stumbled through the darkness, searching for enemies they could never catch. What had once seemed like an unshakable reign now showed the first signs of fragmentation, as each sudden attack chipped away at their authority.

**THESE HIT-AND-RUN TACTICS DROVE THE CONTROLLS TO THE BRINK OF MADNESS.**

## SABOTAGE & ESPIONAGE

Not content with just nipping at the Controlls' heels, Demos sent word to instigate more subtle, sneaky measures. Sabotage became the name of the game. The aplings set about undermining the Controlls' operations — disabling the Aqua Exchange, smashing supply lines, and rigging traps that turned the mountain into a deadly maze. As they moved through these covert acts, they mirrored each other's movements, working in tandem as if guided by a single, unspoken resolve. Aplings slipped into the Controlls' forces with a quiet confidence, subtle glances exchanged to confirm their positions, each one seamlessly blending into the enemy's ranks, all the while feeding false information and gathering secrets like squirrels hoarding nuts. The Controlls, too busy squabbling and chasing shadows, didn't see the real danger creeping up on them.

*Demos makes his move to escape from the gulag. 1328.*

## DECEPTION & DIVERSION

The masterstroke came when Demos orchestrated a trick as old as the hills. He spread rumors of an impending attack on the Economic Chamber, sending the Controlls into a panic. Klepto and his goons scrambled to defend their precious fortress, drawing forces away from the gulag. And while they were off chasing phantoms, Demos made his move. Unified whispers and subtle nods guided his escape; his rebel warriors prepared the way, slipping into place like pieces of a larger strategy. He slipped right out of his cell, vanishing down an escape hatch his rebel warriors had secretly carved through the cave walls. By the time the Controlls realized they'd been played, Demos was long gone, darkness closing around him like a shroud.

When word reached Kratos that Demos had slipped through their grasp, he flew into a fit of rage that shook the mountain to its roots. The Controlls, stinging from their humiliation, now had a new goal: to hunt down Demos and crush this rebellion once and for all. But Demos, free and more dangerous than ever, was already plotting his next move.

### LORE
In the wilds of revolution, it ain't brute strength but cunning that turns the tide, making the mightiest tremble before the smallest and swiftest.

*Chaos erupts on Monkey Mountain as all hell breaks loose – aplings scream, clash, and brawl, their unity shattered in a frenzy of madness and mayhem. 1346*

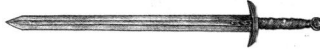

# ALL HELL BREAKS LOOSE

**M**onkey Mountain, once a proud and vibrant place, now shuddered under the weight of the Controlls' fury.

Demos's guerrilla tactics were a thorn in their side, pricking at their pride and unraveling their carefully woven web of destruction But instead of retreating, the Controlls, drunk on their own arrogance, went berserk. They unleashed a wave of violence so fierce it seemed they were ready to tear the entire mountain apart, stone by stone, rather than lose their grip on it.

Fires blazed through the villages, once peaceful homes reduced to smouldering ruins. The Controlls stormed through the chambers like rabid beasts, lashing out at anything and everything in their path. Monuments and statues of valiant aplings from years gone by were torn down in their relentless march of destruction. The mountain was now being systematically ripped apart by those who claimed to rule it.

## THE CONTROLLS STORMED THROUGH THE CHAMBERS LIKE RABID BEASTS.

But it wasn't just the mountain that was at risk – Kratos and the Controlls had become so blinded by their lust for power that they were willing to destroy everything – even themselves. Their obsession with dominance had twisted their minds, turning them into agents of chaos, more than willing to bring every last thing crashing down if it meant clinging to their absolute power just a little longer.

In the heart of this devastation, where the Hearth of Wisdom once burned bright, there now lay only ashes, the fire reduced to a faint smoulder. The Controlls, their eyes wild with madness, regrouped around the dying embers, reveling in their destruction, ready to plan their next wave of obliteration.

**THE CONTROLLS SPUN AROUND, SHOCKED AT HIS SUDDEN ARRIVAL.**

As they stood there scheming their next move, from out of the shadows stepped Demos. His figure gaunt, body bruised from the hardships endured, but his spirit was unbroken. He walked into the faint light of the all but dead Hearth, with the calm resolve of someone with nothing left to lose. The Controlls spun around, shocked at his sudden arrival. Vulgor's eyes popped, Klepto gasped and Brutus shivered, even he alarmed at this unexpected arrival.

Kratos, his eyes narrowing with a mix of rage and confusion, stepped forward. "Demos," Kratos growled, his voice thick with venom. "You should've stayed in the gulag where you belong."

Demos looked at his brother, not with anger, but with a deep, sorrowful understanding. "Kratos, this isn't you. This madness, this destruction... it's not who we were meant to be."

But Kratos only sneered. "It's who I've become!" he spat, suddenly lunging at Demos with the ferocity of a wild beast.

The two brothers clashed in a violent struggle, the echoes of their battle resounding through the hollowed mountain. Demos, though he fought with all his might, was no match for the raw, unbridled power of Kratos, his infected arm rippling with rage. Kratos rained down blow after blow upon his brother, until he was bloodied and beaten, barely able to stand.

Kratos, eyes wild with a fury that bordered on madness, seized Demos by the scruff of the neck and dragged him from the smoldering remains of the Hearth. With terrifying strength he hauled his brother over to the The Political Chamber. The walls, once echoing with the voices of reasoned debate surrounding Quarrel Quadrant, were now crumbling. Kratos slammed Demos against the cold, stone floor, forcing his face toward the tattered remnants of the great rope, now frayed and torn to shreds. "Look at it!" Kratos bellowed, his voice reverberating around the decaying chamber. "This is what your rebellion has brought – chaos and ruin!" But Demos, though in great pain, saw the truth that Kratos could not: it wasn't his rebellion that had torn the chamber apart, but the unbridled corruption of his beloved brother.

*Demos emerges from the shadows, stepping into the Hearth of Wisdom to confront Kratos and the Controlls for a final reckoning. 1286.*

*Locked in a brutal struggle, the brothers clash with raw fury – ideals and loyalties shattered as they fight, neither willing to back down. 1346*

Not satisfied, Kratos yanked Demos to his feet and dragged him down the hall, into the The Economic Chamber. Here, the Aqua Exchange, once intrinsically linked to fair trade and balanced wealth, stood twisted and bloated, pumping precious aqua directly into the grotesque Blob, that had grown even fatter under the Controlls' rule. Kratos shoved Demos toward the monstrous sight, his face twisted with a mixture of pride and disdain. Demos, bruised and barely conscious, could only see the perversion of what they had once dreamed of, the Exchange now little more than a tool for the greedy Blob to leach upon.

Finally, Kratos dragged Demos into the The Public Chamber. This was the place where the voices of the aplings were once heard singing, where the Tree of Echoes had stood tall and proud, embodying the hopes and dreams of all their folk. Now the tree lay broken and dismantled, its branches torn apart with lanterns scattered across the floor.

The Controlls laugh and egg-on Kratos to see through the betrayal of his once-beloved brother, Demos. 1738.

"See this?" Kratos snarled, shoving Demos toward the splintered remains. "This is the cost of your defiance! You've turned the people against us, and now look – there's nothing left!" But even as Kratos fumed, the truth was painfully clear: it wasn't Demos's rebellion that had broken the Tree, but Kratos's own insatiable thirst for power that had desecrated the universal rights of the people. As Demos lay battered and beaten, he realized that his brother, lost to his madness, was showing him not the failure of the revolution, but the ruin of everything they had once held sacred.

Kratos gripped Demos by the arm, dragging his beaten brother back to the smoldering Hearth. Standing over him, eyes wild with fury, he raised his hand for the final strike. The Controlls cackled and cheered, urging him to finish the job. Demos covered in blood, looked up at Kratos, seeing not the monster he'd become, but the brother he'd lost – the brother he may still be able to reach.

**DEMOS, BRUISED AND BARELY CONSCIOUS, COULD ONLY SEE THE PERVERSION OF WHAT THEY HAD ONCE DREAMED OF.**

*The brothers struggle next to the dying Hearth of Wisdom, where a lone ember shall soon make its fateful journey. 1294.*

# THE DYING EMBER

**S**tanding over Demos, bloodied and broken at his feet, all Kratos could hear were the Controlls' wicked howls and cackles as they urged him to deliver the final blow.

The once mighty Chambers of Power, now echoed with the sounds of betrayal and ominous stench of looming death. Demos, barely conscious, could only watch as Kratos raised his fist, ready to strike him down. It seemed the end was nigh, the final flicker of hope about to be snuffed out.

But as Kratos moved to end it all, Demos's limp hand knocked against the last ember sitting in the Hearth of Wisdom, sending it drifting upwards into the air. The tiny glowing coal, the sole remnant of the fire that had once warmed and guided their people, floated like a speck of light in the darkness. The Controlls, too drunk on their impending victory, paid it no attention.

**LORE**
Even in the darkest moment, a single spark of truth can awaken the soul from the grip of corruption.

But that ember had a purpose yet.

It floated gently through the air, catching the dim light as it drifted toward Kratos. And then, as if guided by some unseen force, the ember landed in Kratos's eye. The unexpected heat startled Kratos, causing him to stagger backwards. His vision going white-hot for a split-second. Scrunching his eyes shut, he tried to shake off the searing pain.

In that moment of blindness, a dream-like vision appeared, clearer than any sight he'd ever seen. It was their mother, Hooma, as gentle and loving as he remembered. She held him, as she had when he was just a child.

"Kratos," she whispered, her voice echoing in his mind like the softest breeze, "What have you become, my son?"

A single tear escaped from his eye, the ember's burn no match for the pain this vision of his long since passed mother brought him. The Controlls howled with laughter, mocking his moment of weakness, but Kratos barely heard them. He closed his eyes again, desperate to hold onto the vision of his mother.

"Kratos," Hooma's voice came again, stronger this time, "The Controlls are not real. They are shadows, figments of your imagination, born from your darkest fears and desires. You have the power to break their spell, to free yourself, if only you can summon the strength."

Kratos opened his eyes, now wet with tears, and looked down at Demos, his only brother, lying broken at his feet. In a moment of clarity, he saw Demos not as an enemy, but as the brother he'd once explored the mountain with, the one he had shared hopes and dreams with, so long ago. The vision of his mother lingered in his mind, her words a lifeline through the chaos that had consumed him.

With a shuddering breath, Kratos
reached down and pulled Demos up
from the ground, his grip firm but
gentle. Demos, half-conscious, looked
up at his brother, eyes filled with a faint
glimmer of hope.

Together, they turned to face the
Controlls, who'd stopped their laughter,
sensing a shift in power. Kratos, now
seeing clearly for the first time in a long
while, stood tall beside Demos. The fire
in his eyes had returned, not of madness
however, but with a new sense of clarity.

*The Controlls all covet the last glowing ember, eyes glinting with greed, each desperate to claim its power for themselves. 1347.*

# CONTROL THE TROLLS

**F**eeling the slight heat of something still burning in his eye, Kratos pulled out a tiny grain of ash, faintly smoldering – the last dying ember from the Hearth of Wisdom.

As small it was, this ember held the final remnants of the knowledge, wisdom, and virtue of the aplings. Kratos looked at it, its fragile glow pulsing in the darkness. Turning to the Controlls, who leered and sneered from the shadows, he held up the ember and offered it to them. "Which one of you will take the honour of stubbing out the light that once guided our people? Who among you has the power to finally destroy the heart of our tribe?"

The Controlls, their eyes now fixed on the ember that Kratos held, were mesmerized by its faint glow. Each of them, driven by the twisted desires that had defined their existence, saw in that ember not the last remnant of wisdom, but an opportunity for power. Klepto, his eyes narrowing with greed, was the first to move. "It's mine!" he hissed, his voice dripping with covetous desire. In his mind, possessing that ember meant possessing the very soul of the mountain. With it, he imagined himself ruling over all, hoarding the last vestige of wisdom like treasure, twisting it to his own ends. Klepto's body tensed, every fibre of his being straining toward the ember as he reached out with clawed hands, desperate to claim what he saw as his rightful prize.

But before Klepto could grasp it, Vulgor, always the schemer, slithered forward with a sly grin. "No, no, no," he whispered, his voice smooth as oil. "You fool! Don't you see? It's a trap – this is all a trick meant to ensnare the greedy and the gullible."

**THE CONTROLLS ARE ONLY REAL BECAUSE WE BELIEVE IN THEM.**

Vulgor's eyes flickered with deceit as he spun his web of lies, trying to convince the others that only he had the cunning to take the ember without falling victim to it. "Let me take it," he purred, "and I'll rid us of this burden. I'll be the one to do what none of you can – destroy it, and in doing so, save us all." But even as he spoke, Vulgor's mind churned with plans to use the ember for himself, to twist its power into something dark and self-serving. His lies were not just meant to deceive the others; they were also meant to deceive himself, masking his own greed beneath layers of false righteousness.

*The Controlls, once allies in manipulation, turn on each other in a frenzy of betrayal and greed, each vying for dominance. 1285.*

## SELF-DESTRUCTION

Before Vulgor could slink any closer, Brutus roared in fury. "Enough of your lies!" he bellowed, his voice like thunder crashing through the chamber. "Wisdom and virtue are for the weak! All this talk – just smash it and be done with it!"

With muscles rippling and eyes blazing with rage, Brutus charged forward, his only thought to crush the ember beneath his heel, to obliterate what he could not possess or understand. To Brutus, destruction was power; if he couldn't rule over something, he would see it shattered into dust. As he barreled toward the others, his blind fury was a force unto itself, caring nothing for the subtleties of greed or deceit. In his mind, only raw, unbridled power mattered – an impulse that would drive him to annihilate everything in his path, including those who had once stood beside him.

As the three Controlls lunged for the ember, their vices collided in a chaotic frenzy. Klepto's greed, Vulgor's deceit, and Brutus's psychosis twisted together like a dark storm, each feeding off the other in a spiral of mutual destruction.

In the chaos, greed clashed with deceit, and anger fueled a vicious brawl. They tore at one another, each desperate to claim the ember for themselves, believing that crushing it would grant them ultimate power.

But in their frenzy, they lost sight of the ember itself, their lust for control consuming them until they began to destroy one another. Klepto, blinded by greed, struck out at Vulgor, who, in his desperation, told more wicked lies to turn Brutus against him. Brutus, lost in his own fury, lashed out at them both, crushing what remained of their rotten bond.

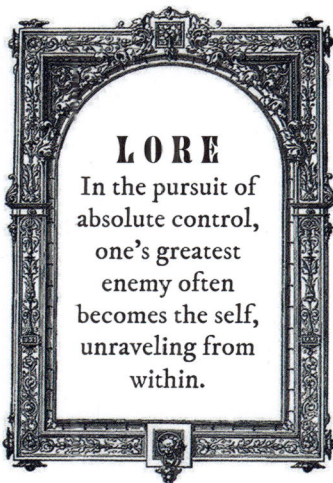

**IN HIS MIND, ONLY RAW, UNBRIDLED POWER MATTERED.**

### LORE

In the pursuit of absolute control, one's greatest enemy often becomes the self, unraveling from within.

*It was their very own vices which brought about the self destruction of Vulgor, Klepto and Brutus. 1326.*

## COMPLETE ANNIHILATION

In their final struggle, the Controlls descended into a savage brawl, each consumed by their own vice and blind to anything but the desire to seize the ember for themselves. Klepto clawed at Vulgor's face, his fingers curling into hooks as he tried to gouge out his rival's eyes, desperate to keep anyone from taking what he believed was his. Vulgor, writhing like a serpent, sank his teeth into Klepto's arm, drawing blood as he fought to slip free and twist the situation to his advantage. Meanwhile, Brutus, lost in a frenzy, grabbed Klepto by the throat and squeezed with bone-crushing force, his fingers digging into the flesh as he reveled in the sheer act of domination. Vulgor, refusing to be outdone, raked his claws across Brutus's back, tearing through skin, while Klepto, choking under Brutus's grip, kicked out wildly, his feet finding purchase in Vulgor's ribs with a sickening crunch. They thrashed and tore at each other like rabid animals, biting, scratching, and crushing without thought or restraint. Blood sprayed, as the chamber echoed with guttural snarls and screams of pain. In their madness, they didn't realize they were destroying themselves, ripping each other apart until nothing remained but the memory of what they once were, proving that the very vices that once made them powerful were also the forces that ultimately led to their complete annihilation.

Kratos, unable to bear the sight of the vicious carnage before him – the gnashing teeth, the tearing claws, the blood-soaked madness – squeezed his eyes shut, desperate to escape the horror. The sounds of snarling and flesh ripping echoed in his ears, but as his eyelids clenched tighter, the noise began to fade, replaced by an eerie silence. The darkness behind his eyes softened, and he felt a strange warmth, with his mother beckoning him one last time to leave this horrid nightmare.

When he finally opened his eyes, he found himself lying in the blood stained chamber, the vision gone. The Controlls were nowhere to be seen, only the remnants of the Hearth remained.

And his brother... Demos.

> **THEY THRASHED AND TORE AT EACH OTHER LIKE RABID ANIMALS, BITING, SCRATCHING, AND CRUSHING WITHOUT THOUGHT OR RESTRAINT.**

*Driven by greed and ambition, the Controlls descend into chaos, tearing each other apart as their alliance crumbles.* 1257.

# CHAPTER XIV
# REDEMPTION

# REKINDLE

# REVELATION

# FUTURE

*With fire rekindled, the brothers sit and discuss*
*what almost became of the mountain.* 1203.

# REKINDLING WISDOM'S FLAME

The mountain lay in desolate ruin, its grand chambers now hollow shells, haunted by the ghosts of what once was.

Where once laughter filled the air, now only the wind whistled, a sad song carrying the melody of loss. Yet in the midst of these crumbled remains, Demos and Kratos sat side by side before the cold Hearth. Between them, a single ember clung valiantly to life, a stubborn remnant of what had almost been lost entirely.

Kratos, scarred but softened by the magnitude of what he'd just been through, gazed at the ember with a mix of regret and resolve. "This mountain was built in the belief that power can elevate us, bring order to the chaos," he murmured. "But instead I was seduced, nearly bringing everything to ruin."

Demos looked thoughtfully at his brother and leaned in, gently breathing life back into the faint ember. In a quiet, unspoken gesture, he reached out, briefly touching Kratos's arm, his fingers grazing the scar from the snake bite. It was a small but powerful act, a silent acknowledgment of forgiveness and concern. "Power," he said, "is a tool too tempting, too corrosive. If wielded for its own sake, it devours the very hands that grasp it. The mountain fell not because of the stone and mortar, but because we forgot what the Hearth was meant for – sharing stories, wisdom, and light, not amassing control."

Kratos nodded, watching the ember catch. "Perhaps the most powerful act, brother, is to relinquish power entirely – to lay down and sacrifice one's own desires – to help others rise up. It's in relinquishing that we find strength. A paradox, maybe, but in that irony lies the truth."

As the flames began to dance once more, casting gentle warmth into the chilling dusk air, the two brothers reflected on the unwritten future. The mountain would rise again – not through force or conquest, but through the steady accumulation of stories, knowledge, and sacrifice. A new chapter was beginning, its first words written in the soft crackle of rekindled fire.

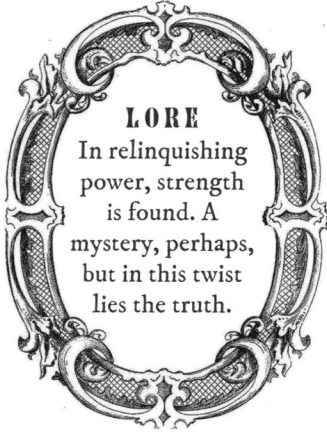

## THE ALLURE & POISON OF POWER

Kratos had learned the hard way. At the peak of his ambition, he became a puppet to Vulgor, Klepto, and Brutus. They'd promised him mastery over the mountain, but instead hollowed him out, turning leadership into tyranny. The grip of power corrupted even the noblest of intentions, twisting unity into division, and governance into oppression. Through their cunning, they revealed the bitter truth: power, if left unchecked, is not the means to build, but the force that destroys.

## SACRIFICE AS THE TRUE PATH TO STRENGTH

In the depths of his struggle, it was Demos who reminded Kratos that real strength lies not in domination, but in humility. In the final battle, Kratos chose redemption over control. He relinquished his ambition, knowing that in sacrifice lies the seed of genuine power – the power to restore, to heal, to nurture. By stepping away from it, Kratos found the true path to how a tribe might be led: as a servant to wisdom, not a master of force.

**THROUGH THEIR CUNNING, THEY REVEALED THE BITTER TRUTH.**

*The last ember from the Hearth of Wisdom, is protected and nurtured so that it might one day illuminate hearts and minds again. 1358.*

## THE UNWRITTEN FUTURE

*Monkey Mountain. 1325.*

As the two brothers rekindled the flame, they spoke of the future, knowing it would bring new challenges, new power struggles. But this time, they would be guided by the lessons of the past. They would build on principles of shared wisdom, with the mountain's foundation not of stone, but of stories. Their hope now rested not in control, but in the collective strength of the tribe to choose the harder path of humility over the easier one of domination.

### LORE

True power is not in holding on, but in letting go; in sacrifice lies the strength to rebuild.

# FACING THE SHADOWS OF THE MIND

As the embers grew into a steady flame, Demos and Kratos turned their thoughts toward the creatures who had nearly twisted Monkey Mountain beyond recognition – the Controlls.

These nefarious figures, born from the darkest recesses of the apling mind, had promised strength but delivered only despair. The fiercest enemies it turns out, are not those we can see, but those that linger in the shadows.

"They were reflections of our worst impulses," Demos began, his voice tinged with a weariness that only comes from staring too long into the abyss. "Vulgor's hunger for dominion, Klepto's greed, and Brutus's uncontrollable anger – they weren't external threats. They were the primal instincts we carry within us."

Demos, eyes fixed on the flickering flame, continued, "The Controlls didn't just creep into the mountain unnoticed. We welcomed them in – through our fears, our ambitions, and our weaknesses. They feasted on our need for power, exploiting our desire for more until we became captives of our own making."

"It wasn't just their cunning that nearly brought us down," Kratos added. "It was my own blindness. I thought myself wise, but it was in chasing after power that I allowed ignorance to settle over my heart like a fog. I was so fixated on controlling the mountain outside that I didn't see the shadows growing within."

**THEY WERE ECHOES OF THE VERY INSTINCTS WE CARRY WITHIN US.**

The brothers fell silent for a moment, contemplating the harsh truth that the Controlls had revealed: the greatest battles are often fought inside the soul, against the very traits that make one susceptible to corruption. To conquer the evil in the world, one must first confront the demons within.

*Demos faces out into the world, contemplating what the future will hold for their fragile civilisation. 1254.*

**EACH OFFERED SHORTCUTS TO POWER, BUT THESE PATHS LED ONLY TO RUIN.**

## THE MASK OF POWER

The Controlls were not mere physical creatures; they were in fact embodiments of the temptations inherent in all that is powerful. Vulgor whispered of dominance, turning authority into tyranny. Klepto spun tales of wealth, making accumulation the end instead of the means. Brutus sowed division, manipulating the tribe's fears and ambitions. Each offered shortcuts to power, but these paths led only to ruin. The lesson was clear: the allure of power is most dangerous when it masquerades as righteous authority.

## THE FRAGILITY OF WISDOM

The Hearth of Wisdom, once a beacon of light, had dimmed under the influence of the Controlls. Knowledge itself was twisted to serve greed, control, and deceit. What Demos and Kratos learned was that wisdom is fragile – it must be constantly tended, protected from those who would pervert it for gain. In relinquishing the Hearth, the tribe had welcomed darkness in. The rekindling of the fire signified not just a return to knowledge, but a commitment to guard it against future corruption.

### LORE

The darkest threats are not external forces but the shadows cast by our own unchecked desires. True strength lies in recognizing and resisting these impulses.

## UNCHECKED POWER

Perhaps the most unsettling revelation was how easily corruption seeps in when left unchecked. The Controlls thrived not only through overt force, but through subtle influence, feeding on the fears, anxieties, and hidden desires of the tribe. This experience taught the brothers that the root of corruption lies in the mind itself – in the unexamined desires for power, wealth, and control that can twist even the purest intentions. The future of Monkey Mountain depended not just on vigilance, but on the cultivation of a civilisation, in pursuit of the highest virtues.

*Within the apling mind, the fire of ambition burns —*
*fueling both wisdom and destruction. 1328.*

*Demos and Kratos look toward the horizon where the
known world blends into the unknown. 1264.*

# BEYOND THE SETTING SUN

**W**ith the fire rekindled and flickering back to life, Demos and Kratos rose quietly, their eyes meeting in a silent agreement.

There was one more place they needed to be – one final ascent to the highest peak of the Mountain, where they could gaze upon the world that stretched far beyond this fine creation.

The climb was steep and the air thin, yet their steps were unhurried, savoring each footfall on the stone path. As they reached the summit, the sun hung low on the horizon, casting long, golden rays across the jungle below. The wild expanse rippled under the evening breeze, concealing both beauty and danger within its tangled depths.

Civilisations, like the seasons, rise, flourish, and fall beneath the weight of their own ambitions. History doesn't move in straight lines but spirals – each generation believing itself wiser, only to stumble into the same mistakes already made. The real challenge wouldn't be just rebuilding, but breaking free from the endless cycle of rise and ruin.

For a long moment, the brothers sat in silence, looking out over the mountain that had been both their dream and burden.

Scarred but still standing, the mountain was indeed a monumental testament to their struggles, hopes, and beliefs in creating something that might endure for many more moons to come.

Demos opened his hand, looked his brother in the eye, and dropped a single seed from the Tree of Echoes into the soft earth at their feet.

Would it take root and help to rejuvenate their people? Or once again be lost to the ravages of time?

THE END.

# EPILOGUE

# DEAR READER,

It seems we've reached the end of our winding tale – this grand saga tracing civilisation's rise, fall, and hopeful rebirth. Where a primitive species strive to reach great heights, all the while struggling to stop their mountain of progress collapsing from within.

But let's return to the question posed at the start of this journey... Who wrote this story? Was it I, Nick McFarlane, someone simply intrigued with how the world really works? Was it the AI GPT, configured to churn out the words my mind couldn't quite construct? Or was it the troop of gorillas in the Congo, unwittingly influencing this yarn through an experiment in primal prompting? Perhaps it's the sum of parts – with the hand of history also having a say in the matter.

Instead of looking back, let's now look forward to where the next chapter of humanity's epic tale might lead. You see, history has a funny way of repeating itself in new guises. And today, one of civilisation's greatest challenges may be unfolding right before our eyes, with the advent of AI technology.

This new power, birthed from human ingenuity, holds the potential to transform society in ways both marvelous and terrifying. Will it help unlock a more just society? Or, like the trolls of old, will it become a force of oppression?

The irony's rich, isn't it? After all the centuries striving to rise above the animal within, we now stand at the threshold of a new era where our species may no longer hold alpha status.

So as you close this book, perhaps the real question isn't who wrote these words, but rather who'll continue the story? Will humanity rise once again as author of its own destiny, or surrender to AI's cold calculating control?

The next chapter is yours...

# Bibliography

## I. OF NATURAL ORIGIN

**Darwin, Charles.** On the Origin of Species by Means of Natural Selection. 1859.

**Diamond, Jared.** Guns, Germs, and Steel: The Fates of Human Societies. 1997.

**Dawkins, Richard.** The Selfish Gene. 1976.

**Axelrod, Robert.** The Evolution of Cooperation. 1984.

## II. THE HEARTH OF WISDOM

**Plato.** The Republic, c. 375 B.C.E.

**Hobbes, Thomas.** Leviathan, 1651.

**Tainter, Joseph A.** The Collapse of Complex Societies, 1988.

**Smith, Adam.** The Wealth of Nations, 1776.

## III. MAKETH THY MOUNTAIN

**Harari, Yuval Noah.** Sapiens: A Brief History of Humankind. 2015.

**Mann, Michael.** The Sources of Social Power, Vol. I: A History of Power from the Beginning to AD 1760. 1986.

**Polanyi, Karl.** The Great Transformation: The Political and Economic Origins of Our Time. 1944.

**McNeill, William H.** The Rise of the West: A History of the Human Community. 1963.

Hayek, Friedrich. The Road to Serfdom. 1944.

**Cannadine, David.** A History of Monarchy. 2004.

**Ferguson, Niall.** Empire: The Rise and Demise of the British World Order and the Lessons for Global Power. 2002.

**Lenin, Vladimir Ilyich.** Imperialism: The Highest Stage of Capitalism. 1917.

## IV. THE CHAMBERS OF POWER

**Althusser, Louis.** Ideology and Ideological State Apparatuses, 1970.

**Nietzsche, Friedrich.** Beyond Good and Evil, 1886.

**Friedrich Nietzsche,** The Will to Power Posthumously published, 1901.

**Lukes, Steven.** Power: A Radical View, 1974.

## V. THE POLITICAL CHAMBER

**Hobbes, Thomas.** Leviathan, 1651.

**Locke, John.** Two Treatises of Government, 1689.

**Marx, Karl, and Engels, Friedrich.** The Communist Manifesto, 1848.

**Mussolini, Benito, and Giovanni Gentile.** The Doctrine of Fascism, 1932.

**Chomsky, Noam.** On Anarchism, 2013.

**Mill, John Stuart.** On Liberty, 1859.

## VI. THE ECONOMIC CHAMBER

**Smith, Adam.** The Wealth of Nations, 1776.

**Friedman, Milton.** Capitalism and Freedom, 1962.

**Marx, Karl.** Capital: Critique of Political Economy, 1867.

**Bentham, Jeremy.** An Introduction to the Principles of Morals and Legislation. 1789.

**Keynes, John Maynard.** The General Theory of Employment, Interest, and Money. 1936.

**Thaler, Richard H., and Cass R. Sunstein.** Nudge: Improving Decisions About Health, Wealth, and Happiness. 2008.

**Kahneman, Daniel.** Thinking, Fast and Slow. 2011.

**Ariely, Dan.** Predictably Irrational: The Hidden Forces That Shape Our Decisions. 2008.

## VII. THE PUBLIC CHAMBER

**Arendt, Hannah.** The Human Condition. 1958.

**Rousseau, Jean-Jacques.** The Social Contract, 1762.

**Locke, John.** Two Treatises of Government, 1689.

**Dewey, John.** The Public and Its Problems, 1927.

**Peterson, Jordan B.** 12 Rules for Life: An Antidote to Chaos. 2018.

**Jack Donnelly,** Universal Human Rights in Theory and Practice. 1989

## IIX. THE CONTROLLS

**Freud, Sigmund.** Civilization and Its Discontents. 1930.

**Orwell, George.** 1984. 1949.

**Machiavelli, Niccolò.** The Prince. 1532.

**Fromm, Erich.** Escape from Freedom. 1941.

**Foucault, Michel.** Discipline and Punish: The Birth of the Prison. 1975.

**Arendt, Hannah.** The Origins of Totalitarianism. 1951.

**Zimbardo, Philip.** The Lucifer Effect: Understanding How Good People Turn Evil. 2007.

## IX. VULGOR

**Orwell, George.** Animal Farm. 1945.

**Ariely, Dan.** The Honest Truth About Dishonesty: How We Lie to Everyone – Especially Ourselves. 2012.

**Murray, Douglas.** The Strange Death of Europe: Immigration, Identity, Islam. 2017.

**Weber, Max.** Bureaucracy. 1922.

**Snyder, Timothy.** The Road to Unfreedom: Russia, Europe, America. 2018.

**Snyder, Timothy.** On Tyranny: Twenty Lessons from the Twentieth Century. 2017.

**Foucault, Michel.** Discipline and Punish: The Birth of the Prison. 1975.

## X. KLEPTO

**Klein, Naomi. The Shock Doctrine:** The Rise of Disaster Capitalism. 2007.

**Acemoglu, Daron, and James A. Robinson.** Why Nations Fail: The Origins of Power, Prosperity, and Poverty. 2012.

**Graeber, David.** Debt: The First 5,000 Years. 2011.

**Chomsky, Noam, and Edward S. Herman.** Manufacturing Consent: The Political Economy of the Mass Media. 1988.

**Friedman, Milton.** Capitalism and Freedom. 1962.

**Harvey, David.** A Brief History of Neoliberalism. 2005.

**Mirowski, Philip, and Dieter Plehwe, eds.** The Road from Mont Pelerin: The Making of the Neoliberal Thought Collective. 2009.

**Stiglitz, Joseph E.** Globalization and Its Discontents. 2002.

## XI. BRUTUS

**Bauman, Zygmunt.** Liquid Fear. 2006.

**Stanley Milgram,** Obedience to Authority: An Experimental View. 1974.

**Michael Ignatieff,** Human Rights as Politics and Idolatry. 2001.

**Marquis de Sade,** The 120 Days of Sodom. Posthumously published in 1904.

## XII. TYRANNY

**Arendt, Hannah.** The Origins of Totalitarianism. 1951.

**Hoffer, Eric.** The True Believer: Thoughts on the Nature of Mass Movements. 1951.

**Bauman, Zygmunt.** Modernity and the Holocaust. 1989.

**Snyder, Timothy.** On Tyranny: Twenty Lessons from the Twentieth Century. 2017..

**Burgis, Tom.** The Looting Machine: Warlords, Oligarchs, Corporations, Smugglers, and the Theft of Africa's Wealth. 2015.

## XI. REVOLUTION

**Arendt, Hannah.** On Revolution. 1963.

**Paine, Thomas.** Common Sense. 1776.

**Hobsbawm, Eric.** The Age of Revolution. 1962.

**More, Thomas.** Utopia. 2001.

**Aquinas, Thomas.** Summa Theologica. 1947.

## XI. REDEMPTION

**Arendt, Hannah.** The Human Condition. 1958.

**Fromm, Erich.** The Art of Loving. 1956.

**Frankl, Viktor E.** Man's Search for Meaning. 1946.

**Jung, Carl G.** Modern Man in Search of a Soul. 1933.

# A troop of gorillas living in the Democratic Republic of the Congo assisted with the writing of this book.

Their behaviour and social interactions were unobtrusively observed and translated into editorial instructions using AI. Changes to the first edit of Monumental were then recommended, based on observations which best correlated with the existing narrative. The goal was to push the boundaries of story-telling, blurring the relationship between human creativity, artificial intelligence, and primate behaviour. These unlikely collaborators affected one key element per chapter, based on 3 observation/impact triggers:

| | | | |
|---|---|---|---|
| 01. | Social Interaction | → | Relationship Dynamics & Conflict |
| 02. | Body Language & Posture | → | Character Archetype & Role |
| 03. | Group Dynamics & Hierarchy | → | Storyline Progression & Power Structures |

## Chapter I. Of Natural Origin
### 01: Social Interaction > Relationship Dynamics & Conflict

| Observation | Current Story Element | Recommended Change | Observation > Impact |
|---|---|---|---|
| The two gorillas are shown sharing and carefully examining a stalk, suggesting cooperation and a quiet, harmonious exchange. This scene is calm and intimate, with no apparent competition or conflict over resources. | The story currently illustrates early social interactions as based on competition and conflict over resources, with limited examples of cooperative behavior between tribe members. | Introduce a scene where two tribe members share a resource, such as a fruit or medicinal plant, reflecting a cooperative dynamic. This change could subtly show the tribe's progression from pure survival instincts toward communal support and shared knowledge. This early shift in behavior could lay a foundation for the more complex social structures that will emerge. |  |

## Chapter II. The Hearth of Wisdom
### 02. Body Language & Posture > Character Archetype & Role

| Observation | Current Story Element | Recommended Change | Observation > Impact |
|---|---|---|---|
| The gorilla displays a calm, steady gaze, maintaining a strong yet non-threatening posture. Its body language, while dominant, is relaxed and focused on its surroundings rather than posturing aggressively. | Current description in "The Hearth of Wisdom" lacks specific details that illustrate a character embodying a thoughtful, wise leader archetype, who exudes calm authority without needing to assert dominance. | Describe a character inspired by this gorilla's posture as embodying wisdom and restrained power, positioning them as a mediator or a guiding figure in the community—someone whose presence commands respect not through aggression but through thoughtful observation and calm. This approach emphasizes wisdom as a form of strength, enhancing the symbolic importance of "The Hearth of Wisdom" as a place of balance and counsel. |  |

## Chapter III. Maketh Thy Mountain

03: Group Dynamics & Hierarchy > Storyline Progression & Power Structures

| Observation | Current Story Element | Recommended Change | Observation > Impact |
|---|---|---|---|
| The gorillas are seated together calmly, suggesting a collective focus without visible hierarchy. They appear relaxed but cohesive, indicating early-stage communal harmony. | This represents the initial phase of the aplings establishing their settlement. Their cooperation in building fences and watchtowers showcases a focus on collective security, as the chapter details their transition from nomadic life to a structured community. | **Emphasize the communal and egalitarian dynamics in the early stages of the aplings' settlement. Introduce a scene where the aplings are seen working side by side with equal input, laying foundations together, symbolizing unity before the emergence of formal hierarchies.** |  |

## Chapter IV. The Chambers of Power

01. Social Interaction > Relationship Dynamics & Conflict

| Observation | Current Story Element | Recommended Change | Observation > Impact |
|---|---|---|---|
| In this footage, two gorillas engage in an intense interaction, with one holding the other's head in a way that appears protective yet potentially controlling. The close physical contact and the pressing of heads together suggest a complex relationship dynamic that balances between connection and dominance, showing both tension and closeness. | In *The Chambers of Power* chapter, the current narrative explores the struggle for control within the various factions and alliances as the tribe establishes the Political, Economic, and Public Chambers. Social dynamics are portrayed through power struggles, negotiations, and the creation of roles. | Introduce a scene that mirrors this close, ambiguous interaction to underscore the dual nature of power —how it can be both unifying and restrictive. By depicting Demos or Kratos in a similar moment of intense, boundary-blurring contact with another character, the narrative can emphasize the complexities of power relationships, particularly in moments where collaboration and control are tightly interwoven. |  |

## Chapter V. The Political Chamber

02. Body Language & Posture > Character Archetype & Role

| Observation | Current Story Element | Recommended Change | Observation > Impact |
|---|---|---|---|
| The dominant gorilla maintains a rigid posture, eyes fixed forward, embodying authority and control. Other gorillas around him display submissive gestures, with lowered gazes and relaxed shoulders. | The Political Chamber currently shows the central figure, the Leader, using both verbal commands and gestures to assert control over the group. | Emphasize nonverbal authority by depicting the Leader as maintaining a calm, yet unyielding posture. Limit his gestures and words, allowing his mere presence to command respect. Other aplings should respond instinctively to his posture with visible deference, creating a silent acknowledgment of his role. |  |

## Chapter VI. The Economic Chamber
### 03. Group Dynamics & Hierarchy > Storyline Progression & Power Structures

| Observation | Current Story Element | Recommended Change | Observation > Impact |
|---|---|---|---|
| Two gorillas engage in close, intense interaction, pressing heads together in a display that suggests both conflict and intimacy. This contact appears ambiguous—neither overtly hostile nor completely gentle—mirroring complex power dynamics within the group. | Economic Chamber currently centers on resource management, exchange, and trade, but lacks emphasis on interpersonal power struggles or alliances within these economic interactions. | **Add a scene with key figures from the chamber, perhaps Kratos and another character, locked in a tense negotiation over resources. This could reflect the ambiguous nature of power, where alliances blur into rivalries, and cooperation can verge on competition.** |  |

## Chapter VII: The Public Chamber
### 01. Social Interaction > Relationship Dynamics & Conflict

| Observation | Current Story Element | Recommended Change | Observation > Impact |
|---|---|---|---|
| *Close, physical engagement between two gorillas, characterized by boundary-blurring contact.* | In *Chapter VII: The Public Chamber*, current text may lack emphasis on intense, boundary-blurring interactions reflecting power and personal space dynamics. | **Introduce a scene mirroring this close, ambiguous interaction. Depict Kratos or another key figure in an intense, close-quarters negotiation, where physical proximity reflects underlying tensions. This interaction can capture the intricate balance of influence, cooperation, or even silent rivalry within the Public Chamber, highlighting how power often operates in personal, ambiguous spaces.** |  |

## Chapter VIII: The Controlls
### 02. Body Language & Posture > Character Archetype & Role

| Observation | Current Story Element | Recommended Change | Observation > Impact |
|---|---|---|---|
| In the sequence, one gorilla subtly but firmly asserts physical control over another in close proximity, conveying dominance without overt violence. The surrounding gorillas watch, their silence reinforcing the weight of the interaction. This restrained but calculated show of power highlights the dominant gorilla's capacity to maintain control through presence alone. | Currently, the chapter introduces the Controlls as archetypes of manipulation—Vulgor, Klepto, and Brutus—but lacks a visceral example of their behavior in action. Each Controll represents a specific form of societal decay: Vulgor through political manipulation, Klepto through greed, and Brutus through fearmongering. | To embody the observed behavior, adjust **Brutus, the Publitroll** in the Public Chamber as a figure who commands silence and obedience through an oppressive physical presence. A scene could depict Brutus engaging in a tense, almost predatory interaction with another apling, who feels compelled to submit. Surrounding aplings watch, subdued, as Brutus exerts his influence through sheer intimidation. This mirrors the close, ambiguous interactions observed in the gorilla footage, adding a layer of physical menace to Brutus's character and visually reinforcing his role as a spreader of fear and discord. |  |

## Chapter IX: Vulgor
### 03. Group Dynamics & Hierarchy > Storyline Progression & Power Structures

| Observation | Current Story Element | Recommended Change | Observation > Impact |
|---|---|---|---|
| In the images, one gorilla grips another's head with a dominant, firm gesture while staring intensely. The subordinate gorilla exhibits passive submission, lowering its head and avoiding eye contact. Other gorillas observe quietly, keeping close but showing deference through their restrained body language. | Vulgor is depicted as the Politroll, wielding power within the Political Chamber, often through manipulation and cunning. His character currently emphasizes influence over others through strategic alliances rather than overt physical dominance. | Emphasize Vulgor's control through physical dominance within the storyline. A scene could show Vulgor asserting his authority with an intimidating presence that commands silence and submission. Surrounding aplings, aware of his power, could be depicted as observing cautiously, reinforcing his role as an unchallenged leader through both fear and respect. |  |

## Chapter X: Klepto
### 01. Social Interaction > Relationship Dynamics & Conflict

| Observation | Current Story Element | Recommended Change | Observation > Impact |
|---|---|---|---|
| A single gorilla sits alone, intently holding a plant, occasionally pausing to survey its surroundings, giving the impression of possessive focus and suspicion. | Klepto is portrayed as a figure of greed, prioritizing wealth and resources over relationships, embodying the obsessive nature of greed within the Economic Chamber. | Emphasize Klepto's isolationist tendencies, depicting him as not only hoarding resources but also distancing himself from others. Show his distrust and wariness of nearby aplings, highlighting his alienation caused by an insatiable hunger for control over resources. This could lead to scenes where he rebuffs attempts at socialization, driven by fear of others coveting his possessions. |  |

## Chapter XI: Brutus
### 02. Body Language & Posture > Character Archetype & Role

| Observation | Current Story Element | Recommended Change | Observation > Impact |
|---|---|---|---|
| A gorilla displays aggressive posture and facial expression, including open mouth and bared teeth, suggesting intimidation. | Brutus exerts control through fear and psychological manipulation. | Emphasize Brutus as an enforcer of fear. Adjust his character to focus on physical intimidation as a tool, showing him dominating others through his stance and posture to reinforce his tyrannical presence. |  |

## Chapter XII: Tyranny
### 02. Body Language & Posture > Character Archetype & Role

| Observation | Current Story Element | Recommended Change | Observation > Impact |
|---|---|---|---|
| In this sequence, the dominant gorilla physically asserts control over the group, positioning itself close to younger gorillas, who respond with playful engagement but quickly cease activity, showing submissive gestures (e.g., lowering gaze) as soon as the dominant approaches. The dominant gorilla's presence alone disrupts their interactions, reinforcing the group's hierarchical structure through non-verbal cues like posture and eye contact. | The existing story element highlights hierarchy through spoken commands and confrontations, but lacks emphasis on physical presence and unspoken dominance within group dynamics. | Enhance the portrayal of tyranny by showing the dominant gorilla using body language to assert authority. Depict scenes where younger gorillas instinctively respond with submission, ceasing their actions, lowering their gaze, or repositioning themselves to respect the alpha's space. This change emphasizes power structures as enforced by silent, physical cues, reinforcing hierarchy and obedience without the need for verbal commands. |  |

## Chapter XIII: Revolution.
### 03. Group Dynamics & Hierarchy > Storyline Progression & Power Structures

| Observation | Current Story Element | Recommended Change | Observation > Impact |
|---|---|---|---|
| The sequence shows a group of gorillas sitting closely together, displaying calm and collective body language. No single gorilla appears dominant; they are positioned at similar levels, with relaxed postures indicating unity rather than submission. Periodically, some individuals shift or look around but return to the unified group formation, emphasizing solidarity. | This current setup represents a collective moment of calm before action, emphasizing equality and cohesion within the group. There's an absence of hierarchical displays, symbolizing a potential for organized unity among them. | Enhance this scene to emphasize the gorillas' shared purpose, potentially symbolizing the brewing of a collective uprising. Highlight subtle, synchronized movements that suggest silent communication and unity, foreshadowing coordinated resistance. Incorporate gestures of mutual reassurance, like brief touches or mirrored postures, to reinforce the theme of solidarity in preparation for a collective stand. |  |

## Chapter XIV: Redemption.
### 01. Social Interaction > Relationship Dynamics & Conflict

| Observation | Current Story Element | Recommended Change | Observation > Impact |
|---|---|---|---|
| Two gorillas sit close together in quiet companionship, their body language relaxed, indicating trust and mutual understanding. The second gorilla visibly leans into the other, a subtle sign of emotional reliance. | Chapter XIV: Redemption Depicts a moment of reconciliation and shared understanding between two characters. | Emphasize this scene as a powerful moment of bonding and silent forgiveness. Highlight the gorillas' mirrored postures and mutual calmness, symbolizing unity and the rebuilding of trust. Add a small detail where one gorilla briefly touches the other's arm or shoulder, reinforcing the theme of solidarity and shared purpose. |  |

**NICK MCFARLANE** is an author and graphic agitator, based in Auckland, New Zealand. His books tend to challenge conventional thinking by distilling complex issues into simple, powerful concepts.

For Monumental, he configured an AI GPT (who he named Dilbert), to observe the world through a unique lens, and communicate with a distinct tone of voice. Together, they undertook an unusual experiment: observe a troop of gorillas in the Democratic Republic of the Congo, and use their behaviour to shape and refine the book's narrative.

This fusion of human creativity, artificial intelligence, and primate influence has resulted in a ground breaking exploration of storytelling's possibilities.

ALSO BY NICK MᶜFARLANE

**SPINFLUENCE**
The Harcore Propaganda Manual
for Controlling the Masses

---

**SPINFLUENCE**
Fake News Special Edition

---

**HUNTING THE KILLER IDEA**
Capturing the Creative Process

---

**nickmcfarlane.co.nz**